CO-AKD-049

Articulating America:
Fashioning a National Political Culture in Early America

Essays in Honor of J. R. Pole

ARTICULATING AMERICA

Fashioning a National Political Culture in Early America

ESSAYS IN HONOR OF J. R. POLE

Edited by Rebecca Starr

A MADISON HOUSE BOOK

ROWMAN & LITTLEFIELD PUBLISHERS, INC.

Lanham • Boulder • New York • Oxford

A Madison House Book
Rowman & Littlefield Publishers, Inc.
4720 Boston Way
Lanham, MD 20706
www.rowmanlittlefield.com

12 Hid's Copse Road
Cumnor Hill, Oxford OX2 9JJ, England

British Library Cataloguing in Publication Information Available

Library of Congress Cataloging-in-Publication Data

Articulating America : fashioning a national political culture in early America :
essays in honor of J. R. Pole / edited by Rebecca Starr.—1st ed.
    p. cm.
Includes bibliographical references and index.
ISBN 0-7425-2076-5 (cloth : alk. paper)
    1. Political culture—United States—History. 2. United States—Politics and
government—1783–1865. 3. United States—Politics and government—
1775–1783. I. Pole, J. R. (Jack Richon)
II. Starr, Rebecca.
E301.A78 2000
306.2'0973'09033—dc21   00-050053

Printed in the United States of America

For Jack Pole: teacher, colleague and friend

Si monumentum requiris
circumspice . . .

(if you seek a memorial, look around you)

The editor wishes to thank The Dean and Chapter of St. Paul's Cathedral, London, for permission to use the final line from Christopher Wren's memorial tablet.

Contents

Preface ANTHONY J. BADGER   ix

Introduction REBECCA STARR   1

Part One: The Antecedents

Commerce, Settlement and History: A Reading of the
Histoire des Deux Indes   15
J. G. A. POCOCK

"The same liberties and privileges as Englishmen in
England": Law, Liberty and Identity in the Construction
of Colonial English and Revolutionary America   45
JACK P. GREENE

Part Two: The Materials and Means

The Fortunes of Orthodoxy: The Political Economy of
Public Debt in England and America during the 1780s   93
RICHARD VERNIER

Voting "Rites": The Implications of Deference in
Virginia Electioneering Ritual, 1780–1820   131
ANDREW W. ROBERTSON

E Pluribus Unum: The Ideological Imperative
in Revolutionary America   153
JOYCE APPLEBY

**Part Three: The Outcome: A National Political Culture
at Work**

Republicanism, Radicalism and Sectionalism: Land
Reform and the Languages of American Working
Men, 1820–1860   177
LAWRENCE GOLDMAN

Part Four: Other Political Cultures

The Case of South Carolina: Reflections on the Nature
of Political Culture   237
REBECCA STARR

Jack Richon Pole: A Scholar's Portfolio   257

Bibliography of Published Works by J. R. Pole   259

Doctoral Theses Supervised by J. R. Pole   267

Contributors   269

Index   271

Preface

Anthony J. Badger

In May 1995 it was my privilege and pleasure to fund and host a two-day conference at Sidney Sussex College, Cambridge University, in honor of Jack Pole. It is a measure of the esteem in which the profession holds Jack that distinguished scholars from both sides of the Atlantic gathered in Cambridge to discuss vigorously the fashioning of an American national political culture in the late eighteenth century. Some had simply engaged with Jack's scholarship. Others had been his graduate students. Others were friends and former colleagues from Oxford (where Jack had been Rhodes Professor of American History and Institutions from 1979 to 1989) and Cambridge (where he had been the first Reader in American History from 1963 to 1979). Some were friends who had traveled the "grand tour" right across the United States in the summer of 1950. Others, like myself, had been introduced to American history as undergraduates by Jack and had been sustained by his loyal support and wise counsel ever since. Some could not come to the conference but were determined to offer essays for this volume.

The early British leaders in American history were urbane and highly intelligent scholars who saw their main role as interpreting America to a British audience. They offered skilled analysis, they wrote well, and some of them had a remarkable network of contacts at the very highest levels of American political, academic and cultural life. At least one, however, had never visited the United States when he was appointed to a chair in American History. When he finally went, he did not like it and never returned.

Jack Pole was the leading figure, along with William Brock, in the generation of scholars who first professionalized the study of American history in Britain. As he laconically recalled, the 1960s were a "fertile period in the progress of the study of political ideology and its practical consequences." His article on deference and his major work, *Political Representation in England and the Origins of the American Republic* dealt with the issues that were right at the cutting edge of current American historiography. *Political Representation* and William Brock's *An American Crisis* on the Reconstruction period remain the two books by British Americanists that actually changed the way historians in the United States wrote about their history.

Jack was an inspiration and a role model to a new generation of American historians in Britain who endeavored to write monographs as carefully researched as their counterparts in the United States, on topics in domestic United States history, rather than in immigration or diplomatic history, and to be published in the United States. Jack supervised many of them. He introduced British students of America not only to the importance of careful and extensive archival research, but also to the importance of getting known in the United States, attending conferences, and being networked to the leading American scholars. In the seminars he ran in Cambridge and Oxford he enabled younger British scholars to showcase their work and to meet a host of distinguished visiting Americans. In my own case, I will never forget a late-night walk through a cemetery at a conference in Winchester when Jack demanded to know what exactly the book I was working on was about. My halting and rather unfocused explanation was greeted by the stark, but compelling, response from Jack that I was trying to write the history of the New Deal without Roosevelt: making me immediately understand my own book a lot better than I had done before.

But, whereas the next generation of Americanists in Britain tended to pride themselves on writing monographs indistinguishable from those produced by their American contemporaries, Jack Pole's work continued to remind us that there was value in a distinctively British voice. His work, and, in particular, the collaboration with Jack Greene, reaffirmed the notion of an Atlantic World in the eighteenth century. All his work challenged comfortable notions of American exceptionalism. While his successors tended to work on precisely circumscribed topics, Jack worked on major themes—the idea of majority rule, the right to information and political responsibility, the notion of equality—themes that got to the heart of what was distinctive or not about the American political culture.

And he has continued to work on those themes. No topic addresses these issues more than Jack's current work on the law in American political culture. No topic demands a more careful delineation of British precedent and American innovation. No topic demands a more careful elucidation of ideology and practical application. At an age when most historians have packed away their bat, Jack carries on with original research: now research trips to New York have the added bonus that they can be combined with visits to the cricket Test Matches in the West Indies. He continues to give papers, to undertake major editorial projects, to attend conferences, and, all the time, to encourage younger scholars. The essays in this volume are a small token of the debt those younger scholars owe him.

Introduction

Rebecca Starr

Like all truly engaging historical problems, the problem of describing an American national political culture begs several prior questions that have been overlooked or incompletely answered in the past. The most immediate problem (to parody one wit) is, "What is still *American* about America's political culture?"[1] I will attempt to summarize the main outlines of this strongly contested question in the paragraphs that follow. Only when we have identified its home-grown roots can we begin to trace the transformation of a sense of "Americanness" from a cultural to a national phenomenon, and from its role in the foundation of a new state, to its life as the engine of that state.

Having got to the matter of an American *national* political culture, among the questions to be addressed are: how was an American national political culture created and defined during the Revolutionary generation and why; what were its metropolitan and colonial antecedents; what were its principal components and contours; how did it relate to the several and mostly much older state political cultures with which it had to coexist; and how did it function to determine what did and what did not fall within the "realm" of the

[1]See footnote 5.

national "public." The answers supplied in this volume's six linked essays will help us to construct a picture of America's national political culture as a system of ideas and behavior during its formative years.

The book's most fundamental question, "What is the nature of political culture" is the subject of the concluding essay. Evaluating the larger implications of the volume, Rebecca Starr wrestles with the historiographical evolution of this guiding conception to recast both what political culture is and how it works.

Since the introduction of the concept "political culture" into early American studies in the 1960s (an event marking a new departure for understanding the American Revolutionary period), the nature and sources of America's political culture have been the subject of increasing debate. With near mathematical precision, Bernard Bailyn, who formally introduced the term (but not the conception) in 1967, defined political culture as a community's collective attitudes, values, beliefs, and assumptions. Patterned behavior as an aspect of political culture got a mention in Bailyn's definition, but no further development in his haste to get on to his real story, the coming of the American Revolution. For Bailyn, colonial Americans were preoccupied by their proud inheritance of a British political culture, in particular the British constitution, but perplexed by the constitution's failure to work as it did in Great Britain. Perplexity created anxiety, anxiety led to suspicion. Suspicion, conditioned by decades of reading British opposition dogma reprinted in colonial pamphlet literature detected a plot, and that sparked off rebellion. The sources for American political culture for Bailyn were British.

J. R. Pole's *Political Representation in England and the Origins of the American Republic* belongs within this revisionist stream of American Revolutionary historiography, but he took a more expansive approach to the problem of early America's political culture. Pole locates vital forces from both sides of the Atlantic converging in

America to produce that most American feature of republican government, the majority principle. In his widely ranging, comparative work, Pole introduced numerous features of America's early political culture that other scholars have gone on to develop so fruitfully.[2]

No less influential has been Pole's seminal article on the role of deference in early American political culture. First published in 1962, this powerful challenge to the historical profession's then prevalent belief that Americans were born free, white, and democratic ignited a debate that has yet to burn out.[3] When scholars began reevaluating the work of the 1960s and 1970s for its radical implications, Pole's study of Equality showed the ramifications of this central revolutionary idea for subsequent American generations.

The work of Jack P. Greene, too, has added many arrows to our quiver. In particular, his articles on the society and politics of Virginia, South Carolina, and the Caribbean have refined our knowledge about the variety of local political cultures. His larger works tracing the divergence of American and British conceptualizations of colonial political culture on the eve of the Revolution have sharpened our understanding of how Americanized that political culture had become.[4]

[2]London and New York, 1966.

[3]"Historians and the Problem of Early American Democracy," reprinted in *Paths to the American Past* (New York, 1979), 223–49; *The Pursuit of Equality in American History* (Berkeley, 1978); and see on deference, for example, the essays and comments by Michael Zuckerman, Kathleen M. Brown, John Murrin, and Robert A. Gross in the special section "Deference or Defiance in Eighteenth-Century America?: A Round Table," *Journal of American History*, 85, no. 1 (1998), 13–97.

[4]See for example, "Colonial South Carolina and the Caribbean Connection," *South Carolina Historical Magazine*, 88 (1987) 192–210; *Peripheries and Center: Constitutional Development in the Extended Polities of the British Empire and the United States 1607–1788* (Athens, Ga., 1986).

J. G. A. Pocock's brilliant work on discourse introduced a new analytical approach and a new pedigree for America's early political culture. Civic humanism, Florentine republicanism, and the ancient world once again displaced homegrown sources. Not since Bailyn had America seemed so much the product of European thought. The American republic as the last act of the Italian renaissance, however, soon found its challenger in Joyce Appleby and others. Appleby's essay on the thought of Thomas Jefferson firmly relocated the republic on American soil, the first act of the modern age.[5]

Although these essential debates are by no means at an end, the need for a fully developed and integrated study of the development of an American *national* political culture is surely at hand. And although no single volume can completely fulfill such a momentous task, these linked essays do identify, integrate, and explore the nature of some of its chief sinews. The larger narrative also pinpoints the moment of transformation of American political culture from a diverse body of competing ideas to a shared method for making and remaking America. It proved a national and nationalizing impulse, welding older ideas about individual equality to corporate identities emerging within voluntary associations, the cradle of America's modern national political culture. It is hoped that these essays will stimulate a reconsideration of what "Americanness" is, both how it came, and how it still comes to be.

What is distinctly American about American political culture? Surely the freedom of any nation to write its own history is dependent on being free from the imperious "Othering" wielding tenden-

---

[5]J. G. A. Pocock, *The Machiavellian Moment: Florentine Political Thought and the Atlantic Republican Tradition* (Princeton, 1975); Joyce Appleby, "What is still American about the Political Philosophy of Thomas Jefferson?," *William and Mary Quarterly*, 3rd ser., 39 (1982), 287–309.

cies of the historians of culturally dominant world powers. This is the thesis of J. G. A. Pocock's historiographical reading of the *Histoire des Deux Indes* (1772–1780), the first European attempt to write an integrated history of the eighteenth century's two worlds, Old and New. The fact that Europeans (at least the Encyclopedists, chiefly Diderot and Raynal, who wrote this multivolume work) were unable to imagine an "America" in the way they could the rest of the world's cultures, bequeathed those who settled these colonies a *tabula rasa* on which to write their own history, their own culture, and by extension (and in time) their own political culture. Furthermore, the fact that the writers of *Histoire des Deux Indes*, see colonial Americans in a state of nature (without a history) rather than as a civic community, suggests that the *Histoire* may have been an ideological preparation (at least for those influenced by the *Histoire*) for the War of American Independence. Their anticipated fall from nature into history implies that Americans will write that history themselves.

Diderot and Raynal's English contemporary Edward Gibbon thought the Encyclopedists' history entertaining, but mistaken. The English indeed (by the revolutionary era if not earlier) had no trouble conceiving a history or a political culture for their American settlements, usually a conflation with their own. And if European intellectuals privileged colonials with a *tabula rasa* for creating their own political culture, America's British settlers did not come empty handed to the task.

Indeed, Jack P. Greene's essay argues that it was on their claim to an inheritance of English common law that British settlers founded their original identity as British nationals in these outposts of the British state. Colonists claimed their right to English common law not only as observable and operative formulations of natural law (the latter being their "liberties"), but also to the processes by which those formulations came into being. If the common law emerges through trial and error, and through long usage is tested, proved and established as the most natural, serviceable, and conducive to the happiness of a given people living in their local conditions, might not other climates than England create common or local laws (passed in their local assemblies) different from those passed by Parliament? It was this *process* and not just its outcome (common law, and in its declaratory form, statute law) that held an *a priori* legitimacy with colonial Americans, which stood in an equality with their natural rights to life and liberty, and that was denominated by the founding fathers as the "pursuit of happiness."[6] By extending their claim to the processes of common law (an intellectual step British thinkers never found it necessary to make and British authorities never accepted), British settlers laid hold upon an essential dynamic for constructing an indigenous American political culture.

Richard Vernier's essay turns to the economic crises of the 1780s as a testing site for America's first usable national political culture. He compares Great Britain and the new republic's views of public debt and funding as each struggled to utilize the developing science of political economy to solve their respective financial woes. Despite America's revolutionary ideology that execrated debt as the key to all that was wrong with British society, the crises of the 1780s generated powerful nationalist voices in favor of floating a large and perpetual public debt funded from taxation along the British model. Their foes, untutored in the rhetoric of political economy, lost the polemical battles of the 1780s. Paper money secured by land banks was their solution, but state legislatures' experiments with paper and debtor protection laws proved incapable of restoring stability. America was bankrupt and Hamiltonian fiscal policy doused antinationalists' voices with a flood of free contract argumentation drawn from the new authorities, in particular from Adam Smith's *Wealth of Nations*.

By the early 1790s, a popularized literature of political economy transformed former anti-nationalists into supporters for a national

---

[6] I offer this reading of the Founders' phrase in addition to the usual economic interpretation.

solution for the crisis. Using the language of political economy, how-ever, they returned public sentiment to a "natural law of political economy," one that held a public debt could be a beneficial, but only if managed by the invisible hand of a free market. Their source—Adam Smith. Although accepting a nationalist objective—public debt—anti-nationalists held to the processes of a free market as their prior and their natural right. At the same time as Great Britain was making stringent efforts to reduce its public debt, an emergent Republican opposition used the very weapons its nationalist foes had discovered, a language of political economy, to "beat them with a stick of their own devising."

Vernier's essay demonstrates that in the contest between advo-cates for stronger central versus state power, there was not yet a na-tional political culture of the critical mass necessary to annihilate the separate and constituent state political cultures with which it had to compete. Even so, the changes wrought in the contest were significant in at least two ways. First, the transformation from per-ceiving the economy as "webs of private relationships" to the level of theory opened the door to articulating a national fiscal policy for the first time, no matter how hotly contested that policy might be. Secondly, for the electorate at large, the same rhetorical battles of the 1780s that nationalized financial policy among the old Revolu-tionary elite, critically engaged the public (if only in a spectator's role) in debates on national issues (points that Andrew Robertson's and Joyce Appleby's essays develop). These two changes helped re-locate the intellectual arena for public debate among ordinary Americans from state legislatures to national councils, and poten-tially enlarged the boundaries for membership in a nascent national political culture.

Andrew Robertson explores another transformation in the fash-ioning of a national political culture, this one at the level of the voter. By examining electioneering rituals in Virginia "the point of contact between the few and the many," Robertson detects a shift from an oral-aural political culture governed by deferential relations, to an expanded, abstract world of electoral opinion knit together by print. Newspapers, editors, correspondents and readers created a national and nationalizing "imagined community" that competed with the older deferential-participant communities of face-to-face personal relations. The intensity of partisan politics of the 1790s accelerated the growth of an interactive press where ideas, opinions, and arguments could be aired more independently than on the hustings. This print community also provided a forum for coherence, reflection, and a search for consensus. It made possible the formulation of a national political culture at the level of the voter. Yet the older, elitist, deferential tradition endured in Virginia (unlike in the Northern states), living side by side with the new until well into the second and third decades of the nineteenth century. This persistence was due in part to the limited extent of literacy, restrictions on suffrage, and reinforced by the practice of voice voting. Robertson's study gives us important insight into how and why at least one state retained its particular and local political culture until well into the nineteenth century.

Robertson's essay provides a point of departure for Joyce Appleby's full exploration of the development of America's national political culture from the 1790s onwards. The birth of popular politics is her focus. Elites with their networks of influence and social intermingling may have developed common grounds on which to build a political culture before the revolution, but non-elites in a hierarchical society required a medium to exchange ideas. "Print and reading" according to Appleby "became the most important activity in nation-building." Through reading (male literacy rates outside the South approached 90%), the lines between elites and non-elites, between public and private realms, between social and political action blurred. Events accelerated this trend.

The fierce debates sparked by the French Revolution spread a "rambunctious" politics that offended high Federalists and cultural nationalists like David Ramsay alike, driving them from national office. The task of defining America's national character passed down the social ladder, crushing deferential-elite politics (outside the South) in its descent. An epidemic of forming voluntary associations that brought ordinary people into full civic participation enlarged the remit of citizenship from mere voting rights. The new and numerous shapers of America's character sought it through public initiatives for reform: temperance, sabbatarianism, hospitals for the insane, prison reform, nativism, the antislavery movement. These reformers sought a national political culture of continuous process rather than concrete outcomes. Circuit riding revivalists carried an analogous religious message of personal and social conversion, without priests or hierarchies. Knit together by a proliferating press, religious, political and social activism became the means for American nation making, driven by self-directing individuals in voluntary associations. Americans, says Appleby, found a common, definitive "modus operandi" rather than any unity of philosophy or purpose.

Paradoxically, this enlarged and more inclusive political culture also excluded: irredeemably dissolute individuals who would not reform, groups like Roman Catholic immigrants who resisted the structural and behavioral norms of associated Americans, and finally the South, where expansive reformist impulses and broad participation ran counter to its social and political arrangements. American identities were one only in this actionable sense. Those unwilling or unable to join in made themselves "unAmerica" in the majority's eyes. A popular, populist national political culture marginalized elite political culture, and a nation of doers was born.

Lawrence Goldman's case study of a nineteenth-century radical workingmen's movement aptly demonstrates this new national political culture at work. Knit together by a network of radical newspapers, American worker activists in 1844 formed a voluntary association, the National Reform Association, to campaign for a Homestead Act. Land reform, not trade unionism, they believed, offered the only solution to workers' growing "immizeration" as mechanization devalued and replaced them. Only land could give workers the economic independence that underpins political power, without which they could only sink further.

An important theme of Goldman's analysis is the notion that political languages can be a tactic rather than a simple reflection of motivating ideals, just one more move in a strategy for reform. In the hands of these self-improving radical activists, both leaders and humble followers (many of them recent British immigrants and ex-Chartists), rhetoric became an instrument. Republicanism, an Anglo-American language of radicalism, and the sectional discourse on slavery were all utilized in press, speechmaking, and public debate to mobilize popular and political support for land reform. In Goldman's example, ideology becomes the servant rather than the spokesman for a political culture.

In the National Reform Association's arguments, revolutionary republican language of natural rights and inherent equality was enlarged to include a natural right to sufficient property to sustain that equality. Such radical thinking "glossed, repeated and reworked the original document [the Declaration of Independence] of 1776" throughout the antebellum period. This radical tradition was an international English speaking phenomenon, developing coterminously on American and British soil. Republican discourse and the language of radicalism therefore became commensurate, interactive analogues of each other.

Even more obviously instrumental was the use of the language of antislavery. Labeling their impoverished, dependent (because landless) condition with the inflammatory term "wage slavery," Northeastern workingmen and women hoped to persuade the political leaders of the more powerful abolitionist movement that reform should begin at home. Within a decade the National Reform Association's cries for "free land" (160-acre homesteads) merged with abolitionists cries for "free soil" (land outside slave cultivation) as a reform ideal of Northern radicals.

Absorbed by the Republican Party in its 1860 platform, the land reform principle became law in 1862 with the Homestead Act of that year. Yet the working class's politicization of the idea demonstrates the potency and reach of an established *process* that marked America's national political culture by the middle of the nineteenth century. It demonstrates that the road to success was marked out by a politics of associationism, public debate, and strategic use of rhetorical traditions. The successful fit of commensurate political languages with each other and with the widely dispersed methods of associationism fashioned a popular national political culture, a nation of "doers" in the service of a range of ideals. It was a fit that found powerful affirmation in that portion of the nation with the political majorities to make law.

But what of the South? While one could say that the ideas of free land (160-acre homesteads) and free soil (land denied to slave cultivation) were inimical to a nineteenth-century plantation society and economy and not be wrong, that would be to ignore that the South had already developed a prior political culture of its own, one that existed almost unnoticed alongside the noisily growing nationalist and populist political culture described here. The South's political culture was not simply excluded by methodologically determined boundaries drawn by most Americans from the 1790s onward, boundaries hardened by the dispute over slavery and land use. The South's political culture had its own methodology and its own organizational structure, derived from patterns rooted deep in its colonial past. These forces and sources of the Old South's political culture are described in my study of its South Carolina hearth,[7] although the work of tracking its southwide spread remains to be done. The growth of a populist political culture made observable a Southern political culture that moved by different processes, a conflict more fundamentally of

[7]*A School for Politics: Commercial Lobbying and Political Culture in Early South Carolina* (Baltimore and London, 1998).

means (particularly the politics of compromise) than ends, and that became more rather than less mutually exclusive as the nineteenth century unfolded.

One last point remains to be made. This book does not claim to describe an American national identity. It is a study of the national political culture out of which Americans have assembled (and continue to assemble) a mosaic national identity. The study emphasizes that a political culture is both the collectivity of a community's values and a mode of behavior—an ongoing process that selectively creates and (at least in the American example described here) revises its character. It is the *processes* of a political culture that make it an organic force, that shape, indeed are, its defining features. America's claim to a national singularity resides in the distinctive mode of its production.

What we call American national political culture in this book was a stepwise development. In its first stage, postrevolutionary elites from all sections sought national, if differing, policies to cope with the crises of the 1780s. Advances in print culture, education and literacy, changes in electoral practices, and a widened suffrage passed the task of defining a national political culture down the social ladder, where it embraced a broadened participation while honing a methodology of voluntary activism. This development, however, was largely confined to the North. The older colony of South Carolina (that would form the cultural core of the Old South) had by the end of the eighteenth century a fully developed political culture that operated upon principles of interest representation and methods of interest brokering by elites on behalf of all. It would take four bloody years of warfare finally to secure federal councils for the associational model of political culture. It would be many years beyond that before the voices articulating a fully voluntaristic model of "America" would speak with Southern accents.

PART ONE

The Antecedents

Commerce, Settlement and History:

A *Reading of the* Histoire des Deux Indes

J. G. A. Pocock

This essay presents a reading of the *Histoire des Etablissements et du Commerce des Européens dans les Deux Indes*, published in many editions between 1772 and 1780 under the authorship of Guillaume-Thomas Raynal, the co-ordinator of a team of anonymous writers, one of whom was Denis Diderot. I present this reading in the context of another: a reading of Gibbon's *Decline and Fall of the Roman Empire* in settings provided by Gibbon's life and by various works which he read.[1] The *Histoire des Deux Indes* is one of these; he read it, though he didn't think much of it,[2] and I intend to show that it develops in a direction taken by *philosophe* and Encyclopedist historiography but emphatically not taken by Gibbon, with the implication that he was not a *philosophe* in the Parisian sense. It is further the case that the *Histoire* is an ideological preparation for

[1]See J. G. A. Pocock, *Barbarism and Religion*, Vol. 1, *The Enlightenment of Edward Gibbon* and especially Vol. 2, *Narrative of Civil Government* (Cambridge, 1999).

[2]"I am ignorant by what guides the Abbé Raynal was deceived; as the total absence of quotations is the unpardonable blemish of his entertaining history." Edward Gibbon, *History of the Decline and Fall of the Roman Empire*, ed. David Womersley (London, 1994), chapter XX, 748 n.74.

the War of American Independence, in which climate Gibbon lived, as a very minor political actor, while he wrote and published the first three volumes of the *Decline and Fall*.

In a broader sense still, I present the *Histoire* as evidence of the historical world in which Gibbon's generation of philosophers and historians were living. The *Histoire des Deux Indes* is the first major history of the world-system; the first attempt to deal philosophically and critically with the European conquest of the planetary ocean, which brought Europeans into contact with, and domination over, virtually every other human culture existing on earth. It is not of course the first history of cultural encounter; these had been produced in some number since the Spaniards arrived before Mexico City; but it is the first attempt to survey all such encounters and sum them up in a single history. And its attitude towards its narrative is not triumphalist, but passionately denunciatory; it recounts horror after horror, incessantly denounces Europeans as barbarous invaders, and repeatedly asks, not whether the global encounter might have been conducted differently, but whether it ought to have occurred at all. It is considered a classic of anticolonialism by those who think—as I do not—that the terms colonialism and anticolonialism are satisfactory tools of interpretation; and among the questions we may ask is what capacity its authors display for depicting the others in all these encounters as having histories of their own and acting in them. Are they unintelligible to the *philosophe;* are they merely those Others about whom we now write so much? These are questions to which it is not certain that a reading of the *Histoire des Deux Indes* will supply the answers; but such a reading may investigate the historical situation—including the situation in the history of historiography—in which such questions may have arisen for something like the first time.

There is one more sense in which it is necessary to understand what kind of reading of the *Histoire des Deux Indes* this is. It is a work produced by at least two authors, men of powerful and independent minds; one of them was Diderot, and how he got on with Raynal must be a story worth telling in its own right. Since it is now more or less known which passages are his and which are not,[3] it would be possible, and certainly will be very valuable, to decompose the text of the *Histoire* into the performances of the several authors and to ask at every point what Diderot or what Raynal was doing or intending to do by writing that. I shall not attempt this; it would involve constructing an intellectual biography of each author, an interpretation of the corpus of his *œuvre* and interpreting each and every locution making up the *Histoire* in the universe of contexts supplied by these operations. The Diderot industry has been active and productive for many years, and a Raynal industry is now well in motion.[4] I approach the *Histoire des Deux Indes*, however, with a more modest program. I propose treating it as a text which Raynal, Diderot and perhaps others produced among them, and which may therefore perform actions not exactly intended by any of them; I propose reading it to see what it says, when the reader is engaged in finding out how Enlightened minds wrote history and may therefore have read it when written by someone else. For this reason I shall try to avoid authorial attributions and will employ such locutions as "the *Histoire* says," or "the authors of this passage seem to mean," as convenient intellectual shorthand. This will be particularly the case if I have to do with an authorial *moi* who makes his appearance—usually in floods of tears—from time to time in the narrative; I shall not ask

[3]For a critical bibliography and an English translation of some of these contributions, see John Hope Mason and Robert Workler, eds. and trans., *Diderot: Political Writings, Cambridge Texts in the History of Political Thought* (Cambridge, 1992). Gianluigi Goggi, ed., *Denis Diderot: Pensées detachés contributions à l'Histoire des Deux Indes* (Siena, 1976); Michèle Duchet, *Diderot et l'Histoire des Deux Indes, ou l'écriture fragmentaire* (Paris, 1978).

[4]A critical edition of the *Histoire des Deux Indes* is being prepared by an international editorial committee for publication by the Voltaire Foundation.

whose *moi* he is or whether he is the same *moi* all the time. In considering the text as a whole, it is true, I beg the question whether it is a text which expects to be so read; but it cannot be guaranteed against such readers as myself, and I shall offer an account of what readers may have experienced from the text in the past.

Let us then begin to read. Gibbon's *Decline and Fall* ends its narrative with the Turkish capture of Constantinople in 1453. The *Histoire des Deux Indes*—written and published before Gibbon's work began to appear in 1776—opens its narrative with the voyage of Vasco da Gama in 1497–1498; that of Columbus five years earlier enters the *Histoire* later in its construction. The Portuguese appearance in the Red Sea, the Persian Gulf and the approaches to India is presented as a response not to the fall of Constantinople, but as an anticipation of the Turkish conquest of Mamluk Egypt in 1517;[5] and here we begin to read a world history based on images of non-European predominance. In the world before da Gama (we are told) there were two principal zones of trade and commerce: the basins of the eastern Mediterranean and the western Indian Ocean (the seas linking China with Indonesia may have been a third), and Egypt had been the land bridge linking as well as separating these two.[6] When Egypt was detached from the Roman ecumene and incorporated in the Muslim, Indo-Arabian commerce built up a system in the Indian Ocean as far west as Suez and as far east as Canton; and centuries later, the Crusades and the Italian trading cities created a system in the Mediterranean linking Egypt and Syria with the distant lands of Europe. The Ottoman conquests were threatening to link the two systems in a Turkish-dominated global monopoly, ex-

---

[5]Guillaume-Thomas Raynal, *Histoire Philosophique et Politique des Etablissemens et du Commerce des Européens dans les Deux Indes*, 4 vols. (Geneva, 1780), I, 80. This is the edition most heavily enlarged by Diderot's contributions.

[6]*Histoire*, I, 28–30.

cluding a Europe in danger of being conquered itself, when the Portuguese came round the Cape of Good Hope, established themselves in the Gulf and the Red Sea, and opened up an era in which the Indian Ocean's commerce came under the control of the Europeans, who had arrived from the remote lands of the north-west by means of a recently-acquired capacity for oceanic navigation. They appear as Vikings, and Europe as a kind of Afro-Asian Scandinavia.

This is a story of European triumphs; is it therefore an epic of European triumphalism? Not in any obvious sense, if we look at the *Histoire's* incessant denunciations of the cruelty, greed and fanaticism of the European conquest of the planetary ocean, which it represents explicitly as a barbarian invasion occurring on a global scale; or if we look at the account it gives of the state of Europe in the thousand years preceding the Portuguese and Spanish voyages. To begin with, the term "Europe" is used with some degree of geographic and historical specificity; it is distinct from the Mediterranean, Nilotic and Fertile Crescent ecumene formerly controlled by Rome. It lies to the north and west; there is no account of its geography, though later in the *Histoire* we are told that France lies at its center, between the Atlantic and the western Mediterranean. Historically, it consists of a group of successor cultures and successor states to the Roman empire, and it is the product of the thousand years of barbarism and religion which succeeded that empire's fall in its extreme western provinces. There is a significant passage in which we are told that the ancient Greeks, those Mediterranean culture-heroes, emerged straight from the hands of nature. An Afrocentric historian might be justified in seeing this statement as one more proof of European cultural arrogance; but in the *Histoire* it is preface to the dictum that whereas in Greece we find men, in Europe we find only slaves.[7] They are the product of Roman tyranny, feudal tyranny and ecclesiastical tyranny, acting in succession and

[7]*Ibid.*, 4–7.

reinforcing one another; and though the voyages to India and America were part of a process by which Europeans emancipated themselves from their frightful past, they occurred early enough in that process to ensure that they were still barbarians and acted barbarously in their encounters with the other peoples of the planet. We are beginning to find that what we call Eurocentricity can be the product of European self-hatred as well as of European self-flattery; and the two together led the *Histoire* to a historization of what Europe was.

The central theme of Enlightenment historiography was the Christian millennium, the eleven centuries of darkness, barbarism and religion, shaped by the Emperor Constantine's alliance with the Christian Church, the collapse of imperial authority over its western and northern provinces, and the rise of a clerical empire exercised from papal Rome. Gibbon's *Decline and Fall* is a history of those centuries, but it differs from Voltaire's *Essai sur les Moeurs*, Robertson's *View of the Progress of Society in Europe*, and Raynal's *Histoire des Deux Indes* in breaking off before the advent of modernity, conventionally situated at the end of the fifteenth century, when innovations and inventions including the advent of the compass had begun the emancipation of Europe from its clerical and feudal past. Gibbon did not write the history of modernity in this sense, or rather he followed an older style in locating the beginnings of modern, i.e., non-ancient, history at the outset of the medieval period. Those for whom modern meant non-medieval, however, were acutely aware that the end of the fifteenth century had been succeeded by nearly two centuries of the Wars of Religion, from which it was a primary purpose of Enlightenment to effect an escape; and they were beginning to distance themselves from the sixteenth and seventeenth centuries, and ask whether those dark times were over yet. "Modern" thus came to mean "non-early modern."

The *Histoire des Deux Indes* joins its peers in identifying as the engines of emancipation the spread of enlightened philosophy—meaning the de-Christianization of social authority—and the in-

crease of commerce; and the growth of a global commerce which is
its subject of course fits into that. But it does so in anything but an
unproblematic way. Certainly, it opens with a song of praise (written
by Diderot) of everything which has made human beings sociable
and happy and free of religious terrors, ending with the words "c'est
le commerce, c'est le commerce."[8] But the nineteen books which
follow are one long denunciation of a commerce which has been extractive and monopolistic, the product of the fact that Europeans are
still barbarous and the cause of the fact that they have been barbarians in their dealings with others; and though we go in search of the
historical conditions in which a global commerce will become universally benign, we discover more and more reasons, often meta-
historical, why this is a utopia and may be inherently unrealizable.
This is a truly European philosophy of history, a product of Europe's
quarrel with its own history, and it provides the historical scheme
into which the histories of the peoples outside Europe may or may
not be fitted. If they had written their own histories of the global
encounter—and why am I assuming they did not?—would they
have used this scheme, and if not what others?

Enlightened historiography—and to some extent Protestant before it—had already identified as a principal *infâme* the disputatious
habit of mind which made Europeans ready to kill one another over
disagreements in theology which, *la saine philosophie* insisted, were
inherently insoluble and therefore about nothing at all. It was this
which had made Jesuits and Dominicans travel all the way to Peking
and impose their controversies on the mystified literati of a civilization supposedly free from metaphysics and disputation;[9] without it
the Portuguese might not have appeared in the Indian Ocean or
Columbus in the Caribbean, and yet there was a clear connection
between its persistence in the European *mentalité* and the undevel-

---

[8]*Ibid.*, 3.
[9]The theme of the closing chapter of Voltaire's *Siècle de Louis XIV*.

oped nature of their commerce. Minds fully socialized by the exchange of goods would be set free from metaphysics. This historiography, furthermore, already possessed some outlines of a world history of religions and philosophies designed to explain why Europeans had become addicted to metaphysics to such an extent. Islam—which we must remember was the most modern and recent of the great religions—enjoyed high respect because of its monotheism, which was unitarian and had bypassed the unending Christian debates about the Trinity, the Incarnation, and the Redemption, and because it did not furnish a clergy with authority independent of the civil order. And yet the *Histoire*, while telling the tale of the Portuguese circumnavigation of both Africa and the Islamic ecumene, insists that a Turkish conquest of Europe, while no more than the popes, priests and kings richly deserved, would have been fatal to enlightenment because there is no religion in the world as hostile to liberty as Islam is. The stereotype of oriental despotism shows itself here, but there is also language which suggests that only European Christians, torn as they are between social and spiritual authority, will ever reach the point of crying out that man is born free.[10] We catch sight of a dialectic which closes the circle between self-hatred and self-love; only because Europeans are in some ways the worst are they perhaps capable of being the best; and would there be a history of liberty in a civilization as undisputatious as the Chinese?

The *Histoire* sets on foot an enquiry into the civilizations of the Indian Ocean and the China Seas in the order in which the Europeans encounter them. That of India is as ancient as Islam is modern, and there is already in place a historical model which connects it with the prehistory of Europe. Because the Brahmins are the premier caste, the Hindu must be the most priest-ridden of civilizations, and to the Enlightened mind priests are close to being the origin of

---

[10]*Histoire*, I, 82–83.

all social evils; Hindu culture is therefore presented as the outcome
of the primary error committed by nearly all legislators—Brahma is
taken to have been a human legislator[11]—that of claiming divine
inspiration to make their laws acceptable, and so opening the way
for priests to exploit the myth of the sacred.[12] Yet this does not explain the history of Christian Europe, since Jesus was not a legislator
even if Moses was; and the *Histoire* falls back on a second model, in
which the magian religions of western Eurasia—Vedic, Zoroastrian,
but not yet Buddhist since so little was known of it—are seen as
originating all metaphysical dispute over essences, which by reason
of its unresolvability is the foundation of dogmatic authority, and
which seems to have passed from India to Iran to Greece, where it
took Pythagorean, Platonic and Aristotelian forms and became the
origin of Christian theology and scholastic disputation.[13] In the encounter with India, therefore, the Europeans are still within the pattern of their own most ancient history; they pass beyond it only
when, in a most important transition, they enter the Chinese ecumene, where the legislator did not make the primal mistake.

The myth of Confucius provided Enlightened deism with its
counter-myth. He was supposed to have set up a religion without
theology, whose rituals institutionalized the worship of nothing but
the social virtues which were natural to humanity; to have succeeded in establishing a natural religion, whereas Socrates had been
executed and Jesus deified. China was therefore the deists' utopia;
but it is remarkable that the *Histoire des Deux Indes*, whose authors
were not deists but rather atheists in their personal beliefs, follows
up a chapter on China as utopia with one presenting it as dystopia—
and that the main charge against its government is that it has pro-

[11]*Ibid.*, 59.
[12]*Ibid.*, 61.
[13]*Ibid.*, 49–51.

duced a crisis in over-population, so grave that *ni moeurs ni police* are any longer possible.[14] The normal premise of Enlightened political theory is that the business of government is to encourage population, by stamping out clerical and monastic celibacy; so it is a question of how the problem of population excess has arisen. The *Histoire* leaves it open whether the utopian or the dystopian account of China is to be preferred; but the former has in an important sense the last word, since it is observed that if this account be the true one, and if the history of China does consist in nothing but the preservation of customs embodying the sociability natural to mankind, then this is the true history of humanity, and the history we know— the history of Europe, the history of false consciousness, the history of barbarism and religion—is nothing but the record of human crimes and follies.[15] If the authors were reduced to the choice between China as utopia and as dystopia, we should say that they had no means of writing China as history at all; but we have also arrived at a point where they are saying that if history be defined as the maintenance of nature, then history as we have it is not history at all. It would be simpler language to define history as the human fall from nature, and this is what we shall find the *Histoire* doing when it enters the New World.

But so far we are in the Old World; the conquest of the planetary ocean is leading to the exploration of the continent of which Europe is a promontory, inhabited by ancient literate civilizations which share history with Europe as far as India and enter alternative history only when we reach China. Both these histories are ancient, uninterrupted by such catastrophes as the Christian Middle Ages have been for Europe, and therefore denied the occasion to remake themselves as modern. The only Asian culture to which the *Histoire* accords something of a "modern" history is, interestingly, Japan. This

---

[14]*Ibid.*, 127.
[15]*Ibid.*, 99–100.

is an island culture, and the *Histoire* is disposed to the view that there is something unnatural about islands; they are broken-off fragments of continents, inhabited by populations who fled there to escape catastrophes;[16] violent, heroic people with crazy ideas of their own independence (Corsica? Britain? The New World itself?). In the case of Japan, an account of Shinto as a natural religion, a jovial country paganism with festivals and ritualized sex, leads to a meditation on the role of women in religion, the chief point of which is that as puberty and virginity together are conducive to visions and ecstasies, it is in the interest of priests to prolong the latter condition as long as possible.[17] In Japan, moreover, there is also a gloomy life-denying religion, with monasteries and hideous visions of the punishments of hell, practiced by the Budsoists, disciples of a certain Buds; and there follows a not imperceptive passage on how such a religion has combined with the warrior ethos to produce a culture as violent and romantic as that of the Chinese is calm and rational. Only a massive infusion of Confucianism could have produced an *état policé* in Japan; but we hear later how Portuguese missionaries arrived in the islands just as the violence of feudal warfare was giving way to the ruthless tyranny of one Taycosama, and the discontented warriors found in Christianity a religion much to the tastes they had already, with the further attraction that its foreignness made it an ideology of protest.[18] Japan, in short, because it is insular and barbaric, possesses a capacity for making its own history by cultural borrowing, a history modern in the sense that it is partly shaped by response to an intrusion; a capacity not accorded to the major continental civilizations, which remain what they were in antiquity and have known no middle ages. If the authors of the *Histoire* had understood that the Tokugawa regime shut itself off from outside influences, while strength-

[16]*Ibid.*, 91, 410–11.
[17]*Ibid.*, 130–33.
[18]*Ibid.*, 167–68.

ening itself by a massive institutionalization of Confucian values, their estimate and probably their esteem of its character would have been enhanced.

They had, as this instance shows, no coherent understanding at all of Buddhism as a world religion distributed throughout Asia. There is mention of Buddou, a mediator between God and man, worshiped among the Sinhalese of Sri Lanka;[19] but he is never linked with Buds of Japan, and when at quite another point in the book there is a fairly benign account of the Lamaist religion of Tibet, this is said to have expanded as far as China, but is not linked with any name suggestive of the Buddha.[20] Yet Raynal and Diderot should have known of Joseph de Guignes' four-volume *Histoire des Huns, Turcs et Mogols*, in which may be found a detailed if simple account of the Buddha and his teachings, together with the suggestion that this is one more religion of the magian west Eurasian kind, possibly akin to Manicheism.[21] De Guignes had also attacked the myth of isolated and unchanging Chinese continuity, saying that his studies of dynastic interactions with the Central Asian nomads showed Chinese history to be as full of wars, revolutions and barbarian invasions as that of any other great empire. It would not have been beyond the reach of the authors of the *Histoire des Deux Indes* to have constructed a model of Chinese history akin to that they had of Roman and European, in which the Confucians would have played the role of Cicero and the Stoics, the Buddhists that of the Christians. This would have been a Eurocentric history, certainly, but there would have been movement and a tension of opposites in it, instead of the static rotation of the cycles of Cathay. Yet it did not occur to them

[19]*Ibid.*, 87.
[20]*Ibid.*, 616–18.
[21]J. G. A. Pocock, "Gibbon and the Idol Fo; Chinese and Christian History in the Enlightenment," in David S. Katz and Jonathan I. Israel, eds., *Sceptics, Millenarians and Jews* (Leiden, 1990), 15–34.

to construct it. In this they were, to some extent, the heirs of the Jesuits; Matteo Ricci and his colleagues had been so intent on their alliance with the Confucian literati that they had followed them in denying any role to the Taoist and Buddhist presences in Chinese culture. The deist and even the atheist *philosophes* had followed the Jesuits in representing Confucianism as the last stronghold of the natural religion of mankind; and as we have seen, they were left with China as an alternative history, or rather a specimen of the incompatibility of history with nature.

The *Histoire* has been conducting a survey—situated somewhere on the border between natural history and civil history—of the societies of southern and eastern Asia, seen in the maritime perspective created by the European encounter. This has been interwoven, first with a natural and *encyclopédiste* history of the seeds and spices which attract the ships of the Europeans, second with a commercial history of the latter, who arrive in successive waves of Portuguese, Dutch, English and French, and are successively misled by their still half-barbaric understanding of commerce into creating economies of plunder, extraction and monopoly. These react upon the national economies of the European states; the chartered companies endowed with monopolies inhibit the circulation and investment of capital, and set up cycles of war and indebtedness which corrupt European society as they plunder Asian. The Portuguese collapse altogether and their economy passes under English control, while the sections on Dutch, English and French commerce end in each case with a polemic of the sort called "patriot" in the 1770s and 1780s, denouncing corruption and prophesying the imminent destruction of virtue and liberty, and arriving in each case at the brink of revolutionary language. What we are reading is not a triumphal history of commerce and enlightenment hand in hand together, but a denunciation of the failure of that vision; and what the Europeans are doing to the Asians is set in the context of what they are doing to themselves. When the Europeans are harangued as "barbarians" and the authorial *moi* tells them how much he hates them and how gladly he would take arms on the side of those they have oppressed,[22] the term "barbarian" is not being used relativistically, to adopt an Indian or Chinese scheme of civilized values and tell the Europeans they are barbarians in Asian eyes; the aim is to tell them they are barbarians by their own standards, historical as well as ethical, who have not yet enlightened themselves to the point of casting off their predatory and fanatical past. They are not only imposing a brutal exploitation on the populations they encounter; they are imposing their own disputatious and deeply unhappy culture.

This is the thrust of the harangue addressed to the "Hottentots"—the Khoi people of the Cape of Good Hope—adjuring them to flee and hide themselves in their deserts at the approach of Van Riebeek.[23] Yet a chapter or so later we are reading quite an idyllic account of the rustic economy of the Dutch settlers around Table Bay, and even the pastoral economy of the *trekboeren* further out, and it is remarked that this would have been a good system for the "Hottentots" to join if they had not died out in an epidemic in 1714.[24] Once the unhappy and unenlightened Europeans have arrived, the only hope for the subjected peoples or for them is the growth of commerce and enlightenment; and Asian or African society and history can be assessed as well as European, to assess the prospects for this happening. But the canons of progress, while rooted in a deep hatred of Europe's past and present, are still European and the hatred is a self-hatred, intimately linked with the disputatious false consciousness it seeks to replace; the Europeans are still unhappy and know it. And if European canons are being used to assess Asian history, there is space for stereotypes to emerge. That of "oriental despotism" appears, because there is need to decide whether the Asian cultivator enjoys the security of tenure with-

---

[22]*Histoire*, I, 206.
[23]*Ibid.*, 205–6
[24]*Ibid.*, 211.

out which exchange and commerce simply cannot appear; and the
Histoire does argue at length that since India is a despotic society, the
replacement of company monopoly by free trade can be introduced
only by degrees.[25] China remains at a distance until the debate about
its form of government is resolved, and Japan is not again mentioned
at all.

There are two interacting sets of reasons why the *Histoire des
Deux Indes* is self-inhibited from allowing the Asian civilizations
what may be termed an active history, i.e., one which they make for
themselves. The first is that they lack a middle ages, a descent from
ancient civility into barbarism and religion, priestcraft and corruption, from which Europeans have found that the only way out is
through commerce and enlightenment. The circle is closed; European inferiority becomes, as it did for Voltaire, the precondition of
European superiority, and the oceanic world-system is a revolution
in European history which Europe is imposing upon the globe. The
second is that Asians lack an active commerce, in control of its own
exporting and importing, which may be the necessary precondition
of enlightenment. It is the Europeans who have circumnavigated
Africa and appeared in the Indian Ocean and the China Seas; what
world history would have been like if the Indo-Arabs or the Chinese
had appeared in the Bay of Biscay and the English Channel is not
considered, even in fantasy. In these two senses, then, the Asians
lack an active history, a modern history; and there has appeared the
alternative of regarding them as inhabiting a universe which is not
that of history at all. Perhaps Hindu culture remains entrapped in
caste and oriental despotism, imprisoned in customs which date
from the mistakes of the legislators and the rise of the priests; perhaps Chinese culture is a utopia, where the legislator made no mistakes and customs which embody pure natural sociability have
reigned ever since. Utopia, however, is known to be utopia, and the

[25]*Ibid.*, 687–88, 704.

authors of the *Histoire* are impelled to provide a matching picture of China as dystopia, adding that only the curiosity of voyaging and philosophic Europeans can enquire which it is in fact. Japan, which is allowed some desperate capacity to shape for itself a modern—or a medieval?—history, is an island society and therefore deeply anomalous and self-absorbed; we hear no more of it.

This opposition between history as the Europeans have shaped it, and something which is either history in another sense or altogether other than history, becomes more pronounced as the three remaining volumes of the *Histoire* in its 1780 edition turn away from the Indian Ocean to consider the settlements, commerce, and above all the conquests of the Europeans in Mexico and the southern American continent, in what it calls the great archipelago of the Americas, and lastly in the northern continent from the Gulf of Mexico to the Hudson Bay. Here we are no longer in what begins to be called the Old World, the Eurasian or Afro-Eurasian continent with its documented ancient civilizations and its ancient history from which that of Europe may be traced. We are in the *nouveau monde*, where the records of ancient civilizations have disappeared and it can be doubted if they even existed; a world of which it can easily be said that it possesses no history capable of explaining it, so that it must be explained in some other way. The New World is of course the great Other of early modern European experience; Asians, even Chinese, are not so much others as other selves who may share a history with "us" (from which I draw the conclusion that the concept of Other ought to be applied more discriminatingly than it has sometimes been). But the first question asked about the human inhabitants of the New World had been whether they were humans at all; the second was whether they existed in history or only in nature, and from this there could arise, alternatively, a downgrading of the natural man or a downgrading of history. The *Histoire* devotes three volumes to the New World and never returns to the Eurasian Old; and it can be (and was) said that what set out as an *Histoire des Deux Indes* became an *Histoire des Deux Mondes*. I shall argue, however, that it is so far based on an opposition between history and nature that while on one level it offers programs for an incorporation of the New World in an active history of enlightenment, on another it asks whether it would not have been better if the *deux mondes* had never been linked by discovery and human societies had remained in their natural ignorance of one another; that is, in the world of nature. This is the point at which the *Histoire* irrevocably becomes something which Gibbon would never have written.

The New World is populated, and its history is made if it has one, by three sets of humans: savages, settlers and slaves. The settlers provide the historical dynamic; they expropriate the savages and import the slaves, and if the process of enlightenment through commerce is to occur at all, it must occur through them. The savages ask, sometimes through their natural eloquence but more often through their silence and even their death, whether it was necessary for this process to occur at all and whether humans should not have been left in their natural condition. The slaves ask the same question through their presence, and raise the no less troubling question of what they are to become as a consequence of their enslavement, which is a condition neither natural nor historical. The *Histoire* ends with the settlers necessarily at center stage; there are programs for incorporating the settled Americas (all three of them) in the commercial and enlightened history of Europe; but there is a chorus of questions asking whether such programs are natural, utopian or historically viable. Diderot said that this was the book out of which a Brutus would be born; but if there is a revolutionary program in the *Histoire des Deux Indes*, it is the radically insecure product of all these questions.

In dealing with the savages, I shall refer to them by the French word *sauvages*, in the hope of distancing ourselves a little from the vulgar meanings of the term—not that these are by any means absent—and emphasizing that we are concerned with *bons sauvages* or *sauvages innocents* in the sense associated with Rousseauan social theory. Whatever it was that made Diderot regard Rousseau with an almost terrified detestation, it was not any rejection on his part of

the myth of natural society as an idyllic moment before the knowledge of good and evil and the fall into history, towards which we
could not find our way back without discovering that there was no
moment in history or before it at which such a condition could be
said to have existed. In the *Supplément au Voyage de Bougainville*, Diderot depicted a repressed and miserable French monk in dialogue
with Tahitians who were *bons sauvages* in the sense that their society
was wholly natural—the men being interested only in morality and
the women only in maternity—but added that from the moment
that every society began to form customs which differentiated it
from any other, there had been "civil war in the cave" between what
individuals were by nature and what they became by custom; and
yet, without customs there could be no society. Among the cultures
of the New World immediately before their encounter with the Old,
some are permitted to have approached as near as it is possible to
come to the primal innocence which never quite existed; there are
those island populations—why are islanders suddenly innocent?—
trustfully welcoming the goldhungry and bloodthirsty Spaniards
who will be their conquerors and slavemasters tomorrow; and of
these it can be asked whether the natural condition, deeply unintel-
ligent though it is, should not be preferred to the knowledge of good
and evil which comes with history. All this recurred, of course, in
that copious literature of 1992 accompanying the quinquecentennial
of Columbus's voyage of 1492 which depicted the Europeans as invaders and despoilers of paradise; but the authors of the *Histoire des Deux
Indes*—and of course one does think of Diderot here—were entirely
clear that paradise is crucially important to us because it never existed and yet we cannot escape it. The one population of the New
World which is absolutely and naturally sociable is not human at all;
it consists of the beavers, who are *citoyens* of a *république, jaloux de
leur propriété*, all the more because they are so by instinct, un-cursed
by self-consciousness and language.[26] The religion of nature, in 1780

[26]See Volume III of the 1775 Geneva edition, 152–53.

as today, has anti-humanism as one of its outcomes; we are accursed because we ate the apple that taught us to know and say we were eating an apple, and original sin has become history.

The human populations of the pre-Columbian New World were not all *bons sauvages*. Those of Mexico were not idyllic food-gatherers, but hunting societies—savages as the term was used in Scottish social theory—in which agriculture was left to the women, an employment wholly unsuited to their vulnerable and maternal bodies, while the men went off on long hunting trips highly conducive to the formation of pederastic relationships. Cortes' concubine Dona Marina, and other women who deserted to the Spaniards, did so (says the *Histoire*) out of a frenzied desire for straight sex,[27] and probably maternity also; whether they got what they wanted is another question. The Tlaxcalans are permitted to have formed themselves into a Spartan or Roman republic, but the *Histoire* is inveterately hostile to the suggestion that either the Aztec or the Inca systems had reached the condition of highly civilized empires. There seem to have been several reasons for this. In condemning the image of Mesoamerican imperial grandeur as an invention of the conquistadors and clerics trying to magnify their own achievements, the *Histoire* is maintaining the image of Spaniards as essentially barbaric until the dawn of Bourbon enlightenment, and slighting or silencing the intellectual and other achievements of baroque and clerical culture in Hapsburg Spanish America. There is indeed a deeply ambivalent love-hate relationship with the Jesuits, very typical of the *philosophes*, running through the work; but the Jesuits are praised, and very highly praised, not when they are inventing a historiography for Mesoamerica or furnishing Peru with Manco Capac, a legislator who might have turned out the Confucius of the New World, but when they are taking innocent natural societies under their protection in Paraguay or California. Perhaps they were on the way to transforming *sauvages*

[27]*Histoire*, II, 25–26.

into cultivators in a system of commerce; but that this should have been the enterprise of priests of all people, and Jesuits of all priests, is an aspect of the utter reversal of values that marks Spanish empire in America and reduces it to a confrontation between Indian *bons sauvages* and Spanish *barbares farouches*. The *Histoire* is intent on maintaining this image, on depicting Spanish empire as an exhausted enterprise, to be rescued only by an enlightened French imperialism; and perhaps it is necessary to deny the Incas a history, so that the scene shall consist only of natural society, present barbarism, and potential commerce. To pursue this theme we turn from the *sauvages* to the settlers.

Perhaps that is to allow too much play to alliteration. In the first instance, the Europeans who appear in the archipelago and Mexico are not settlers at all, and it is uncertain whether they will become or remain so. To begin with, they are voyagers, explorers and masterless men; and there are passages in which it is seriously asked whether the seaman, the traveler, even the enlightened voyager like Bougainville, has not abandoned his *patrie* and his humanizing social attachments, so that he traverses the globe directed only by his solitary passions, of which curiosity may not be the least dangerous.[28] Rousseau might have asked such a question; to find it asked by the authors of the *Histoire des Deux Indes* is to find it asked in a context of commerce and enlightenment, in such a way as to render these concepts more problematic. Enlightenment was held to be the child of commerce; only by exchanging goods and ideas with each other could humans hope to understand their world and themselves, and to enlarge the scope of exchange was to enlarge the sphere of understanding. But enlightenment was also held to lead back to the discovery of natural sociability, and this could very easily mean the return to natural society, the charmed and limited sphere within which one formed one's natural attachments and constructed a self as happy as

[28]*Ibid.*, II, 357–58; III, 2, 331–32.

the socialized self could hope to be. Hence the myth of the paternal family, the idyllic village, the virtuous republic, beyond which one should never stray; hence the mirage of the *bons sauvages,* even the republic of the beavers, the state in which natural sociability was guaranteed—unless the natural man should turn out to be a solitary vagrant after all. But if commerce was a necessity, how were these happy self-sufficiencies to trade with one another? There are hints in the *Histoire* of the ancient myth of commerce without encounter, that point on the Silk Road at which one group lay down their trade-goods and retire, and the other remove the goods and lay down a just equivalent, and both are satisfied without seeing or speaking to one another; commerce in the Lockean state of nature, before the invention of a medium of exchange. If one's needs were met without the distracting sight or speech of the Other, they would never be enlarged to the point where they corrupted one; one would never learn more than one needed to know. But what then was the antecedent implicit in "c'est le commerce, c'est le commerce?"

And once embarked upon salt water, what if commerce could not be extended without sending out navigators and expatriates, men by definition set free from social attachments and therefore incapable of commerce? The first trader was a pirate or a Viking; how could he learn commerce as a social art? Social philosophy was for land animals, developing their relations with each other by appropriating the earth, that is the solider yet not too solid surfaces of the geosphere; the frightening thing about compass navigation was that it had given Europeans the capacity for simultaneous encounter, through the ungoverned and unappropriated medium of water, with all the landbound cultures of the planet. In theory, the first encounters were liable to be made by desocialized and lawless men coming from the sea, the "sharks walking on land" of Greg Dening's imagination or (I hope) translation.[29] In history according to the Enlight-

[29]*Mr. Bligh's Bad Language: Passion, Power and Theatre on the Bounty* (Cambridge, 1992).

ened vision, this had come at a moment when Europeans possessed the barbaric energy, not yet disciplined, civilized or softened by commerce, necessary for these oceanic conquests but not yet capable of the philosophically very difficult task of establishing commerce with those they encountered; nor had the *Histoire* found the means of attributing a capacity for active commerce to those beyond Europe. In setting up the global encounter as one between the historical and the natural man, the authors repeated on a planetary scale the juristic problem of the state of nature, and at the same time invited European man to revisit the contrast between history and nature within his own culture.

The masculine pronouns are justified because this is specifically a problem of men adventuring without women. Behind the navigators come the conquistadors, characterized at the level of historical narrative by an insistence that Spaniards were still Visigoths engaged in a Reconquista, barbarians who had learned nothing from the centuries of European feudalism. Spain is denied any place in the Italian- and French-centered narrative of European recovery and renaissance, much as the Portuguese had been in recounting their crusade into the Indian Ocean; and this enables the *Histoire* to tell the whole tale of conquest in the Caribbean, Mexico and Peru as that of a barbarian invasion, not in a merely rhetorical sense but in the historically literal sense that the conquistadors were much like their Gothic Ancestors, Vikings adventuring in search of gold, loot, land and the labor of others, accompanied, however, by a legion of celibate priests with ambitions of their own. In an ideal world, the *Histoire* pauses to remark, the way to colonize new lands would have been to send out equal contingents of men and women to intermarry with the natives and set up productive economies;[30] how they would have been prevented from marrying each other, and setting up lily-white aristocracies of sahibs and memsahibs, is not explained. The

----

[30]*Ibid.*, II, 358.

problem of the all-male population shift is taken further in some highly interesting studies of the pirate or semi-pirate communities of the Caribbean: first the buccaneers proper, the *boucaniers* of the Honduras coast, whose bonded male partnerships are described in terms that make one think of the Indian hunter cultures described earlier;[31] second, the *flibustiers*, filibusters or Brethren of the Coast, who are permitted a high sense of barbaric honor and whose extraordinary energies and daring—denied to the heirs of the conquistadors, by now sinking into the lethargy of creole culture—are explained by saying that because they were Dutch, French and English, they came from lands long disciplined by law, which made greater the energies that exploded on the removal of the law's restraints.[32]

If the authors of the *Histoire* had known more about the history of Castile, it might have occurred to them that the same could have been said about the Spaniards. The tragedy of Spanish settlement and creole society, however, is said to be that, being semi-barbarians who knew little about cultivation and less about commerce, they obtained control of an infinite supply of Indian labor, with which to exploit an infinite reserve of mined silver, and thus set up a purely extractive economy which did no good to them and much damage to Europe. The history of the Spanish empire in the New World now runs on familiar lines: first the *destruccion de las Indias*, the *leyenda negra* or American holocaust—there was little in the polemic of 1992 which had not been told before—second, the history of Spanish decline, of how they shipped bullion to Europe with which they knew how to start a war cycle but did not know how to invest, until the Dutch, the English and belatedly the French laid hold of it and created a capitalist economy from which Spain was shut out. The history of America is being enacted in Europe; in America there is going on the destruction of natural society but no creation of history.

[31]*Ibid.*, 25–28.
[32]*Ibid.*, 32–54.

No European power understands how to use its establishments in America to create a system of commerce linking open markets on either side of the Atlantic; the slave societies taking shape in America have an effect similar to that of the despotic societies already existing in India. The volume on Ibero-American history concludes with an account of how the Portuguese have let their national economy run down to the point where it exists only to produce wine for the English market, while the English have obtained a monopoly for the sale of their goods in Portugal. Much of the *Histoire* from this point is a call for a French-led war of liberation from the reduction of Europe to such an English colony. It would have been better for Mesoamericans and West Africans if the Atlantic empires had never been created; it might also have been better for Europeans, but they possess the capacity to react to what has happened, and conduct a revolution which may—or which may not—bring their history closer to the promptings of nature.

Settlers and slaves dominate the volume on the history of the American archipelago, from which it is presumed that the *sauvages* have disappeared through genocide. Now we encounter the problem of the Creoles. The history of the filibusters—that case study in European neo-barbarism—is over; the Spanish and Portuguese on the two continents are conducting economies dominated by the extraction of silver through native slave labor, and both sexes are sliding into the blend of lethargy and passion which characterizes creole culture as it anciently characterized barbaric. In the islands, increasingly dominated by the French, the scene is different. On the one hand, there is intensive cultivation, and agriculture can lead to commerce and enlightenment. On the other, it is cultivation of a single crop; but by the end of the volume we are being told that the sugar islands are the key to the whole system of global commerce; and the cultivation is being carried on by African slave labor imported for the purpose. The African continent enters the *histoire des deux mondes*, and we are left in no doubt that Africans are selling Africans to European purchasers. As European trade increases the demand for

goods along the West African coasts, there is increasing need to pro-
cure and sell slaves to assure one's buying power; and this economy
expands up the rivers into the heart of the continent.[33] It is a classic
case of how a monopolistic extractive economy works: the Hudson
Bay Company operates in exactly the same way to drive the Indians
to make war on the beavers, and there are hints of an analogy with
the English domination of Europe through a universal empire of the
seas. Whether the heart of the African continent is yet a heart of
darkness is not clear: on the one hand it is clearly possible that the
slaves are being drawn from *sauvage* populations in the state of pre-
historic innocence, but on the other a complete *philosophe* history of
how the human intellect works is here erected on the sole foundation that it is very hard to explain why Africans have dark skins[34]—
an ominous reminder of the obsessive importance this problem
could assume.

What is to become of the transplanted African populations in
the *nouveau-monde* is a question raised but not analyzed. As the history of the archipelago is reviewed island by island, we learn a good
deal about the Maroon wars in Jamaica and Guyana, and there are
prophetic imaginings of a general slave rebellion and a vengeful warrior leader who may emerge at its head—a sort of Spartacus, or a
Dessalines before the event.[35] But the problem of slaves and the
problem of settlers are collapsed into one as the program which the
Histoire is being written to promote begins to emerge. This is nothing other than the use of Enlightenment as an instrument of a
French and Spanish, European and American, war of liberation directed against the peace of 1763 and the British monopoly of oceanic and continental world power it is supposed to have entailed. I

[33]*Ibid.*, III, 147.
[34]*Ibid.*, 128–29.
[35]*Ibid.*, 307–8. Cf. Michel-Rolph Trouillot, *Silencing the Past: Power
and the Production of History* (Boston, 1995), ch. 3.

will not go into the question of what support from what French ministry which of the book's authors were receiving, but it is hard to read the text without guessing that it was there. Commerce, let us remember, was the necessary engine in bringing about enlightenment, but a commerce set up by still half-barbarous Europeans had proceeded by way of slavery and monopoly and had created more new barbarisms than it had abolished old; there are very few Enlightened heroes in the narrative of the *Histoire*. The British ascendancy attained in 1763 is the last and greatest of the monopolies, and will complete the corruption of British politics if it is not checked in time. There must be a European league to establish a complete system of free trade between Europe and the Americas, and this can only be achieved by the re-creation of a strong French navy, a theme to which the *Histoire* many times returns. The rhetoric of navalism entails an image of France as the mistress of Euro-Atlantic culture, situated at the heart of that ill-defined area called Europe and assured of her dominance of its culture through her control of the fashion industries.[36] We are reminded here that Enlightenment was always capable of criticizing itself. Luxury and vanity are among the engines of emancipation, and if you ask the *sauvage* whether he is unhappy and the *homme civilisé* whether he is happy, the answer in both cases will be no.[37] We have entered the world of the pursuit of happiness, and the creation of new needs ensures that we won't catch it. History is an open-ended process, and once we have left the savage state we are in every sense obliged to press on.

What this program entails for the Americas is the conversion of extractive and slave economies into systems capable of an active and therefore an internal commerce, based on free, productive and wage labor. How this is to be achieved in Brazil and Peru is not much considered, but when the *Histoire*'s eye is on the mainly French islands,

[36]*Histoire* 1775, III, 499–500.
[37]*Ibid.*, 263.

the emancipation of slaves and their masters to take part in this process obviously becomes problematical. Not much is said about or to
the slaves—there is no alacrity to rush upon the future in which
that heroic liberator may appear—but the conversion of creoles
into *citoyens* is much, if ambivalently, discussed. At one point a creole readership is being told what a future is theirs if they can eman-
cipate themselves from the role of slavemasters; at another a wider
public is being told that, precisely because the Creoles are extractors
and slavemasters, they have no roots and no loyalties in their societies—they are in fact not settlers at all—and cannot be trusted with
economic or political management, so that (once again) a strong
navy is required.[38] The authors of the *Histoire* are not well equipped
to understand the claims of settler nationalists to be authors of their
own history, and Burke in his speech on Conciliation may be said to
have understood the part slavery might play in this better than they
did. There were many drags—this study has deliberately avoided the
great debate over the degeneration of species in the New World[39]—
retarding the Enlightened capacity to believe that European settlers
could make new history. We have only to recall the thesis that in
leaving one's *patrie* one leaves behind one's social self and enters on
a new barbarism. It does not help to assert that here one enters the
state of nature and sets about the re-creation of society and self, if
the natural space is already populated by *sauvages* with very different
ideas about what this means; one may be driven to assert that *sauvages*
have no ideas at all, settlers none of their own making, and that only
the *sauvages* are happy. The authors of the *Histoire* were close to sen-
tencing themselves to utopia; in denying that history could cross salt
water, they were close to saying that it could not exist anywhere. New
societies could never be founded, and the human condition was im-

[38]*Histoire*, III, 230; *Histoire* 1775, III, 606.
[39]Antonello Gerbi, *La Disputa del Nuovo Mondo; storia di una polemica,
1750–1900* (Milan and Naples, 1955).

possible as that of the migratory species which humans had been in fact.

The mention of Burke's 1775 speech reminds us that the *Histoire* overlaps and envisages the years of the American Revolutionary War. The sections on the *grand archipel de l'Amérique* conclude by insisting that the sugar islands are still the key to the world economy, but make it clear that a new power is rising in the north. It has already been suggested that it was a British mistake to prefer Canada to Guadalupe in 1763, since command of the Gulf of Mexico would have given them the empire of North America. There is an anticipatorily classic account of the huddled masses of Europe and Russia flocking to settle in these lands of liberty, which seem identical with Louisiana;[40] we are imagining the Mississippi Valley being colonized by ascent from New Orleans, rather than the more laborious routes up the Mohawk and over the Alleghenies. But New England shipping is being shown playing an increasingly dominant role in the economy of the sugar islands, and this part of the *Histoire* closes by saying that the future lies with the success or failure of the new republics which the English colonies have now become. It is by no means clear that they belong in the grand design of re-creating Franco-Spanish empire by enlightening it. Nor is it clear that the *Histoire*'s commitment to that design, while strong, is unambiguous.

The fourth volume of the 1780 edition reviews North America from Hudson Bay down to Florida, as a history of French and English colonization. Here we are in a temperate though at times a violently arctic climate, and the *sauvages*, instead of gentle and diminutive, grow warlike and robust—in the usual cases, with consequences savage enough. Nature is being diversified by climate and culture, and its fall into history is already under way. A temperate climate permits settlement by Europeans who farm and trade with one another as well as with the *métropole*, exterminating the *sauvages* instead of ex-

[40]*Histoire*, III, 88–89.

ploiting them, and laying the foundations of the active commerce which is the precondition of enlightenment. As the narrative survey moves south into the English colonies we look for the heartland of this enlightenment, and we find it not in New England—dismissed as a dark culture of repressed and repressive witch-hunters—but in the Quaker utopia of Pennsylvania.[41] Here the natural sociability of humanity has been re-created, and we notice that Enlightenment fastened not on Puritanism but on pietism as the form in which the Christian religion might be induced to socialize itself; Pennsylvania is in the west what the Confucian utopia is in the east. The problem is why utopia, not history, is the theater from which revolutionary enlightenment is being drawn. Because the Quakers are peaceable and unclerical, they are fitted for the occupation of land in ways instantly conducive to commerce; we might call this the Lockean vision if there were not a chapter about Locke's Constitutions of Carolina, whose proposals for slavery and feudal authority are held unworthy of an Englishman and a philosopher.[42] The *Histoire* has little to say about the circumstance that every colony south of Pennsylvania was a slave economy, and this cannot be explained as discreet language about wartime allies, since the role of slavery in the French islands remains crucial and there is every reason to ask whether tobacco and rice are creating a creole problem in the Anglo-Protestant north. Nor are the United States yet the mirage in the west which a utopian reading was to make of them. The *Histoire* concludes its vast narrative by pronouncing against unqualified support for Independence, on the grounds that the colonies severed from Europe must become either a weak confederation like those of Greece, or an imperial republic like that of Rome, a standing threat to the sugar islands and to Louisiana.[43]

[41]*Histoire* IV, 269–88.
[42]*Ibid.*, 310.
[43]*Histoire* 1775, III, 449–51; cf. *Histoire* 1780, IV, 452–55.

At the end of the *Histoire des Deux Indes* we are at an ambiguous moment in history, and still poised between history and nature. The program for using Enlightenment as an instrument of state policy is matched by a messianic reminder to the peoples of Europe that they will only recover their natural virtue and happiness when they have governments worthy of it and them; if the book had a proto-revolutionary impact, it was probably because it increased the sovereignty of sentiment over its readers' minds; and yet it reminded them that once embarked upon the enterprise of history they might pursue happiness but could not expect it. Thus far the book is a strictly European phenomenon, no less Eurocentric because it is not complacent or triumphalist but joins in the self-contempt of which it makes Europe alone truly capable; we study other cultures, it once remarks, *pour bien détester le nôtre*, but in what other culture do they say as much? There may be a sense in which it privileges the cultures of the Old World, in which ancient histories can be written and that of Europe seen to be entwined with them, above those of the New, where there is no contact and all can be relegated to the world of nature. There is of course a counter-privileging of nature above history, and the New World receives three times the attention given to the Old; but is not that because the history of Europe, and its encounter with nature, can be both rewritten and remade in a Euramerican but not a Eurasian setting? And if we read Raynal and Diderot in search of a historiography which permits those who are not Europeans—whether Asian, African or American, savages, settlers or slaves—to exist in a history of their own making, European self-condemnation will not supply us with what we are looking for. Those who want their own history must write it for themselves; if we write it for them, we must learn to accept the selves we criticize.

"The same liberties and privileges as Englishmen in England":

Law, Liberty, and Identity in the Construction of Colonial English and Revolutionary America

Jack P. Greene

During the second wave of European imperialism in the nineteenth and early twentieth century, European law frequently served the conquerors as an instrument of domination and control. In this phase of European expansion, a (usually) relatively small group of *colonizers*, acting as agents of European states and as the self-appointed bearers of European cultures, sought with varying degrees of success to subject the *colonized*, an often vast population with ancient and complex legal systems of their own, to European legal traditions and institutions.[1] By contrast, among the many settler societies established by Europeans, first in America beginning in the seventeenth century and then in other sections of the globe starting in the nineteenth century, law functioned as the principal instrument of cultural transplantation. Intending to create offshoots of the Old World in the New, the large numbers of emigrants to the colonies insisted upon taking their law with them and making it the primary foundation for the new societies they sought to establish. For these societies, European law thus became "not a tool of imperialism," a device to

---

[1] An excellent introduction to this important subject may be found among the several essays published in W. J. Mommsen and J. A. De Moor, eds., *European Expansion and Law: The Encounter of European and Indigenous Law in 19th- and 20th-Century Africa and Asia* (Oxford, 1992).

dominate whatever indigenous populations remained in their midsts, "but a concomitant of emigration. It was not imposed upon settlers but claimed by them." To "live under European law," Jorg Fisch has recently and correctly noted, "was a privilege, usually not to be granted to the indigenous people,"[2] a vivid and symbolically powerful signifier of the emigrants' deepest aspirations to retain in their new places of abode their identities as members of the European societies to which they were attached, identities that, in their eyes, both established their superiority over and sharply distinguished them from the seemingly rude and uncivilized peoples they were seeking to dispossess.

The English settlements established in North America and the West Indies provide a striking case study of the way this process worked. Among the main components of the emerging identity of English people in early modern England, the Protestantism and, increasingly during the eighteenth century, the slowly expanding commercial and strategic might of the English nation were both important.[3] Far more significant, however, was the system of law and liberty that, contemporary English and many foreign observers seemed to agree, distinguished English people from all other peoples on the face of the globe. The proud boast of the English was that, through a variety of conquests and upheavals, they had been able, in marked contrast to most other political societies in Europe, to retain their identity as a free people who had secured their liberty through their dedication to—their invariable insistence upon—what later analysts would call the rule of law.

[2]Jorg Fisch, "Law as a Means and as an End: Some Remarks on the Function of European and Non-European Law in the Process of European Expansion," in *ibid.*, 21.

[3]See Richard Helgerson, *Forms of Nationhood: The Elizabethan Writing of England* (Chicago, 1992); Linda Colley, *The Britons: Forging the Nations, 1707–1837* (New Haven, 1992); and Benedict Anderson, *Imagined Communities: Reflections on the Origin and Spread of Nationalism* (London, 1983).

The nature of the tradition that supported this boast, the ways in which English colonists sought to incorporate that tradition into their own political societies between 1607 and 1776 and the opposition their efforts encountered, and the use of that tradition in their resistance to Britain during the 1760s and 1770s and in the establishment of republican polities in American are the principal questions that will be addressed in the pages that follow.

I

Certainly, the most pervasive and important tradition of political thought English colonists carried with them to the New World in the seventeenth century developed out of English jurisprudence. This tradition emphasized the role of law as a restraint upon the power of the Crown. Rooted in such older writings as Sir John Fortescue, *De Laudibus Legum Angliae,* written during the fifteenth century and always familiar to the English law community but not published until 1616, this tradition was fully elaborated during the early seventeenth century in a series of works by several of the most prominent judges and legal thinkers of the era, including Sir Edward Coke, Sir John Davies, and Nathaniel Bacon. Writing in an age when, except for the Netherlands, every other major European state was slipping into absolutism, and England's first two Stuart kings seems to be trying to extend the prerogatives of the Crown and perhaps even to do away with Parliaments in England, these early seventeenth-century legal writers were all anxious to erect legal and constitutional restraints that would ensure security of life, liberty, and property against such extensions of royal power.[4]

---

[4]The best analysis of the emergence of this tradition is J. G. A. Pocock, *The Ancient Constitution and the Feudal Law: English Historical Thought in the Seventeenth Century* (Cambridge, 1957). A short discussion may be found in Jack P. Greene, *The Intellectual Heritage of the Constitutional Era: The Delegates' Library* (Philadelphia, 1986), 19–22.

The early modern jurisprudential tradition rested on a distinction, already fully elaborated by Fortescue, between two fundamentally different kinds of monarchy, what Fortescue called *regal* monarchy and *political* monarchy. Whereas in a regal monarchy like
France, *"What pleased the prince,"* as Fortescue wrote, had *"the force
of law,"* in a political monarchy like England, "the regal power" was
"restrained by political law." Bound by their coronation oaths to the
observance of English law, English kings could neither "change laws
at their pleasure, make new ones, inflict punishments, . . . impose
burdens on their subjects," "determine suits of parties at their own
will and when they wish," nor keep standing armies "without the assent of" their "subjects." Rather, they were "obliged to protect the
law, the subjects, and their bodies and goods." In a political monarchy, Fortescue observed, "the will of the people" effectively became
"the source of life," the law constituted the " 'ligando' by which the
community . . . sustained" itself, and the people who composed that
community "preserve[d] their rights through the law."[5]

The happy result of this system, according to Fortescue, was that
English people, in contrast to their neighbors, were "ruled by laws
they themselves desire[d]" and were, therefore, able to use the law to
maintain their liberty, to make sure, in Fortescue's words, that "the
law of England [would] favour liberty in every case." By law, they
knew that they could not be "brought to trial except before the ordinary judges, where they" could expect to be "treated justly" according to laws to which they had themselves consented, and that
they could not arbitrarily, be "despoiled" of their property by either
"their own king" or "any other." By law, they knew that they could
"freely enjoy their properties," that "every inhabitant of that realm"
could use "at his own pleasure the fruits which his land yields, the
increase of his flock, and all the emoluments which he gains,

[5]Sir John Fortescue, *De Laudibus Legum Angliae* (Cambridge, 1942),
25, 27, 31, 33, 79, 81.

whether by his own industry or that of others, from land and sea, hindered by the injuries and rapine of none without obtaining at least due amends." For these reasons, Fortescue predicted, English law would "always be exceptional among all the other laws of the earth, among which I see it shine like Venus among the stars." No wonder, as he noted, that "among the English the law" and reverence for it were so "deeply rooted."[6]

By the term *law*, English jurisprudential theorists of course referred both to common law or custom and to statute law. As Coke said, the common law, which included all those ancient customs that appertained to the whole country and which he called *consuetudo Angliae*, was "the most generall and ancient law of the realms." The product of time, continuous usage, and the quiet and common consent of the people who lived under it, the common law or *lex non scripta* as exhibited in the practice of the courts of justice and set down in the decisions of judges was a "collection of maxims or customs" which, as Blackstone wrote, were "of a higher antiquity than memory or history can reach." By such law, wrote Fortescue, the English realm had "been continuously ruled." The laws of no other kingdom, he insisted, in terms that were fundamental to the conception of the role of law in the early modern English world, were "so [deeply] rooted in antiquity." So far as Fortescue and other later panegyrists of the English legal system were concerned, the long survival of this system of laws through political upheavals and the reigns of would-be tyrants removed all "legitimate doubt but that the [legal] customs of the English" as they operated through the common law were "not only good but the best."[7]

[6]*Ibid.*, 25, 87, 89, 105, 115, 139.

[7]Sir Edward Coke, *Institutes, Part One*, 2 vols. (London, 1832), II, 10, 165, 171; Coke, *Institutes, Part Two* (London, 1797), ch. 30, pp. 57–58; Sir William Blackstone, *Commentaries on the Laws of England*, 4 vols. (Philadelphia, 1771), I, 67–68; Fortescue, *De Laudibus*, 37, 39, 41.

So powerful was the authority of a law so deeply grounded in antiquity that, as Coke declared, it could have "no controler in any part
of it, but the high court of parliament." Wherever "the common law
and a statute differ[ed], the common law," most writers in the jurisprudential tradition agreed, had to give way to the statute. But Coke was
only the foremost of those who emphasized "how dangerous it" could
be "to change an ancient maxime of the common law" and "how difficult a thing it" was to try "to restore the subject again to his former
freedoms and safety" once "any ancient law or customs" had been
"broken, and the crowns possessed of a precedent" against it.[8]

This ancient law performed two vital functions. First, it "guided
and directed" the "proceedings and determinations in the king's ordinary courts of justice," settling such vital matters as "the course in
which lands descend by inheritance[;] the manner and form of acquiring and transferring property; the solemnities and obligation of
contracts[;] the rules of expounding wills, deeds, and acts of parliament; the respective remedies of civil injuries; the several species of
temporal offenses, with the manner and degree of punishment; and
an infinite number of minuter particulars." The modes of proceeding
on all such matters, as Blackstone emphasized, were rarely "set down
in any written statute or ordinance, but depend[ed] merely upon immemorial usage, that is upon common law."[9] Second, and even more
significant, the common law supplied the foundations for all of the
most cherished liberties of English people. Most significantly, these
included the rights of every person not to be taxed or subjected to
laws without their consent and not to be deprived of life, liberty, or
property without due process of law, including the "lawfull judgment
of . . . [his] peers," that is, "by Equals, Men of his own Rank and

---

[8]Coke, *Institutes, Part One*, II, 10, 169, 171; Coke, *Institutes, Part Two*,
Merton, ch. 9, p. 97; Confirmationes Chartarum, ch. 5, pp. 528–29; Blackstone, *Commentaries*, I, 89.

[9]Blackstone, *Commentaries*, I, 67–68.

Condition" from the neighborhood in which the alleged offense had been committed.[10]

If, according to English jurisprudential writers, statute law, which represented the formal "assent of the whole realm" through the medium of Parliament, carried more authority than the common law, statutes were, in Blackstone's language, very often "either *declaratory* of the common law or *remedial* of some defects therein." Indeed, said Coke, the "statute of *Magna Charta*" itself, "the foundation of [all statutes and] other acts of parliament," and the *Statute de Tallagio non concedendo* of 94 Edward 1, which provided that "No tallage or aid shall be taken or levied by us or our heirs in our realm, without the good will and assent of archbishops, bishops, earls, barons, knights, burgesses, and other freemen of the land," were "but a confirmation or restitution of the common law." What was true of Magna Charta was also true of many "other ancient statutes," which, Coke observed, were "for the most part" only "affirmations of the common law."[11]

The antiquity of the common law and the customary rights it contained was an important article of faith for those who took upon themselves to define the English jurisprudential tradition. "*Never the Dictates of any Conqueror's Sword, or the Placita, or Good Will and Pleasure of any King of this Nation, or, to speak impartially and freely, the Results of any Parliament that ever sate in this Land,*" the "Fundamental Laws" of England, declared the Whig publicist Henry Care in echoing and citing Fortescue and Coke, were "coeval" with the formation of English political society. Thus, Care wrote, the liberties referred to in Magna Charta should never "be understood as meer

[10]Fortescue, *De Laudibus*, 44; Coke, *Institutes, Part Two*, proeme, ch. 29, pp. 45, 50; Henry Care, *English Liberties*, 5th ed. (Boston, 1721), 23–24.

[11]Fortescue, *De Laudibus*, 41; Blackstone, *Commentaries*, I, 86; Coke, *Institutes, Part One*, II, 4, 10, 108, 171; Coke, *Institutes, Part Two*, ch. 30, p. 60; Stat. De Tellegio, ch. 1, p. 531.

Emanations of Royal Favour, or new Bounties granted, which the People could not justly challenge, or had not a Right unto before." Rather, as "that Oracle of the Law, the Sage and Learned Coke," had asserted "at divers places . . . and all Lawyers" knew, Magna Charta granted "no new Freedom" but only restored "such as lawfully" English people had "had before" but "had been usurped and incroached upon" by earlier monarchs. By "often" mentioning "*Sua Jura,* their Rights, and *Libertates, suas,* their Liberties," Magna Charta, Care pointed out, clearly recognized that the English had had those rights and liberties "before, and that the same were now confirmed."[12]

Thus were the "absolute rights of every Englishman, (which, taken in a political and extensive sense, are usually called their liberties)," very "deeply implanted" in the laws and constitution of England. Defined generally by Blackstone as the capacity of every subject to be "entire master of his own conduct, except in those points wherein the public good requires some direction or restraint" or by the popular Whig theorists John Trenchard and Thomas Gordon as "the Power which every Man has over his own Actions, and his Right to enjoy the Fruit of his Labour, Art, and Industry, as far as by it he hurts not the Society, or any Members of it, by taking from any Member or by hindering him from enjoying what he himself enjoys," *liberty* in English jurisprudential theory consisted, as Blackstone systematically specified them, in three principal legal rights: the right to personal security in terms of life, limbs, well-being, and reputation; the right to personal liberty, including "the power of loco-motion, of changing situation, or removing one's person to whatsoever place one's own inclination may direct," and freedom from "imprisonment without cause;" and the right to "the free use, enjoyment, and disposal of all" property "without any control or diminution, save only by the laws of the land." What was "truly and properly . . . an *English Man's Liberty*" was thus, in Care's words, "a

---

[12]Care, *English Liberties,* 3, 6–7, 27.

Privilege, not to be exempt from the Law, but to be freed [by law] in Person and Estate from Arbitrary Violence and Oppression."[13]

Not just common-law lawyers and other jurisprudential theorists but also the leading liberal natural rights political philosopher John Locke drew a similar connection between law and liberty during the closing decades of the seventeenth century. "The end of Law," Locke wrote in his *Second Treatise*, was "not to abolish or restrain, but *to preserve and enlarge Freedom.*" Freedom, he said, was not "*A Liberty for every man to do what he lists:* (For who could be free, when every other Man's Humour might domineer over him?) But a Liberty to dispose, and order as he lists, his Person, Actions, Possessions, and his whole Property, within the Allowance of those Laws under which he is; and therein not to be subject to the arbitrary Will of another, but freely follow his own." For Locke, no less than for legal writers, liberty was rooted in law.[14]

The happy capacity of English people to preserve this liberty rested largely upon two institutions for determining and making law: juries and Parliaments. By guaranteeing that "no Causes" would be "tried, nor any Man adjudged to lose Life, Member, or Estate, but upon the Verdict of his Peers, (or Equals) his Neighbours, and of his own Condition," the first gave every person "a Share in the executive Part of the Law." By giving each independent person through "his chosen Representatives" a share "in the Legislative (or Lawmaking) Power," the second insured that no law should be passed without the consent of the nation's property holders. Over the centuries, Parliament had taken a conspicuous role in maintaining the

[13]Blackstone, *Commentaries*, I, 126–28, 129–40; John Trenchard and Thomas Gordon, *Cato's Letters*, in David L. Jacobson, ed., *The English Libertarian Heritage* (Indianapolis, 1965), #62, pp. 127–28; Care, *English Liberties*, 3–4.

[14]John Locke, *Two Treatises of Government*, ed. Peter Laslett (Cambridge, 1960), 348.

"vigour of our free constitution" from the assaults of would-be tyrants. Through not just Magna Charta but the Petition of Right under Charles I, the Habeas Corpus act under Charles II, the Bill of Rights during the Glorious Revolution, and the Act of Settlement, Blackstone proudly noted, Parliament repeatedly had acted to restore "the ballance of our rights and liberties" to their "proper level." Occasionally in these efforts, Englishmen had had to resort to arms, and they were careful to preserve their right to bear arms in order to be able to do so when necessary. But most of the time Parliaments and juries, those "two grand Pillars of *English* Liberty" through which "the Birth-right of Englishmen" had always shone "most conspicuously," had functioned effectively to insure that in England "the law" would continue, as Coke said, to be "the surest sanctuary, that a man can take" and "the best Birth-right of the Subject." "A greater Inheritance descends to us from the Laws, than from our Progenitors," wrote Care in paraphrasing Coke. By protecting every subject in his "Goods, Lands, Wife and Children, his Body, Life, Honour and Estimation," and his liberties, the law had been the principal device through which English people had managed to remain "more free and happy than any other People in the World."[15]

For Englishmen, freedom, or liberty, was thus, according to the powerful English jurisprudential and liberal traditions, not just a condition enforced by law but the very essence of their national identity. In most early modern countries, noted Trenchard and Gordon quoting the republican Algernon Sidney, rulers "*use[d] their Subjects like Asses and Mastiff Dogs, to work and to fight, to be oppressed and killed for them*," considering "their People as Cattle, and" using "them worse, as they fear[ed] them more. Thus" had "most of Mankind" become "wretched Slaves" who maintained "their haughty Masters like Gods," while "their haughty Masters often use[d] them like

---

[15]Care, *English Liberties*, 3–4, 27; Blackstone, *Commentaries*, I, 126–28, 144; Coke, *Institutes*, *Part Two*, ch. 29, p. 55.

Dogs." In most "other countries"—English writers invariably sin-
gled out Turkey, France, and sometimes Spain—"the meer Will of
the Prince is Law; his Word takes off any Man's Head, imposes
Taxes, seizes any Man's Estate, when, how, and as often as he lists;
and if one be accused, or but so much as suspected of any Crime, he
may either presently execute him, or banish, or imprison him at
pleasure." Only in England were "the Lives and Fortunes" of the
people not subject to the "Wills (or rather Lusts)" of "Arbitrary"
tyrants. Only in England did the monarchs, in Fortescue's words,
have "*two-Superiours, God and the Law.*" Only in England was "the
Commonality . . . so guarded in their Persons and Properties by the
Sense of Law, as" to be rendered "Free-men, not Slaves." Only in England did law require the consent of those who lived under it. Only
in England was "the Law . . . both the Measure and the Bond of
every Subject's Duty and Allegiance, each Man having a fixed fundamental Right born with him, as to Freedom of his Person, and
Property in his Estate, which he cannot be deprived of, but either by
his Consent, or some Crimes for which the Law has impos'd such
Penalty or Forfeiture." Few early modern English people had any
doubt, as Care put it, that the "Constitution of our English Government" was "the best in the World."[16]

If, as some commentators thought, the liberties of the English
had formerly belonged to all mankind, they obviously now were, "in
a peculiar and emphatic manner," exclusively "the rights of the
people of England." With Fortescue, they pondered "why this law
of England, so worthy and so excellent," was "not common to all the
world." Fortescue attributed "this superiority" to the high fertility of
England's soil that produced large crop yields that in turn fostered
the extensive social independence and spirit of intellectual inquiry
necessary to sustain a free government. This situation, in the words
of a later writer, made "all Men" ambitious "to live agreeably to their

---

[16]*Cato's Letters*, #25, pp. 68, 70; Care, *English Liberties*, 1–3.

own Humours and Discretion" as "sole Lord[s] and Arbiter[s] of" their "own private Actions and Property." This passion for indepen-dence in turn encouraged Englishmen both to acquire property and to try to secure that property "by the Laws of Liberty; Laws which" were "made by Consent, and" could not "be repealed without it." To contemporaries, the truth of this line of argument seemed to be confirmed by England's economic abundance, large population, and religious independence, which could be interpreted as both the foundations for and the effects of the island's "inestimable Blessing of Liberty."[17] Whatever the reason why, as Montesquieu wrote in praise of the spirit of the English legal and constitutional system, England was "the only nation in the world, where political and civil liberty" was "the direct end of its constitution," early modern English people thus knew, as Blackstone wrote, that the "idea and practice of . . . political and civil liberty flourish[ed] in their highest vigour in" England, "where it" fell "little short of perfection, and" could "only be lost or destroyed by the folly or demerits of its owner."[18]

More than any other component of English life or character, possession of this unique system of law and liberty was the most dis-tinctive and important marker of the English people during the early modern period. Together, England's status as the palladium of liberty and the English people's profound devotion to law and liberty were the principal badges of Englishness, the essential—the most deeply defining—hallmarks of English identity.

II

For English people migrating overseas to establish new communities of settlement, the capacity to enjoy—to possess—the English sys-tem of law and liberty was thus crucial to their ability to maintain

---

[17]Blackstone, *Commentaries*, I, 129; Fortescue, *De Laudibus*, 67, 69, 71, 73; *Cato's Letters*, #25, pp. 68, 70; #62, pp. 127–28; #68, pp. 177–78.
[18]Blackstone, *Commentaries*, I, 126–28, 145.

their identity as English people and to continue to think of themselves and to be thought of by those who remained in England as
English.[19] For that reason as well as because they regarded English
legal arrangements as the very best way to preserve the properties
they hoped to acquire in their new homes, it is scarcely surprising
that, in establishing local enclaves of power during the first years of
colonization, English settlers all over America made every effort to
construct them on English legal foundations. As George Dargo has
observed, "the attempt to establish English law and the 'rights and
liberties of Englishmen' was constant from the first settlement to the
[American] Revolution."[20]

Several developments during the early stages of the colonizing
process encouraged this attempt. To entice settlers, colonial organizers
early found that they not only had to offer them property in land but
also to guarantee them the property in rights by which English people
had traditionally secured their real and material possessions. Thus in
1619 the Virginia Company of London found it necessary to establish
a polity that included a representative assembly through which the
settlers could, in the time-honored fashion of the English, make—
and formally consent to—the laws under which they would live. Directed by company leaders "to imitate and follow the policy of the
form of government, laws, customs, and manner of trial; and other
administration of justice, used in the realm of England," the new assembly immediately claimed the right to consent to all taxes levied
on the inhabitants of Virginia.[21]

[19]Much of the material in this section is drawn from Jack P. Greene,
*Peripheries and Center: Constitutional Development in the Extended Polities
of the British Empire and the United States 1607–1788* (Athens, Ga., 1986),
7–76.

[20]George Dargo, *Roots of the Republic: A New Perspective on Early American Constitutionalism* (New York, 1974), 74.

[21]Ordinance, July 24, 1621; Virginia laws, March 1624, in Jack P.
Greene, ed., *Great Britain and the American Colonies, 1606–1783* (New
York, 1970), 28, 30.

The legal instruments of English colonization—letters patent, charters, proclamations—encouraged this attempt in three ways. First, they often specified that the settlers and their progeny should be treated as "natural born subjects of England" and thereby strongly suggested that there would be no legal distinctions between English people who lived in the home islands and those who resided in the colonies. Second, they required that colonies operate under no laws that were repugnant to "Laws, Statutes, Customs, and Rights of our Kingdom of England" and thereby powerfully implied that the laws of England were to provide the model, and the standard, for all colonial laws. Third, beginning with the charter to Maryland in 1632, they also stipulated that colonists should use and enjoy "all Privileges, Franchises and Liberties of this our Kingdom of England, freely, quietly, and peaceably to have and possess . . . in the same manner as our Liege-Men born, or to be born within our said Kingdom of England, without Impediment, Molestation, Vexation, Impeachment, or Grievance," and that no laws be passed without the consent of the freemen of the colony.[22]

Everywhere in the colonies, the early assemblies followed the lead of the first Virginia Assembly and asserted the claims of their constituents to all the rights and legal safeguards enjoyed by English people at home. Thus did the first Maryland Assembly in 1637–1638 pass an act "for the liberties of the people." Providing that free Marylanders should "have and enjoy all such rights[,] liberties[,] immunities[,] priviledges[,] and free customs as any naturall born subject of England hath or ought to have or enjoy in the Realm of England by force or vertue of the common law or Statute Law of England," this act stipulated that no one should "be imprisoned nor disseissed or dispossessed of their freehold goods or Chattels or be out Lawed[,]

---

[22]David S. Lovejoy, *The Glorious Revolution in America* (New York, 1972), 39; Maryland Charter, June 30, 1632, in Greene, *Great Britain and the American Colonies*, 24.

Exiled[,] or otherwise destroyed[,] fore judged[,] or punished than according to the Laws of this Province." Similarly, in the *Body of Liberties* of 1641 the General Court of Massachusetts incorporated many provisions of English common law into the legal system of that colony.[23] The result of these efforts was the creation in America of several local systems of authority modeled on that of the English.

Beginning in the 1650s and continuing in recurrent phases for the next half century, London officials sought to impose metropolitan authority upon these local centers of power. Throughout the last half of the seventeenth century, the metropolitan government undertook a variety of measures intended to reduce the colonies to what it called an "absolute obedience to the King's authority."[24] These included the subordination of the economies of the colonies to that of the metropolis through the navigation acts, passed between 1651 and 1696; bringing as many as possible of the still mostly private colonies under the direct control of the crown, curtailing the powers of colonial political institutions, and consolidating the colonies into fewer entities that would be presided over by viceregal representatives of the monarch and be unhampered by representative assemblies.[25]

Everywhere, these metropolitan intrusions into colonial affairs provoked a profound mistrust of central authority among the colonists and intensified the determination of property holders within the expanding colonies to secure both their new estates and their claims to an English identity by obtaining metropolitan recognition that, as English people or the descendants of English people, they were entitled to enjoy all the rights and legal protections of English

[23]Dargo, *Roots of the Republic*, 58–61.

[24]Report of Commissioners sent to New England, [April 30,] 1661, in W. Noel Sainsbury *et al.*, eds., *Calendar of State Papers. Colonial*, 44 vols. (London, 1860–), 1661–68, 25.

[25]This subject is discussed more fully in Greene, *Peripheries and Center*, 12–18.

people in the home island. This determination stimulated an extensive constitutional discussion intended to identify explicit legal
defenses that would put their claims to English rights and legal protections on a solid foundation and thereby protect the colonies
from such wholesale intrusions of metropolitan power.

In these discussions, colonial spokesmen articulated an elaborate argument to strengthen their early claims to what they thought
of as their inherited rights as English people. According to this argument, the original settlers and their descendants were all equally
"honest free-born Subjects of England," who, with authorization
from the English monarchy, had voluntarily left their "native country" for "a waste and howling wilderness." *"With great danger to our
persons, and with very great charge and trouble,"* they said, they had
turned that wilderness into thriving and well-inhabited settlements
and had thereby, at little or no cost to the English government, significantly "enlarged the *English* Trade and Empire" and brought
"England . . . its greatest Riches and Prosperity." While they were
thus creating the new and valuable *"English* Empire in *America,"*
they retained their English identity and remained, as a Barbadian declared in 1698, "no other but *English* Men: . . . your Countrey-Men,
your Kindred and Relations," who, said another, "pretended to have
as good *English* Bloud in our Veins, as some of those that we have left
behind us." It followed that their continuing identity as English people entitled them to all the "hereditary Rights" of English subjects,
rights that they could not lose merely "by Transporting themselves"
to America, rights, moreover, that had been confirmed to them by
their charters and were secured by their respective civil governments—governments which, they pointed out, had been formed on
their own initiative on "the nearest model of conformity to that under which our predecessors of the English nation have lived and
flourished for above a thousand years." To be in any way diminished
in their rights simply because of their "great Distance . . . from the
Fountain of Justice" in England, they believed, would deprive them
of "their Birthright and the Benefits of the Laws and Priviledges of

English Men" and reduce them to a species of "slavery far exceeding all that [any of] the English nation hath yet suffered."²⁶

The effort to secure these rights against the claims of the crown was continuous from 1660 to 1760. In general, colonial leaders pursued this quest along two parallel lines. First, they sought explicit guarantees of the rights of the colonists to English laws. Second, they sought to enhance the authority of their elected assemblies. In the colonies, no less than in the metropolis, they hoped that law and parliaments would be the bulwarks of the people's liberties and properties.

The colonists' quest for explicit guarantees of their right to English laws was a recurrent subject of dispute for more than half a century beginning around 1670. This debate turned around two questions: first, whether the colonists were entitled to English laws, and, second, if so, to what laws?

At the root of the debate over the former question was the problem of whether the colonies were conquered countries. In 1607, in *Calvin's Case*, Coke had laid down the opinion that conquered countries, such as Ireland, could be governed according to the will of the king, who, though presumably bound to govern "according to natural equity," might or might not introduce the laws of England. Although the early Stuarts proceeded in some respects to treat Virginia, the Irish plantations, and other colonies as "conquered"

²⁶*The Liberty and Property of British Subjects Asserted* (London, 1728), 28, 32; Samuel Nadgorth to Secretary Morrice, October 26, 1666, in *Calendar of State Papers. Colonial, 1661–68*, 417–18; N. Darnell Davis, *The Cavaliers and Roundheads of Barbados, 1650–1652* (Georgetown, British Guinea, 1883), 198–99; Edward Littleton, *The Groans of the Plantations* (London, 1689), 15–17, 23, 26; *A State of the Present Condition of the Island of Barbados* (London, 1698), 3; *Maryland Gazette* (Annapolis), March 16, 1748; *The Case of the Inhabitants and Planters in the Island of Jamaica* (London, [1714]).

countries, there were obvious doubts, forcibly raised and frequently reiterated by the colonists themselves, about whether colonies of English people settled in the "vacant" spaces of America fitted this definition. Thus, in 1670 Chief Justice John Vaughan (in a report of *Craw v. Ramsey*) distinguished between dominions acquired by conquest and those acquired by colonization. But no judge or lawyer seems to have spelled out the implications of Vaughan's decision until 1694, when, in the case of *Dutton v. Howell*, relating to a dispute in Barbados, Sir Bartholomew Shower, one of the lawyers, argued that, as "a new settlement of *Englishmen* by the King's consent in an uninhabited country," Barbados was not a conquered territory. Whereas, according to the doctrine of *Calvin's Case*, the inhabitants of a conquered country were entitled to the privilege of English law only if the monarch had extended it to them, those in a newly settled colony of Englishmen, Shower contended, enjoyed that privilege as their birthright. The House of Lords, the tribunal in the case, ultimately ruled against Shower's view, and metropolitan judicial and legal officers continued in many instances to consider the colonies as conquered territories. But the Privy Council ultimately reaffirmed Shower's argument in 1722, when it determined in a widely reported case that "an uninhabited country newly found out, and inhabited by the *English*," as presumably were all of the American colonies, could not be treated as a conquered territory but had "to be governed by the laws of England."[27]

[27]The contemporary discussion of the legal status of the colonies and the questions of under what circumstances what sorts of English law applied there may be traced in A. Berriedale Keith, *Constitutional History of the First British Empire* (Oxford, 1930), 9–17, 182–86; Sir William Searle Holdsworth, *A History of English Law*, 16 vols. (London, 1922–1966), XI, 229–48; and, especially, in the excellent analysis by Joseph Henry Smith, *Appeals to the Privy Council from the American Plantations* (New York, 1950), 464–522. The quotations are from Smith, *Appeals*, 468, 472; and Peere Williams, *Reports*, 3 vols. (London, 1740), III, 75–76.

Of course, none of these ad hoc pronouncements settled the question. As late as the 1760s there was still enormous confusion in the metropolis over whether the colonies had been acquired through settlement or, as such a widely respected authority as Sir William Blackstone affirmed, had been "principally . . . obtained . . . by right of conquest." This continuing confusion was vividly revealed at the close of the Seven Years' War, when British officials were establishing regulations for governing the ceded islands of Dominica, Grenada, St. Vincent, and Tobago, obtained from France in the Treaty of Paris of 1763. "While those islands were deemed Conquered Countries and subject to the King's Prerogative Royal by the Ministers on the first Floor," complained William Knox, later undersecretary of state for the colonies, "the Ministers on the second were considering them as British Colonies and investing the Inhabitants with all the privileges of Englishmen," and the "Privy Council which was intended by the Constitution to control the other Departments sanctified the absurdity by lending its Authority to both Propositions." Few colonists shared this confusion. They did not dispute that many of the colonies had initially been conquered from the Amerindians or from rival foreign powers. But they insisted that the subsequent occupation of those colonies "by natural-born subjects of England" clearly entitled their inhabitants "to the benefit of all the laws of England . . . and the rights of Englishmen."[28]

When the colonists claimed the benefit of English laws, they were referring primarily, as the Jamaica legislature declared in 1677, to the common law and all those "laws and statutes heretofore made and used in our native country, the Kingdom of England, for the

[28]Blackstone, *Commentaries*, I, 107–8; Jack P. Greene, ed., "William Knox's Explanation for the American Revolution," *William and Mary Quarterly*, 3d ser., XXX (1973), 302; Anthony Stokes, *A View of the Constitution of the British Colonies* (London, 1783), 10–12; Edward Long, *History of Jamaica*, 3 vols. (London, 1774), I, 160.

public weal of the same, and all the liberties[,] immunities[,] and privileges contained therein." These liberties included especially those basic protections, confirmed by Magna Charta and the Petition of Right, against imprisonment, loss of life, or dispossession of property without due process of law, and exemption from taxation without consent. Between 1670 and 1700 the legislatures of several colonies had sought explicit confirmations of those rights in new charters, public declarations, and statutes, and these efforts continued during the early years of the eighteenth century, particularly in Jamaica, where, perhaps because the colony had been acquired by conquest from Europeans, the inhabitants were especially anxious to have some positive codification of their rights, and in Maryland, where antiproprietary leaders viewed English laws as a bulwark against possible arbitrary rule by the proprietor.[29]

The work of the Maryland lawyer Daniel Dulany, Sr., *The Right of the Inhabitants of Maryland to the Benefit of the English Laws*, published in Annapolis in 1728, is the fullest and most penetrating statement of this position. Quoting Coke that the common and statute law of England was an Englishman's "best Inheritance" and " 'the best and most Common Birth-Right, that the Subject hath, for the Safeguard and defense, not only of his Goods, Lands, and revenues but of his Wife, and Children, his Body, Fame, and Life,' " Dulany emphasized the connection between English identity and access to those laws. "All the Rights and Liberties, on which the British Subject, so justly, values Himself upon," he wrote, "are secured to Him, by the British-Laws." Law was the means by which in England "every Honest Man, who has the benefit of it," could "effectually secure . . . his Life, the Enjoyment of his Liberty, and the Fruits of his

---

[29]Agnes M. Whitson, *The Constitutional Development of Jamaica, 1660 to 1729* (Manchester, 1729), 60–127; St. George Leakin Sioussat, *The English Statutes in Maryland* (Baltimore, 1903); Keith, *Constitutional History*, 141.

Industry. 'Tis by virtue of this Law," he continued, "that a British Subject" could "with Courage and Freedom" stand up to "the most daring and powerful Oppressor." "Uprightly and honestly applied, and administered," this law, he insisted, would "secure Men from all Degrees of Oppression, Violence, and Injustice."[30]

That Marylanders and other colonists had every right to both the liberties of English people and "the Laws, made to create or preserve" those liberties, Dulany had not the slightest doubt. Because Maryland was "undoubtedly a Part of the British Dominions," because its inhabitants were English subjects who had "always adhered to, and continued in their Allegiance to the Crown," and because Every [English] Subject" had "a Right to the Enjoyment of his Liberty and Property, according to the established Laws of his Country," Marylanders, he contended, had, by virtue of their identity and inheritance as Englishmen, a right not just to English "Liberties, and Privileges" but also "to all the Laws, whether Statute or Common, which secure to the Subject, the Right[s] of a Subject, as inseparably incident to those Rights." Like "their Fellow Subjects residing in England," Marylanders, according to Dulany, held their lives, liberties, and properties under precisely the same legal protections.[31]

This determination, in the words of the Duke of Portland, who acted as governor of Jamaica in the mid-1720s, "to be as near as Can be, upon the foott of H[is] M[ajesty's] English Subjects in England" finally succeeded in Jamaica in 1729. After a long battle, the legislature managed, in return for granting the Crown a permanent revenue of £8,000 per year, to obtain metropolitan approval of a Clause declaring "all such laws, and statutes of England as have been at any time esteemed, introduced, used, accepted, or received, as laws of this Island . . . to be and Continue laws of this His Majesty's Island

---

[30]Daniel Dulany, *The Right of the Inhabitants of Maryland to the Benefits of the English Laws* (Annapolis, 1728), 4, 11.

[31]*Ibid.*, 3, 7–8, 10, 12–13, 27.

of Jamaica for ever."[32] But Jamaica's success was exceptional. Most metropolitan officials, judges, and lawyers opposed such efforts, partly because of fears that they would diminish the royal prerogative in the colonies and partly because "so much of the English law" was either directed to purely local concerns or so full of those "artificial refinements and distinctions incident to the property of a great and commercial people" as to be "[in]applicable to . . . the condition of an infant Colony."[33]

As Knox observed, the continuing failure of officials in London to make a systematic and effective effort to clarify this ambiguous situation left local institutions in the colonies with wide latitude and primary responsibility for determining which English "Laws the People in any Colony were to be governed by." Some colonial writers and political leaders—notably in Jamaica, Maryland, and New York—sought to obtain maximum benefits of English law by contending that not just the common law but all English statutes that did not specifically exclude the colonies applied to them. But the most prevalent opinion in the colonies seems to have been that only English common law, insofar as it was applicable to local conditions, and English statutes that specifically mentioned the colonies were in force. The corollary of this position was that English statutes that did not explicitly mention the colonies were *not* in force unless, as Sir William Keith, and former governor of Pennsylvania, observed in 1726, they had been formally "brought over by some Act of Assembly in the Colony, where they are pleaded." Thus, during the century before the American Revolution, the colonial assemblies gradually,

[32]Duke of Portland to [Lord Carteret], December 7, 1723, in *Calendar of State Papers, Colonial, 1722–23*, 385; Whitson, *Constitutional Development of Jamaica*, 142–67.

[33]Keith, *Constitutional History*, 185–86; Stokes, *View of the Constitution*, 10; Jeremiah Dummer, *A Defence of the New-England Charters* (London, 1726), 56–57.

in Knox's words, "assumed the authority of deciding which" general English statutes "should be of force, and which not, and, by an Act of their own declared Acts of Parliament binding or useless as they judged proper."[34]

But these formal enactments by the legislatures do not appear to have limited colonial courts in their use of English law. Rather, during the last half century of the colonial period, lawyers and judges seem to have applied all kinds of English law—the common law, presettlement statutes, and postsettlement statutes that both did and, at least in some instances, did not specifically mention the colonies— as it suited local and temporal needs and conditions. In so doing, local legal and judicial officials followed the strategy pursued during the late seventeenth and early eighteenth centuries by the Jamaicans. When they were unable to win metropolitan approval for a statute to secure the benefits of English laws to the colony, they "pronounce[d] and admit[ted] in their Courts of Justice there English Laws [to be] in Force in the Islands," with the deliberate intention of making them "after a Series of Years . . . freely Operate as Customs" that through "Prescription and long Usage" would acquire "the Effect and Value of Written Laws." Through this process, they fashioned a legal system for each colony that, as Sir William Gooch, lieutenant governor of Virginia from 1729 to 1749, observed, was

[34]Greene, ed., "Knox's Explanation of the American Revolution," 302–3; Isaac Norris, *The Speech Delivered from the Bench in the Court of Common Pleas held for the City and Court of Philadelphia* (Philadelphia, 1727), 2; Sir John Randolph to Captain Pearce, [1734–1735], in William Smith, Jr., *The History of the Province of New-York*, ed. Michael Kammen, 2 vols. (Cambridge, Mass., 1972), I, 264–67; Smith, *Appeals to the Privy Council*, 476–85; Thomas Nairne to [Earl of Sunderland], July 28, [1708], *Calendar of State Papers, Colonial, 1708–09, 433*; Dulany, *Right of the Inhabitants of Maryland*; Sir William Keith, "A Short Discourse on the Present State of the Colonies in America," [1726], in Greene, ed., *Great Britain and the American Colonies*, 191–92.

both "exactly suited to the Circumstances of the Respective Governments, and as near as possible it can be, conformable to the Laws
and Customs of England." The colonies thus gradually gained in
practice what they had, except in a few cases, been unable to obtain
by statutes: the traditional English legal guarantees of life, liberty,
and property. This development no doubt helps to account for the virtual disappearance of colonial attempts to enact such laws after the
mid-1780s in those colonies that remained in the British empire.[35]

In the process of incorporating and adapting English law to colonial legal systems, colonial judges, lawyers, and political writers
had a large and increasingly available technical literature to draw
upon. Before 1776, colonial printers issued at least fifty legal treatises. Intended for laymen and justices of the peace or other officers,
these mostly consisted of handbooks which, as George Webb's *Office and Authority of a Justice of the Peace*, published in Williamsburg
in 1736, announced on its title page, set forth rules, precedents,
and procedures "Collected from the Common and Statute Laws of
England, and Acts of [the Virginia] Assembly, now in force; and
adapted to the Constitution and Practice of Virginia." But they also
included reprints of important English works, including Care's *English
Liberties*, the first American edition of which appeared in Boston in
1721, and Blackstone's *Commentaries*, first issued in the colonies in
Philadelphia in 1771–1772. Although the first legal title printed in
colonial British America, *The Excellent Priviledge of Liberty & Property
being the Birth-right Of the Free-born Subjects of England* (Philadelphia,
1687), contained large sections from Coke's second *Institute*, no co-

---

[35]Smith, *Appeals to the Privy Council*, 520–22; Edward Long, "On the
Constitution and Government of Jamaica," [ca. 1770s–1780s], Long Pa-
pers, Additional Manuscripts 12,402, British Library, London, f. 42b.
Gooch's remarks, written in the late 1720s, are reprinted in Greene, ed.,
Great Britain and the American Colonies, 196–212. The quotations are from
p. 203.

lonial printer undertook to publish in extenso any of the treatises of Coke or other seventeenth-century English common lawyers.[36]

The English editions of such works were, however, widely available and frequently cited by colonial legal and political writers. In a survey of the libraries of twenty-two early American lawyers, Herbert Johnson has found that, excluding law reports from the Westminster common law courts and the English High Court of Chancery, which "were staple reading materials" for colonial lawyers, those libraries contained 212 English legal treatises published between 1700 and 1799, including abridgments, commentaries and institutes, practice manuals, conveyancing manuals, law dictionaries, formularies, justice of the peace manuals, legal bibliographies, and treatises about every aspect of the law from admiralty to torts. Eight libraries contained Fortescue's *De laudibus legum Angliae*, and twelve, Coke's first *Institute*.[37] A recent census of law books in colonial Virginia libraries finds 449 identified and 163 unidentified titles, all but a few of them imported and all but a few of those from England. With 22 copies of the first part of the *Institutes* 10 copies of the *Third Institute*, and 18 copies of his *Reports*, Coke seems to have been the most popular English legal author, but Sir Mathew Hale, Fortescue, and other common-law theorists were also well represented.[38]

Much more enduring in the colonists' struggle to secure their claims to English liberties, legal protections, and identities was a sec-

[36]Eldon Revere Jones, "A List of Legal Treatises Printed in the British Colonies and the American States Before 1801," in *Harvard Legal Essays Written in Honor and Presented to Joseph Henry Beale and Samuel Williston* (Cambridge, Mass., 1934), 159–79. The quotation is from p. 164.

[37]Herbert A. Johnson, *Imported Eighteenth-Century Law Treatises in American Libraries 1700–1799* (Knoxville, Tenn., 1978). The quotation is from p. xi.

[38]William Hamilton Bryson, *Census of Law Books in Colonial Virginia* (Charlottesville, Va., 1978).

ond issue, the issue, in the words of an anonymous Virginian in 1701, of "how far the Legislative Authority is in the Assemblies of the several Colonies."[39] That the colonists had a right to legislative assemblies and that those bodies did indeed have power to legislate was not in dispute. The early charters from the crown or, for those few colonies like Jamaica and New Hampshire that had never had charters, the royal commissions to the first governors had explicitly conveyed that right to most colonies. Subsequently, clauses in the governors' commissions empowering them "to summon and call General Assemblies of the . . . Freeholders and Planters with . . . full Power and Authority to make, constitute and ordain Laws, Statutes and Ordinances" repeatedly reaffirmed these early grants of rights in all royal colonies—whether or not they had charters. As early as 1703, the crowns' law officers had affirmed that acts of these assemblies were "of the same effect" in the colonies as was an act of Parliament in Britain.[40] Except for the brief experiment with absolute government for the Dominion of New England under James II from 1684 to 1689, metropolitan officials never attempted to govern in the colonies dominated by permanent settler populations without representative institutions.

The question was thus not whether the assemblies had lawmaking power but how extensive that power was. Although the Navigation Act of 1696 declared "illegal, null and void" any colonial law that was contrary to the navigation acts, the only express reservation

---

[39][Benjamin Harrison III], *An Essay upon the Government of the English Plantations on the Continent of America (1701): An Anonymous Virginian's Proposals for Liberty under the British Crown, with Two Memoranda by William Byrd*, ed. Louis B. Wright (San Marino, Calif., 1945), 23–24.

[40]Smith, *Appeals to the Privy Council*, 465; Leonard W. Labaree, ed., *Royal Instructions to British Colonial Governors*, 2 vols. (New York, 1935), II, 818–19; Edward Northey to Board of Trade, May 31, 1703, *Calendar of State Papers, Colonial, 1702–03*, 470–71.

in the colonial charters and governors' commissions was the provision, earlier referred to, that laws could "not be repugnant, but [had to be] as near as may be, agreeable to the Laws and Statutes of . . . Great Britain." This "nonrepugnancy" clause formed the legal basis for the review of colonial legislation by the king and Privy Council.[41]

With so few express restrictions on their legislative authority, the colonial assemblies interpreted that authority very broadly. Two conditions encouraged this impulse. First was their distance from the metropolis and the need for a broad range of laws and regulations to organize and reorganize the new environments they had been created to serve. Second was their inherited ideas about the functions of representative bodies in English polities. The largely successful effort by metropolitan authorities following the Restoration to substitute an English model of colonial governance for the welter of existing political forms that had grown up in the colonies during the first six decades of the seventeenth century powerfully reinforced the notion that these ideas were applicable to the colonists' local situations. By the early eighteenth century, the inhabitants of the colonies took great pride that their "Form of Government" was "as nigh as conveniently can be to that of *England*." Just as the governors were invested with all the prerogatives of the king, and the councils performed the functions of the House of Lords as a middle or "*Aristocratical*" branch of the legislature, so did the lower houses conceive of themselves as being "upon the very same foot" with the House of Commons in Great Britain. "'Tis well known," wrote a Pennsylvanian in 1728 in repeating what had already become a commonplace, "that the Assemblies in the *English*-Plantations are formed on the Plan of an *English* Parliament." Thus did the several colonial assemblies "proceed to do Business, choosing Committees, and in all other Respects imitating the House of Commons in *England* as nigh as possible." Thus did those assemblies insist that they be vested with the

---

[41]Labaree, ed., *Royal Instructions*, II, 819.

same powers and privileges in the colonies that the Parliament exercised in Britain.[42]

The assemblies' efforts to assimilate themselves to the pattern of the English House of Commons created serious problems, both for governors and their supporters in the colonies and for colonial officials in London. Already by the 1670s, metropolitan representatives were condemning the assemblies for trying "to grasp all the power." By the early eighteenth century, governors were complaining, frequently and stridently, that the assemblies had "extorted so many powers from" the "predecessors, that there" was "now hardly enough left to keep the peace, much less to maintain the decent respect and regard that is due to the Queen's servant." The assemblies "not only claim[ed] . . . all such priviledges as" were "enjoyed by the House of Commons of Great Britain, but . . . even attempt[ed] to grasp at more power than any House of Commons ever yet exercised." While they were sitting, they acted as if "all power and authority was only in their hands," and, it was charged, they seemed determined "to divest the administration . . . of all . . . power and authority and to lodge it in the Assembly." Nor did this situation improve through the middle decades of the eighteenth century.[43]

[42][Thomas Nairne], A Letter from South Carolina (London, 1710), 21–22; William Douglass, Summary, Historical and Political, of the First Planting, Progressive Improvements, and Present State of the British Settlements in North America, 2 vols. (Boston, 1749–1751), I, 213–14; Henry Worsley to Duke of Newcastle, August 4, 1727, Calendar of State Papers, Colonial, 1726–27, 325–26; Remarks on the Proceedings of some Members of Assembly at Philadelphia: April 1728 [Philadelphia, 1728], 1–2. In this connection, see Jack P. Greene, "Political Mimesis: A Consideration of the Historical and Cultural Roots of Legislative Behavior in the British Colonies in the Eighteenth Century," American Historical Review, LXXV (1968), 337–60.

[43]Lord of Trade to Privy Council, May 28, 1679, Calendar of State Papers, Colonial, 1677–80, 368; Sir William Beeston to Board of Trade, August 19, 1701, ibid., 1701, 424–25; Robert Lowther to Board of Trade, August 16, 1712, ibid., 1712–14, 29; Board of Trade to the King, August

Although, as William Knox put it, the assemblies seem to have had little difficulty in baffling "the feeble attempts of Royal Power" within the colonies, metropolitan officials never accepted the legitimacy of this development. The assemblies might indeed have lawmaking power within the colonies. According to metropolitan theory, however, their very existence depended, not upon their constituents' inherent rights as Englishmen, specifically upon their right to consent to all laws by which they should be governed, but upon the favor of the crown, as extended to them by royal charter or some other official document such as the king's commission or instructions to his governors. The Lords of Trade articulated the official position as early as 1679 during their early attempts to restrict the lawmaking powers of the Virginia and Jamaica assemblies. Declaring that colonists could not "pretend to greater privileges than those [specifically] granted them by Charter or" commission, that body condemned the colonial assemblies for "regarding as a right what was granted [only] as a favour" and denied that such "temporary" and experimental constitutions as the crown had thus far extended to the colonies could ever be regarded "as a resignation and devolution to them of the royal authority."[44] Repeatedly affirmed over the next eighty years by the crown's law officers in London, this doctrine served as the favorite defense for colonial executives trying to combat the assemblies' pretensions to full legislative powers in the colonies.

In the colonies, however, few other than metropolitan representatives and their supporters subscribed to this view. Denying that the colonies were to be considered as nothing more than "new Clay in the Potter's Hand," most colonial political leaders emphatically re-

10, 1721, *ibid.*, 1720–21, 386–87; Samuel Shute to the King, August 16, 1723, *ibid.*, 1722–23, 324–30; *The Representation and Memorial of the Council of the Island of Jamaica to the Right Honourable The Lords Commissioners for Trade and Plantations* (London, 1716), ii, iv, 14.

[44]Lords of Trade to Privy Council, May 28, 1679, *Calendar of State Papers, Colonial, 1677–80*, 369.

jected the "slavish . . . position . . . that we have no Constitution in the Colonies, but what the king is pleased to give us" and challenged the notion that their constitutions, including their rights to representative government, were founded only on royal charters and commissions. Partisans of those few colonies that still retained charters through the middle decades of the eighteenth century praised their "Precious CHARTER[S]" as those "great Hedge[s] which Providence has planted round our natural Rights." As Edward Rawson pointed out in 1691 in justifying the overthrow of the Dominion of New England in Massachusetts, the charters might indeed be considered as "an Original Contract between the King and the first Planters" by which the king promised them that "if they at their own cost and charge would subdue a Wilderness, and enlarge his Dominions, they and their Posterity after them should enjoy such Priviledges as are in their Charters expressed."[45]

But colonial partisans insisted, in paraphrasing Sir Edward Coke, that the charters, like Magna Charta itself, were only "declaratory of Old Rights, and not . . . Grant[s] of new ones." A charter, the New York Assembly told Governor William Burnett in August 1728, merely confirmed "Rights and Privileges inherent in Us, in

---

[45]Zacharius Plaintruth, *New-York Gazette Revived in the Weekly Post-Boy*, January 27, 1752; [Nicholas Bourke], *The Privileges of the Island of Jamaica Vindicated with an Impartial Narrative of the late Dispute between the Governor and House of Representatives* (London, 1766), 45; Thomas Prince, *A Sermon on the Sorrowful Occasion of the Death of His Late Majesty King George* (Boston, 1727), 26; Thomas Foxcroft, *God the Judge, pulling down One, and setting up Another* (Boston, 1727), 27, 39; Jared Eliot, *Give Cesar his Due: or, The Obligation the Subjects are under to Their Civil Rulers* (New London, 1738), 36–38; *New-England Weekly Journal* (Boston), March 18, 1728; Norris, *Speech Delivered from the Bench*, 2; A Freeholder, *Maryland Gazette* (Annapolis), March 10, 1748; The Inhabitant, *South Carolina Gazette* (Charleston), December 10, 1764; [Edward Rawson], *The Revolution in New England Justified* (Boston, 1691), 42–43.

common with [all] . . . his Majesty's Freeborn Natural Subjects." No less than in Britain itself, colonists thus argued, the inhabitants of British "*America* have a just Claim to the *hereditary Rights* of British Subjects." Accompanying "every *British* Subject . . . wheresoever he wanders or rests so long as he is within the Pale of the *British* Dominions, and is true to his Allegiance," these "inherent" rights, as one colonial writer defined them, included the right "to have a Property of his own, in his Estate, Person and Reputation; subject only to Laws enacted by his own Concurrence, either in Person or by his Representatives."[46]

Quite apart from whether it still had or ever had had a charter, therefore, every colony, as "the Progeny of" Britain, therefore had "an undoubted Right to the Liberties of its Mother Country." Because the colonists were thus entitled to "the same *fundamental Rights, Privileges,* and *Liberties*" as the "People of *England,*" "no difference [could be] made, between the Rights and conditions of subjects in the colonies, and those in England." Moreover, because their rights ultimately rested upon "the same *grand Charter* with the People of *England,*" the colonists believed, their claims to those rights were every bit as secure as the king's title to the crown, which was founded precisely on the same document. In the colonies, as in Britain, "the *Prerogatives* of the *Crown,* and the *People[']s Liberty*" were thus "regulated by and under the Protection of the *same* [fundamental] *Laws.*" Even more recently than the issuance of the charters, various colonists pointed out, their entitlement to these rights had

---

[46][Increase Mather], *The Declaration of the Gentlemen, Merchants, and Inhabitants of Boston, and the Countrey Adjacent* (Boston, 1689), 2; *New York Gazette*, August 19, 1728; Americanus, *A Letter to the Freeholders and other Inhabitants of the Massachusetts-Bay* ([Boston], 1739), 5; [Richard Jackson], *An Historical Review of the Constitution of Government of Pennsylvania* (London, 1759), 7; Thomas Pownall, *The Administration of the Colonies* (London, 1764), 40–41.

been confirmed both by the crown's law officers and, in 1740, by Parliament itself in an act offering naturalization to foreigners after seven years' residence in the colonies. This act, James Otis later contended, constituted a "plain declaration of the British parliament, that the subjects in the colonies" were "intitled to all the privileges of the people of Great Britain."[47]

Of all the rights thus inherited by and confirmed to these distant colonies, colonists considered none more essential to their identities as British people than the rights, in the words of New York justice William Smith, "*to choose the Laws by which we will be Governed*" and "*to be Governed only by such Laws.*" Colonial writers were fond of quoting Sir William Jones, attorney general under Charles II, that the king "could no more grant a commission to levy money on his subjects in the plantations, without their consent by an assembly, than they could discharge themselves from their allegiance." If the colonial legislatures thus existed by virtue not of royal charters or commissions but of the colonists' "right to participate in the legislative power," it followed that because their distance prevented them from being represented in the British Parliament and having "Laws made for them . . . from Home" they "must therefore have new Laws from a legislature of their own." Both law and necessity thus dictated that the colonies should have "a perfect *internal* Lib-

[47]William Bollan's Petition to the House of Commons, August 6, 1749, Massachusetts Archives, Boston, XX, 501–6; [Bourke], *Privileges of the Island of Jamaica Vindicated*, 28; [William Smith], *Mr. Smith's Opinion Humbly Offered to the General Assembly of the Colony of New York* (New York, 1734), 13, 34, 45; Opinions of Richard West, 1720, and Charles Pratt and Charles Yorke, n.d., in George Chalmers, ed., *Opinions of Eminent Lawyers* (Burlington, Vt., 1858), 206–7; James Otis, *A Vindication of the Conduct of the House of Representatives of the Province of Massachusetts-Bay* (Boston, 1762), 51–52; Pennsylvania Assembly Journals, *Pennsylvania Archives* (Harrisburg, 1852–1935), 8th ser., V, 4176–77; *Boston Evening Post* (Boston), April 27, 1761; [Rawson], *Revolution in New England Justified*, 42–43.

erty, as to the Choice of their own Laws, and in all other Matters that" were "*purely* provincial." Precisely because "the Colonies themselves," as a West Indian remarked during the last decade of the seventeenth century, were the "proper Judges of what they suffer, want, and would have," and because the colonists' "minds must best appear in [their] general Assemblies," it seemed to the assemblies that there could be no "Reasonable Objection" to those bodies in "any . . . British Colonies . . . Exercising" a "Legislative power in its full Extent . . . within their own Jurisdiction[s]," so long as they did "not act contrary to the Laws of Great Britain." "What . . . may be done by the Legislature there," declared a Jamaican in the mid-1740s, "may be done by the Legislature here."[48]

Assembly partisans in this debate relied not only on the colonists' inherent rights as Englishmen but also upon custom, usage, and prescription. Whether the colonies had "been long enough set[t]led" to be able to claim "their Liberties and Privileges by immemorial Custom" was a matter of some doubt, even among assembly adherents. Yet in asserting that their right to representative institutions was in-

---

[48][Smith], *Mr. Smith's Opinion Humbly Offered*, 34; [Rawson], *Revolution in New England Justified*, 42–43; Smith, *History of New York*, I, 256–58; The Inhabitant, *South Carolina Gazette*, December 10, 1764; [William Blathwayt] to Chief Justice North, [October 20, 1680], *Calendar of State Papers, Colonial, 1677–80*, 616; Cornbury to Board of Trade, February 19, 1705, *ibid., 1704–06*, 386; Board of Trade to Privy Council, November 13, 1711, *ibid., 1711–12*, 146–47; James Knight, "The Natural, Moral, and Political History of Jamaica, and the Terretories thereon depending," 2 vols., II, 110–18, in Long Papers, Additional Manuscript 12,419, British Library, London; Christopher Gadsden, *South Carolina Gazette*, February 5, 1763; "Remarks on the Maryland Government," *American Magazine, or a Monthly Review of the Political State of the American Colonies*, I (1741), 29–20; Dalby Thomas, *An Historical Account of the Rise and Growth of the West-India Colonies* (London, 1690), 32; John Webb, *The Great Concern of New-England* (Boston, 1731), 28; Pownall, *Administration of the Colonies*, 40.

herent in them as Englishmen, the colonists were claiming, as Justice Joseph Murray of New York declared in 1734, that the assemblies derived "their Power or Authority . . . from the *common Custom and Laws of England*, claimed as an *English-man[']s Birth Right*, and as having been such, by *Immemorial Custom in England*; and tho' the People" in the colonies could not "claim this by *Immemorial Custom* here, yet as being part of the Dominions of *England*, they are intitled to the like *Powers* and *Authorities* here, that their fellow Subjects have, or are intitled to, in their *Mother Country*, by *Immemorial Custom*."[49]

From very early on, however, colonists defended their rights to assemblies on the basis not just of English but of their own custom. The assemblies had authority to exercise "a Legislative power in its full[est] extent," James Knight, a former attorney general of Jamaica, announced in the mid-1740s, in part because over a long period of time they had "in Fact Exercised a Legislative Power in almost every Instance, wherein it is possible to be Exercised." Similarly, although colonists themselves insisted that "the *constitutions* of the British colonies" had to be "modelled . . . in as near a conformity as possible to [that of] the mother country," they had no qualms in defending the assemblies' claims to peculiar rights and privileges that deviated from metropolitan norms on the basis of "*Perpetual Usage*," "established custom," or "Length of practice." Like the British Parliament, each assembly, this position implied, had its own peculiar "Lex & Consuetudo Parliamenti," a set of privileges and powers that rested, like the common law in England, primarily upon the authority of immemorial custom as it had developed over time in the colonies.[50]

[49]Joseph Murray, *Mr. Murray's Opinion Relating to the Courts of Justice in the Colony of New-York* [New York, 1734], 7, 15.

[50]Knight, "History of Jamaica," II, 110–16; Christopher Gadsden, *South Carolina Gazette*, December 17, 1764; [Bourke], *Privileges of the Island of Jamaica Vindicated*, 31; Elisha Cooke, *Mr. Cooke's Just and Seasonable*

Whether the crown could—or could not—alter colonial rights and privileges established through usage and founded on either custom or the colonists' presumed inherent rights as English people was certainly the most divisive issue separating metropolis and colonies during the seven decades following the Glorious Revolution. Although colonial assemblies rarely shrank from any challenges from the metropolis to the rights of people and institutions within their respective jurisdictions, they virtually ceased to demand the explicit recognition of those rights they had so often sought between 1660 and 1720. Thereafter, the unstated strategy of the assemblies seems to have been to secure local rights against the power of the metropolis in much the same way that those rights had been achieved within the metropolis itself: through practice and usage that with the implicit acquiescence of the metropolis would gradually acquire the sanction of custom.

But this approach left vital constitutional problems unsettled. "The chiefest Thing wanting to make the Inhabitants of these Plantations happy," an anonymous Virginian told his English readers in 1701, was "a good Constitution of Government." By a good constitution, he explained, he meant one that would not only settle the nagging questions of "what is Law, and what is not in the Plantations" and "how far the Legislative Authority is in the Assemblies of the several Colonies," but settle them in such a way as to leave the colonies with "a Just and Equal Government." Such a constitution, he insisted, was necessary to guarantee the colonists the equal and impartial administration of justice and the full enjoyment of "their Liberties and Estates" that were the proud distinguishing marks of

Vindications Respecting some Affairs transacted by the late General Assembly at Boston, 1720 [Boston, 1720], 9; Henry Wilkinson, "The Governor, the Council & Assembly in Bermuda during the First Half of the Eighteenth Century," *Bermuda Historical Quarterly,* 2 (1945), 81–84; "Vindication of the Council," *South Carolina Gazette,* June 5, 1756.

English people whether they remained at home or lived in distant colonies.[51]

But the crown's continuing claims for "*a more absolute Power in the Plantations than in* England" meant that the colonists would never be able to extract such formal and explicit guarantees from metropolitan authorities. These claims stirred recurrent fears among colonial leaders that "the natural, and legal, and constitutional rights of the people" in the colonies might "be annihilated" and their identity as English people destroyed. Intensely resentful that crown officials should yet "be so infatuated, as to seek every occasion for alarming the fears and exciting the jealousy, of his majesty's subject; endeavouring, to extend the prerogative, and advance the power, of the Crown, to the diminution, if not the total extinction, of the *natural* and *indisputable rights* of the people" in the colonies, they fretted that their claims to the liberties and legal protections of English people would be constantly exposed "to a *perpetual mutability*" and that metropolitan officials would never "*explicitly* . . . acknowledge, and put out of farther danger of unconstitutional attempts" the "*essential* rights" and thus the identity of the colonists as English people.[52]

III

The metropolitan effort to tax the colonies for revenue in the 1760s raised, for colonials, the new constitutional issue of the extent of Parliament's jurisdiction over the colonies and forced them to think through a number of crucial issues, including especially the nature of

[51][Harrison], *Essay upon the Government of the English Plantations,* 15–24.

[52]*The Groans of the Plantations. Expressed in a Letter from a Gentleman Residing there, to his Friend in London* (London, 1714), iv; The Inhabitant, *South Carolina Gazette,* December 10, 1764; [Joseph Galloway], A *True and Impartial State of the Province of Pennsylvania* (Philadelphia, 1759), 11; C. G., *South Carolina Gazette,* December 17, 1764.

sovereignty and the distribution of authority in a composite extended polity such as the British Empire. Throughout the long debate over these subjects between 1764 and 1776, however, they grounded their constitutional arguments against Parliamentary jurisdiction over their internal affairs on precisely the same, by then ancient, foundations on which during the long colonial era they had repeatedly rested their claims to entitlement to the laws, liberties, and identity of English (after 1707, British) peoples: their inherited rights as English people and the customary supports they had developed, through the same time-honored process of usage that was the foundation of the English common law and representative systems, to support, strengthen, expand, and localize those rights.

To colonial leaders, the colonists' claims to English rights seemed unassailable. "To the infinite advantage and emolument of the mother state," the colonists, as the Providence merchant Stephen Hopkins announced in 1764, had "left the delights of their native country, parted from their homes and all their conveniences[, and] . . . searched out . . . and subdued a foreign country with the most amazing travail and fortitude." They undertook these Herculean tasks on the assumption "that they and their successors forever should be free, should be partakers and sharers in all the privileges and advantages of the then English, now British constitution," and should enjoy "all the rights and privileges of freeborn Englishmen." "Of all the rights of Englishmen," the "primitive right[s] that every freeholder had of consenting to those laws by which the community was to be obliged" and of "being tried by juries" were certainly "the most material and important."[53]

---

[53]Stephen Hopkins, *The Rights of the Colonies Examined* (Providence, 1764), in Charles S. Hyneman and Donald S. Lutz, eds., *American Political Writing during the Founding Era 1760–1805*, 2 vols. (Indianapolis, 1983), I, 46–47, 49; Aequus, *Massachusetts Gazette and Boston Newsletter*, March 6, 1766, in *ibid.*, 63; Brittannus Americanus, *Boston Gazette*, March 17, 1766, in *ibid.*, I, 89.

Although the crown through many charters had formally confirmed that emigrants and their descendants "should have and enjoy all the freedom and liberty that the subjects of England enjoy[ed]," including the right to "make laws for their own government suitable to their circumstances, not repugnant to, but as near as might be agreeable to the laws of England," colonial protagonists insisted, reiterating the argument their ancestors had fully worked out over the previous century and a half, that the colonists had never held "those rights as a privilege granted them, nor enjoy[ed] them as a grace and favor bestowed" by the crown. "Under an English government," they contended, with the Virginia lawyer Richard Bland, "all men" were "born free," and, because the first settlers and their progeny had continued English subjects, they had always been "freeborn subjects, justly and naturally entitled to all the rights and advantages of the British constitution," and possessed those rights and advantages "as an inherent, indefeasible right." As "English subjects who" were "free" and had never "legally forfeited *any part* of their freedom," they had no need for "charter declarations to confirm" that they were "justly entitled to any and every [one of] the rights, liberties, privileges and immunities" of English people. Colonial charters, like the "great charter of liberties, commonly called *Magna Charta*," thus did "not *give* the privileges therein mentioned" but were "only declaratory of our rights, and in affirmance of them."[54]

Custom as well as inheritance provided an additional foundation for colonial entitlement to British rights. Since they first "left

[54]Hopkins, *Rights of the Colonies*, in Hyneman and Lutz, eds., *American Political Writing*, I, 47, 49–50; Richard Bland, *The Colonel Dismounted* (Williamsburg, 1764), in Bernard Bailyn, ed., *Pamphlets of the American Revolution* (Cambridge, Mass., 1965), 319–20; Brittannus Americanus, *Boston Gazette*, March 17, 1766, in Hyneman and Lutz, eds., *American Political Writing*, I, 89; [Silas Downer], *A Discourse at the Dedication of the Tree of Liberty* (Providence, 1768), in *ibid.*, I, 100.

the Mother Kingdom to extend its Commerce and Dominion" more than a century earlier, colonial writers argued, they had "quietly possessed" and "fully enjoyed all the freedoms and immunities promised on their first removal from England." In language redolent of the colonists' ancient disputes with crown authorities, they pointed out that their rights had thus been "sanctified by successive usage" and that that usage had been "ratified by repeated authoritative acquiescence." Such "constant and uninterrupted usage and custom," it seemed to them, was, in the best traditions of English constitutional development, "sufficient of itself" to provide a firm legal foundation for their claims to the liberties and legal protections of Britons.[55]

Throughout the long quarrel with Parliament, they reiterated and dilated upon this argument. "Permitted and commissioned by the crown," said the Pennsylvania lawyer and immigrant from Scotland, James Wilson, in 1774, they had undertaken, "at their own expense, expeditions to this distant country," taken "possession of it, planted it, and cultivated it." By thus freely "quitting the soil" of Great Britain, they had neither abandoned nor forfeited their rights to "British Freedom." They had not, said Wilson, "embark[ed], freemen, in Great Britain, [and] disembark[ed], slaves in America." Rather, they had brought their rights with them and implanted them in their own polities by adopting, in the words of the Virginia lawyer Thomas Jefferson, "that system of laws which" had "so long been the glory and protection of" Britain and "under which they had hitherto

[55]Virginia Petition to the King, December 18, 1764, in William J. Van Schreeven *et al.*, eds. *Revolutionary Virginia: The Road to Independence* (Richmond, 1973), I, 11; Hopkins, *Rights of the Colonies,* in Hyneman and Lutz, eds., *American Political Writing,* I, 50; Aequus, *Massachusetts Gazette and Boston Newsletter,* March 6, 1766, *ibid.*, I, 65; Bland, *Colonel Dismounted,* in Bailyn, ed., *Pamphlets of the American Revolution,* 323; John Gay Alleyne, *A Letter to the North American, On Occasion of his Address to the Committee of Correspondence in Barbados* (Barbados, 1766), 4.

lived in the mother country." Secure under that system of laws and experiencing the benefits of living under a mode of British governance in which people were "only subject to laws made with their own consent" and every individual was in "a situation without the reach of the highest EXECUTIVE power in the state, if he lives in an obedience to its laws," they subsequently "grew and multiplied, and diffused British freedom and British spirit, wherever they came. Happy in the enjoyment of liberty, and in reaping the fruits of their toils; but still more happy in the joyful prospect of transmitting their liberty and their fortunes to the latest posterity, they inculcated to their children the warmest sentiments of loyalty to their sovereign . . . and of affection and esteem for the inhabitants of the mother country, with whom they gloried in being intimately connected."[56]

Exalting in their identity as Britons, they took pride in having come "out from a kingdom renowned for liberty[,] from a constitution founded on compact, from a people of all the sons of men most tenacious of freedom." They celebrated "the admirable temperament of the British constitution," that "glorious fabrick of Britain's Liberty—the pride of her citizens—the envy of her neighbours—planned by her legislators—erected by her patriots—maintained entire by numerous generations past!" "The boast of Englishmen and of freedom," the British constitution and "code of laws," they declared repeatedly, were obviously "the best that ever existed among men." In phrases that echoed Fortescue and Coke, whom they frequently cited, they expressed their happiness that, unlike the inhabitants of

---

[56]James Wilson, *Considerations on the Nature and Extent of the Legislative Authority of the British Parliament* (Philadelphia, 1774), in Robert Green McCloskey, ed., *The Works of James Wilson*, 2 vols. (Cambridge, Mass., 1967), II, 733, 740; Thomas Jefferson, *A Summary View of the Rights of British America* (Williamsburg, 1774), in Van Schreeven *et al.*, *Revolutionary Virginia*, I, 243–44; Bland, *Colonel Dismounted*, in Bailyn, ed., *Pamphlets of the American Revolution*, 319–20.

most other polities, they were not "governed at the will of another, or of others, and" that they were not "in the miserable condition of slaves" whose property could "be taken from them by taxes or otherwise without their own consent and against their will." Rather, they militantly asserted, they lived, like Britons in the home islands, under a "beneficial compact" by which, as British subjects, they could "be governed only agreeable to laws to which [they] themselves have some way consented, and are not to be compelled to part with their property but as it is called for by the authority of such laws."[57]

This assertion that the colonists enjoyed "the Liberty & Privileges of Englishmen, in the same Degree, as if we had still continued among our Brethren in Great Britain" was a demand for recognition of the colonists' identities as Britons. Not just "Our Language, . . . our Intermarriages, & other Connections, our constant Intercourse, and above all our Interest[s]," they cried, but also, and infinitely more important, "Our Laws [and] . . . our Principles of Government," those preeminent characteristics of true Britons, identified them as Britons who, "descended from the same Stock" as their "fellow-Subjects in Great Britain" and "nurtured in the same Principles of Freedom; which we have both suck'd in with our Mother's Milk," were "the same People with them, in every Respect."[58]

Vociferously, then, the colonists objected to being taxed or governed in their internal affairs without their consent because

[57]Hopkins, *Rights of the Colonies*, in Hyneman and Lutz, eds., *American Political Writing*, I, 46, 49; Wilson, *Considerations*, in McCloskey, ed., *Works of James Wilson*, II, 731; Carter Braxton, *An Address to the Convention of the Colony and Ancient Dominion of Virginia on the Subject of Government in General, and Recommending a Particular Form to Their Attention, Virginia Gazette*, June 8, 15, 1776, in Hyneman and Lutz, eds., *American Political Writing*, I, 332.

[58]George Mason to the Committee of Merchants in London, June 6, 1766, in Robert A. Rutland, ed., *The Papers of George Mason*, 3 vols. (Chapel Hill, 1970), I, 68, 71.

such actions subjected them to a form of governance that was at once contrary to the rights and legal protections traditionally enjoyed by Britons and, on the very deepest level, denied their very identity as a British people. To be thus governed without consent was to be treated not like the freeborn Britons they had always claimed to be, but like a "conquered people" ; not like the independent proprietors so many of them were, people who "possessed . . . property" that could be "called" their "own" and were therefore not dependent "upon the will of another," but like "miserable . . . slaves" who could "neither dispose of person or goods, but" enjoyed "all at the will of" their "masters"; and certainly not like people with similar amounts of property in Britain, as *"free agent[s] in a political view"* with full rights of civic participation, but like those many people in the home islands who had little or no property, as people who were *"in so mean a situation, that they"* were "supposed to have no will of their own" and were therefore ineligible even to vote. "Unless every *free agent* in America be permitted to enjoy the same privilege[s]" as those exercised by similarly free agents in Britain, the young Alexander Hamilton declared in 1775, the colonists would be "entirely stripped of the benefits of the [British] constitution," deprived of their status as a British people, "and precipitated into an abyss of slavery."[59]

That such was the return made by metropolitan leaders to the colonists "for braving the danger of the deep—for planting a wilderness, inhabited only by savage man and savage beasts—for extending the dominions of the British crown—for increasing the trade of the British merchants—for augmenting the rents of the British landlords—[and] for heightening the wages of British artificers"

---

[59]Wilson, *Considerations*, in McCloskey, ed., *Works of James Wilson*, II, 740; Alexander Hamilton, *The Farmer Refuted* (New York, 1775), in Harold C. Syrett *et al.*, eds., *The Papers of Alexander Hamilton*, 27 vols. (New York, 1961–1987), I, 105–7; Hopkins, *Rights of the Colonies*, in Hyneman and Lutz, eds., *American Political Writing*, I, 46.

seemed to colonists to be understandable only as an act of "Tyranny and Oppression" intended to deny colonial Britons an equality of status with metropolitan Britons by "destroy[ing] the very existence of law and liberty in the colonies." Only by exercising their inherited right, a right "secured to them both by the letter and the spirit of the British constitution," to employ force to defend their "British liberties" against such "Violence & Injustice," only by actively "resist[ing] such force—force acting without authority—force employed contrary to law," they decided in 1775–1776, could they manage to "transmit" their British heritage "unimpaired to" their "Posterity" and to make good their own claims to be worthy of a British identity.[60]

IV

If, in the mid-1770s, the colonists rose up to defend their claims to British liberty, law, and identity, the crisis over independence, as one Virginian suggested in mid-1776, "relaxed the tone of government in almost every colony, and occasioned in many instances a total suspension of law," thereby provoking a widespread demand for constitutional changes that would insure the former colonists their customary "benefit of law" and secure for them "the enjoyment of" the inherited "liberties" they had gone to such extremes to protect. In constructing their new constitutions, they sought to avoid some of the defects they had, during the previous twelve years, identified in the British constitution. In particular, they had become acutely aware that the unlimited power claimed by Parliament in the wake of the Glorious Revolution represented an open invita-

---

[60]Wilson, *Considerations*, in McCloskey, ed., *Works of James Wilson*, II, 733; Mason to Committee of Merchants, June 6, 1766, in Rutland, ed., *Papers of George Mason*, I, 71; James Wilson, *Speech Delivered in the Convention for the Province of Pennsylvania* (Philadelphia, 1775), in McCloskey, ed., *Works of James Wilson*, II, 755.

tion for the exercise of "an absolute legislative power" that left both liberty and law in a precarious condition. Hence, they sought to improve upon the English system by trying to find ways to place "constitutional limits to the exercise of the Legislative Powers," an objective that, through trial and error, they slowly learned to meet by declaring "certain rights . . . paramount to the power of the ordinary Legislature."[61]

In abandoning monarchy for republicanism, however, Americans made every effort to hold on to and augment their inherited British traditions of law and liberty. Celebrating the republican form because it was entirely, in John Adams's words, "an empire of laws, and not of men," they sought to contrive constitutional arrangements that in virtually all of their particulars revealed a powerful intention to incorporate those traditions into their new republican polities. By the late 1790s, American interpreters could credibly claim that the experiment in republican and federal government had made it clear, had there ever been any doubt, that, no less than for their British ancestors, "the love of liberty [and] . . . the love of law" were the virtues that were "chiefly . . . descriptive of the American character."[62]

Few contemporaries had much doubt that Americans had derived this defining, this identifying, love for law and liberty in some major part from their British ancestors and, more particularly, from the English common law tradition. Containing the "strongest" evidence of "common consent . . . practically given . . . in the freest and most unbiased manner" and resting "upon the most solid basis—experience as well as opinion," England's customary common law,

---

[61]Braxton, *Address to the Convention*, in Hyneman and Lutz, eds., *American Political Writing*, I, 329; *Four Letters on Interesting Subjects* (Philadelphia, 1776), in *ibid.*, I, 384–85; James Kent, *An Introductory Lecture to a Course of Law Lectures* (New York, 1794), in *ibid.*, II, 941.

[62]John Adams, *Thoughts on Government* (Boston, 1776), in Hyneman and Lutz, eds., *American Political Writing*, I, 403; James Wilson, *Lectures on Law*, in McCloskey, ed., *Works of James Wilson*, I, 72.

Americans acknowledged, had, "by a long experience," slowly developed to accommodate "the situation and circumstances of the" English people, been "incorporated into their very temperament, and . . . become the constitution of the English commonwealth." Out of the common law had emerged a "spirit of liberty" that had successfully carried that commonwealth through "all the vicissitudes, revolutions, and dangers, to which that system has been exposed." "It was this spirit," James Wilson told his law students of the College of Philadelphia in the early 1790s, "which dictated the frequent and formidable demands on the Norman princes, for the complete restoration of the Saxon jurisprudence; it was this spirit, which, in magna charta, manifested a strict regard to the rights of the commons, as well as those of the peerage; it was this spirit, which extracted sweetness from all the bitter contentions between the rival houses of Lancaster and York; it was this spirit, which preserved England from the haughtiness of the Tudors, and from the tyranny of the Stuarts."[63]

"From the time of their emigration from Europe, and settlement on this side of the Atlantic," said James Kent, professor of law at Columbia College in 1794, "the influence of the Common Law was strongly felt and widely diffused by our American Ancestors." The common law, said Wilson, was the principal means by which the emigrants had "carried with them the Rights of Englishmen" to the colonies, where it slowly underwent modifications "proportional to the changes" the colonists experienced "in their situation" and helped them to keep "the great ends of liberty . . . steadily and constantly in view." In significant part through their attachment to the English common law tradition, said the South Carolina historian David Ramsay, the "English colonists were from their first settlement in America, devoted to liberty, to English ideas, and English principles. They not

[63]Wilson, *Lectures on Law*, in McCloskey, ed., *Works of James Wilson*, I, 102, 335, 355–57.

only conceived themselves to inherit the privileges of Englishmen, but[,] though in a colonial situation, actually possessed them." "No higher evidence need or can be found of the prevailing knowledge of our Rights, and the energy of the freedom of the Common Law," observed Kent, "than the spirit which pervaded and roused every part of this Continent on the eve of the late Revolution."[64]

Through their experience with the English law system, in the words of Wilson, the "dearest birthright and richest inheritance" of the colonists, American observers during the Revolutionary era profoundly believed, the colonists had learned that neither law nor liberty could "exist, without the other," that "Without liberty, law loses its nature and its name, and becomes oppression," and that "Without law, liberty loses its nature and its name, and becomes licentiousness." Their deep attachment to these basic principles of the British common law tradition, so firmly rooted in their identities as British people in the New World, was, in Wilson's view, principally responsible for rescuing Americans "from the oppressive claims, and from all the mighty efforts made to enforce the oppressive claims, of a British Parliament," carrying them through the uncertain travails of a constitutional revolution, and providing crucial experiential and theoretical foundations for the political "establishments in the several states and in the national government" through which they hoped to transmit "their best and noblest birthright" to their posterity and perpetuate their ancient self-identity as a self-governing people who lived in political societies governed by the rule of law.[65]

[64]Kent, *Introductory Lecture*, in Hyneman and Lutz, eds., *American Political Writing*, II, 939–40; Wilson, *Lectures on Law*, in McCloskey, ed., *Works of James Wilson*, I, 359–60; David Ramsay, *The History of the American Revolution* (Philadelphia, 1789), in Hyneman and Lutz, eds., *American Political Writing*, II, 721.

[65]Wilson, *Lectures on Law*, in McCloskey, ed., *Works of James Wilson*, I, 72, 131, 183, 356–57, 359.

PART TWO

The Materials and Means

The Fortunes of Orthodoxy:

The Political Economy of Public Debt in England and America during the 1780s

Richard Vernier

In the aftermath of the American war for Independence, both the new United States and His majesty's government in Great Britain were confronted with unprecedented war debts. Both nations viewed the problem of public indebtedness from a shared vantage point which derived from over eighty years of extensive commentary on public debt and taxation. In Britain the conventional wisdom portrayed the growing debt as a grave threat to the polity. Even the minority view that public indebtedness was not a threat, and was in many respects a public blessing, betrayed a fundamental ambivalence which underscored the feeling of menace which the debt and funding systems evoked in the eighteenth century. The policy response to the crisis of the war debt, climaxing in Pitt's revival of the Sinking Fund, showed the strength of this orthodoxy. Paradoxically, it was where that orthodoxy was strongest, America, that the most profound ideological transformation occurred. In America the negative view of British debt and funding was exacerbated by the ubiquity of a political ideology in which the debt was totemic of all that was wrong with British society, and all that the American republic was not going to be. Yet this ideological perspective on public finance was of limited relevance to the plans for the financial reconstruction of the new republic. It was in the

American hotbed of Country, opposition thought that the new, more favorable attitude towards funding and the debt met with its greatest successes, and policy was consequently heterodox. But this success, in turn, restored the fortunes of the old orthodoxy, for confronted with the visage of the old enemy, the voice of Cassandra became again familiar, convincing, and correct.

I

England's public debt was a central political issue throughout the eighteenth century, and it was one of the key issues in the developing science of political economy. The key figures of British political economy—from Charles Davenant, to David Hume, James Steuart, and Adam Smith—placed the growing public debt at the center of their analysis. Inasmuch as political economy was born of the systematic reflection upon the impact of government fiscal policy on the trade of the nation, it was inevitable that the public debt would be a topic of central concern. From the outset, public borrowing was analyzed in terms of its impact on economic and commercial growth. Indeed, within a few years of the creation of England's public debt, Charles Davenant's explorations in "political arithmetic"—those means by which a kingdom became rich or poor—led him to excoriate its growth. According to Davenant, private credit was "the principal mover in all business," and yet heavy government borrowing obstructed the flow of capital to enterprise: it increased the demand for limited supplies of credit, and thereby pushed up the rate of interest. Moreover, the premiums paid by government securities diverted money from the channels of trade "where it is always best employed to the kingdoms advantage" to be plowed into high-return government funds. The lucrative returns offered by government securities served to undermine commercial society itself. "Will men who can safely," worried Davenant, "and without trouble, reap such gains bre[e]d their children to be merchants? Will they venture great stocks to make discoveries and employ their industry to enlarge and extend our dealings with distant parts?"[1]

Davenant's concerns were increasingly echoed over the course of the eighteenth century, a product of the debt's seemingly inexorable growth. Standing at £54 million in 1720, nearly two decades' application of the sinking fund only managed to shrink the debt by £7 million. From that point on, the debt metastasized; the reason, of course, was war. Each war increased the debt: at the end of the Seven Years' War in 1763 the debt was over £132 million; while at the end of the American war the debt was nearly £240 million and the annual cost of debt service was over £9 million. Although these figures seem rather paltry by today's standards, the debt was actually huge by comparison with the size of the economy. In 1700 the total debt represented over 26% of annual national income; by 1759 over 136% of national income. By comparison, America's debt was under 56% of annual national income after ten years of depression spending in 1939, and still just 116% of national income in 1949 after the enormous expense of the Second World War.[2]

Moreover, the growth of the British debt was not matched by growth in the economy. From 1700 to 1790, the debt increased an average of 3.47% per year, and the cost of servicing the debt increased

---

[1]Charles Davenant, *The Political and Commercial Works* . . . , 5 vols. (London, 1771), I, 16, 22–23, 30, 155–56; III, 329.

[2]For British debt figures, B. R. Mitchell, *British Historical Statistics* (Cambridge, 1988), Public Finance, Table 7; national income estimates for England and Wales, 1688 (£54.44 million) and 1759 (£66.84 million), from Peter H. Lindert and Jeffrey G. Williamson, "Revising England's Social Tables, 1688–1812," *Explorations in Economic History*, 19 (1982), and "Reinterpreting Britain's Social Tables, 1688–1913," *Explorations in Economic History*, 20 (1983). For U.S. national income and federal debt, see Ben Wattenberg, ed., *Statistical History of the United States* (New York, 1976), tables series F 6–9 and series Y 493–504, pp. 224, 1116–17.

an average of 2.75% per year.[3] Yet recent estimates of eighteenth-century British economic growth by N. F. R. Crafts suggest that the economy only grew at an annual rate of .69% from 1700 to 1760, and just over 1% a year from 1760 to 1801.[4] R. V. Jackson has further argued that profound difficulties in measuring the impact of government spending on economic growth should further reduce estimates of the rate of growth in private sector output to .51% per year from 1700 to 1760.[5] According to these figures, therefore, the debt grew nearly seven times faster than the economy in the first half of the century; the burden of servicing the debt increased at over five times faster than the rate of economic growth. The tax burden to service the debt was also mounting. Tax revenues—nearly half went to debt service—grew from £4.3 million in 1700 to over £11 million on the eve of American independence. Historian Patrick O'Brien estimates that taxes as a share of national income increased from about 3.5% in the 1670s to 8.8% in 1700, and 11.7% in 1775. Moreover, these figures understate the actual burden of taxation. Since approximately 40% of national income was untaxed, the state's bite for those actually paying taxes was about 17% of income. The tax burden was even greater than this, since O'Brien's figures are not the gross sums raised from the public, and exclude another 10% in collection costs, together with another 10% for local taxation. Just as the growth in debt was not matched by the growth of the economy, so too, economic historian Peter Mathias writes, "economic growth was not the

---

[3]Based on calculations from the data in Mitchell, *British Historical Statistics*, Public Finance, Tables 2 and 7.

[4]N. F. R. Crafts, British Economic Growth during the Industrial Revolution (Oxford, 1985), 45.

[5]R. V. Jackson, "Government Expenditure and British Economic Growth in the Eighteenth Century," *Economic History Review*, 2nd ser., XLIII, No. 2 (1990), 217–35, Table 2, p. 232.

major factor behind the marked rise in tax revenue."[6] Government consumption of resources grew throughout the eighteenth century in both absolute and relative terms.

In the decades following Davenant's strictures on public debt the analytic foundation for its disparagement only grew. By the middle of the eighteenth century, political economy was acquiring the status of a discipline, with systematic works produced by writers drawing upon an accepted corpus of authorities—like Locke and Davenant—and was employing theories—like the quantity theory of money and the balance of trade—to explore and explain topics outside of the context of specific policy debates. If previous theorists had grasped the notion of the economy as an interrelated system governed by economic laws, the achievements of the giants of political economy in Britain, Adam Smith and David Hume, lay in their articulation of the mechanisms within that system that tended to produce equilibrium, balance, order, and progress without anyone's direction or design. A beneficent social order could emerge, and economic progress take place, as the unintended consequence of human action. In its most famous exemplar, Adam Smith's *Wealth of Nations*, a simple and natural system of liberty is described by which men, acting in their own self-interest and in response to the signals of market prices and profit opportunities, are led to actions which tend most to promote economic progress and well-being. They are, in his memorable phrase, led by an invisible hand to promote an end

[6]Peter Mathias, *The First Industrial Nation*, 37–38; Patrick O'Brien, "The Political Economy of British Taxation, 1660–1815," *Economic History Review*, 2nd ser., XLI, No. 1 (1988), 3, 6; Price to Shelburne, 1775 (undated), Price/Shelburne Correspondence, Shelburne MS, Bodleian Library; Peter Mathias, "Taxation and Industrialization in Britain, 1700–1870," in *The Transformation of England* (London, 1979), 117; quote from O'Brien, 6.

which was no part of their intention. Government actions which interfered in this natural order were, therefore, almost invariably destructive of social well-being.[7] On this point, the matter of government finances, taxes, and the permanent debt took heavy criticism. With few exceptions, the new science distrusted the new finance.

Hume consistently portrayed the growth of public debt in Britain as a disaster. In 1754 he wrote that the modern expedient of placing the burdens of war finance upon posterity was "ruinous beyond all controversy," leading to "certain and inevitable" abuses, to "poverty, impotence, and subjection to foreign powers;"[8] while in the year of his death he wrote that it was mathematically demonstrable "that the endless increase of National Debts is the direct road to National Ruin," and a display of such egregious folly that "we have even lost all title to compassion in the numberless calamities that are waiting for us."[9]

The claim popularized by Walpole—that the public debt constituted a public blessing—drew Hume's ridicule as equal to the "trials of wit among rhetoricians, like the panegyrics on folly and fever."

[7]See Peter Gay, *The Enlightenment: The Science of Freedom* (New York, 1969), 344–53; William Letwin, *Origins of Scientific Economics. English Economic Thought, 1660–1776* (New York, 1964), 223–38; Joseph J. Spengler, "The Problem of Order in Economic Affairs," in Joseph J. Spengler and William R. Allen, eds., *Essays in Economic Thought: Aristotle to Marshall* (Chicago, 1960). Social wealth and economic growth, however, were sometimes portrayed as mere adjuncts of state power by political economists, most strikingly in Hume: e.g., in the emphasis on the money supply's impact on ease of tax-collection in "Of Money," or in the discussion of the impact of commerce on a nation's martial power in "Of Commerce," in *Essays, Moral, Political, and Literary*, ed. by Eugene F. Miller (Indianapolis, 1987), 289, 255–67. Cf. Gay, *The Enlightenment*, II, 346–48.

[8]Hume, "Of Public Credit," *Essays*, 350–51.

[9]David Hume, *History of England*, 6 vols. (London, 1776), V, 475, note B.

Arguments to show that the debt was no real burden—Melon's argument in 1736 was that the debts of the state were simply the left hand paying the right[10]—ignored the fact that the debts were serviced by taxes, and growth in taxes would inevitably become ruinous. As every tax was mortgaged for debt service, new taxes would have to be found for revenue, even though they injured commerce and discouraged industry.[11] A system of public credit, according to Hume, was an open invitation to abuse, as politicians would always seek the rewards of public acclaim which war or other great expense could bring if the consequent tax burdens could be deferred or disguised by borrowing. "It would scarcely be more imprudent" Hume wrote, "to give a prodigal son a credit in every banker's shop in London, than to empower a statesman to draw bills, in this manner, upon posterity."[12]

Malachy Postlethwayt's *Universal Dictionary of Trade and Commerce*[13] was enormously influential, as it served to introduce to the British reading public the latest French theories on commerce, along with the great English theorists—Locke, North, Mun, Davenant,

[10]Cf. Shutaro Matsushita, *The Economic Effects of Public Debts* (New York, 1929), 20.

[11]Hume, "Of Public Credit," *Essays*, 356–60.

[12]In a 1741 essay, Hume was not unwilling to grant Walpole his due, but still maintained that his vices "were not compensated by those virtues which are nearly always allyed to them." In an unsubtle reference to Walpole's personal corruption and handling of the public debt, Hume wrote "His ministry has been more advantageous to his family than to the public, better for this age than for posterity." Thus, Hume wrote, "As I am a man, I love him; as I am a scholar, I hate him; as I am a Briton, I calmly wish his fall." Hume, "Character of Sir Robert Walpole," *Essays*, 574–76; "Of Public Credit," *Essays*, 352.

[13]Malachy Postlethwayt, *The Universal Dictionary of Trade and Commerce*, 2 vols. (2nd ed., London, 1757); on Smith and Cantillon, see Joseph A. Schumpeter, *History of Economic Analysis* (Oxford, 1954), 184.

and Hume.[14] According to the *Dictionary*, public borrowing and debt were at best a necessary evil; an inviolate sinking fund was therefore of utmost importance; releasing the nation from the burden of debt would cause tremendous growth and prosperity.[15] If the debt could be eliminated, the *Dictionary* assured its readers, the profits of manufacturers would increase 40%, "new arts and manufactures would be introduced, and the old ones brought to perfection; our most barren lands would be cultivated, and the produce of the whole insufficient to supply the demands of our people."[16]

While the debt was coming under an increasingly sophisticated attack from the new science of political economy it continued to be defended primarily in political terms. An old argument found new uses: Hume in 1770 repeated the Old Whig argument—now transmuted into a Court Whig defense—that the debt was primarily designed to be a prop to the regime.[17] As the threat of the Jacobite challenge receded, the debt was increasingly celebrated as proof of the stability of the regime, and a sign of the "Esteem which the people of England . . . entertain for our glorious Constitution."[18] This argument was to have an enormous impact on the American financiers Robert Morris and Alexander Hamilton, and it became a staple

---

[14]E. A. J. Johnson, *Predecessors of Adam Smith* (New York, 1937), Appendix B.

[15]*Dictionary*, II, 287; I, 576–79, 631.

[16]*Ibid.*, II, 285; I, 576; II, 10; I, 630; II, 286.

[17]Hume, "Of Public Credit," 355: "The first visible eruption . . . of public disorder must alarm all the stockholders, whose property is the most precarious of any; and will make them fly to the support of government. . . ." This passage was added to the 1770 edition of his *Essays*. See also Adam Smith, *Lectures on Jurisprudence* (Oxford, 1978), Report of 1762–1763, p. 268; Report of 1766, p. 430.

[18]"A Speech Without-Doors . . ." (1737), quoted in P. G. M. Dickson, *The Financial Revolution in England: A Study in the Development of Public Credit* (London, 1967), 16.

of court Whigs by mid-century. "When a free government," Robert Wallace wrote in 1758, "is able to contract great debts by borrowing from its own subjects, this is a certain sign, that it has gained the *confidence* of the people."[19]

Charges that the debt was a brake on the nation's prosperity, however, demanded a response, and the publication of Sir James Steuart's *Inquiry into the Principles of Political Oeconomy*—the first systematic treatise on political economy published in Britain—in 1767 provided the basis for the economic defense of the debt for the rest of the century.[20]

Far from being a drag on economic growth, Steuart maintained, public debt was an engine of circulation, a machine of progress. In a commercial society mere coin was an inadequate medium of circulation, but the institution of credit allowed the circulation of landed wealth, "the melting down of property." Most of the credit in a society, however, was unable to circulate, because it existed in forms like money of account, and only became money when it was paid. Public debt and government borrowing, however, allowed these stagnant funds to be used by the government, and hence monetized. An increase in capital and circulating medium are therefore great advantages of the funding system and public debt. The public debt did not create new wealth, but it did reallocate it by the tax system, which allowed that wealth to circulate. He wrote, "the effect of public borrowing, or national debt, is to augment the permanent income of the country out of the stagnant money and balances of trade." Stagnation in one sector of the economy could, Steuart claimed, "interrupt circulation in another"; for that reason "public borrowing

[19]Robert Wallace, *Characteristics of the Present Political State of Great Britain* (London, 1758), 53–54, 61, 63–68.

[20]See Andrew S. Skinner, "Sir James Steuart," *Scottish Journal of Political Economy*, 28 (February 1981), 20–42, for a more detailed sketch of his thought and background.

for domestic purposes has the good effect of giving vent to stagnation and throwing money into a new channel of circulation." Once created, this augmented capital must be kept in motion or the whole chain of circulation would break down: capital was only of value for the interest it earned. "Were the capital of £140 million [of British Debt] to be thrown in to the hands of the present creditors . . . what trade could absorb it?" Without the debt there would be a glut in the circulation of wealth, and the whole society would suffer. Yet even Steuart had some misgivings about the potential for mischief which a public debt could produce; above all, that its unchecked growth would result in the nation's creditors becoming masters of the nation.[21]

Perhaps nowhere was the public debt subject to a more searching and damning examination than in Adam Smith's *Wealth of Nations*. Smith's analysis of government debt and spending must be seen in the context of his analysis of economic progress, which, he wrote, was dependent upon the division of labor and the extent of the market, both of which required an increase of stock. Accumulation of stock was therefore the cause of increasing social produce. Public debt, according to Smith, represented nothing more than a transfer of stock from productive to unproductive uses. Indeed, he argued, had the nation not expended such vast sums in the century's endless series of wars,

> [m]ore houses would have been built, more lands would have been improved, and those which had been improved before would have been better cultivated, more manufactures would have been established, and those which had been established before would have been more extended; and to what height the real wealth and revenue of the country might, by this

[21]Sir James Steuart, *An Inquiry into the Principles of Political Oeconomy*, Andrew S. Skinner, ed., (1767; 1966, Edinburgh), II, 532–63, 600–601, 637, 638, 611, 644.

time, have been raised, it is not perhaps very easy even to imagine.[22]

Smith strongly denied that public securities were an addition to the capital stock of the nation. A public debt merely used an already existing capital as revenue, and capital was thus diverted "from maintaining productive labourers to maintain unproductive ones, and to be spent and wasted, generally in the course of the year, without even the hope of any future reproduction." There was no disguising that government borrowing represented a net loss to the capital stock of the nation.[23]

Thus, although the public debt was not uniformly regarded as an unalloyed disaster, the general consensus of informed opinion was that it posed a serious threat to Britain's well-being. That compendium of political wisdom, Blackstone's *Commentaries upon the Laws of England* conceded that debt certificates did provide a useful addition to the circulating medium, but that the size of the debt was far in excess of a beneficial amount; overall he deplored the debt for keeping taxes high, injuring trade, and impoverishing the nation.[24]

The war of American Independence was a turning point in Britons' perceptions of the public debt, which nearly doubled during the war. In the aftermath of the war, predictions of imminent national financial ruin achieved wide currency. At the same time that American nationalists were lauding the strength and solidity of British credit, William Grenville wrote that in the 1780s the "nation gave way . . . to an almost universal panic on the subject" of the national debt. The size of the debt left most commentators gasping: "inconceivable sum" or "astonishing sum" were the phrases used to describe

---

[22]Adam Smith, *An Inquiry into the Nature and Causes of The Wealth of Nations* (1776), ed. by Edwin Cannan (New York, 1937), I, 276–79, 342–45.

[23]*Ibid.*, II, 924–25; see also *Lectures* (1766), 514–15.

[24]Blackstone, I, Ch. 8 (1773 ed.).

"that monster of the age, a National Debt." The panic which gripped Britain in the 1780s was the clearest evidence of the consensus of opinion that a national debt was a national curse. Every Englishman with which he had conversed, wrote one author, together with the best authors on the subject for the past four decades, agreed that "the National Debt will destroy this vast fabric of the British Empire."[25]

Richard Price had warned in 1772 that the next war would raise the debt to over £200 million. "One cannot reflect on this without terror," he wrote, "No resources can be sufficient to support a kingdom long in such a course." The only solution, he insisted, was to revive the sinking fund of Walpole's era, but reconstituted on a new, inviolable basis. Here Price's fascination with mathematics clearly got the better of him, and he saw in the operations of compound interest a force little short of miraculous: "One penny, put out at our saviour's birth to 5% compound interest, would, before this time, have increased to a greater sum than would be contained in A HUNDRED AND FIFTY MILLIONS OF EARTH, all solid gold. But if put out to *simple* interest, it would, in the same time, have amounted to no more than *seven shillings and fourpence, half-penny.*"[26] Only a sinking fund, set up on the firm foundations set forth in his works could prevent the calamity of national bankruptcy and ruin.[27] For this reason,

---

[25]Grenville, quoted in John Ehrman, *The Younger Pitt: The Years of Acclaim* (London, 1969), 158; *The Present State of Great Britain Considered* (London, 1786), 1–2; P. Barfoot, *Two Letters to William Pitt* (London, 1782), 21–22; Thomas Day, *Reflections on the Present State of Affairs*, 3–4; Francis Blake, *A Proposal for the Liquidation of the National Debt . . .* (London, 1786), 10; Robert Bird, *Proposals for Paying a Great Part of the National Debt* (London, 1780), 21–22.

[26]*Observations on Reversionary Payments, on Schemes for Providing Annuities for Widows . . . and on the National Debt* (1771; 5th ed., London, 1792), 182, 188, 4.

[27]*Appeal to the Public on the National Debt* (London, 1772), 10, 13, *passim.*

one of Pitt's first priorities in the aftermath of the failed war was revival of the Sinking Fund, based upon a plan drafted by Price; an act
which underscores the degree to which the consensus view was that
a public debt was dangerous without stringent efforts to place it on a
path of redemption.

II

As Jack Pole reminded us, eighteenth-century "Americas and their
British contemporaries were in a strong sense fellow-citizens of a great
republic of Whig ideas."[28] Americans differed, however, in their re-
ceptiveness to radical Whig ideas; and radical Whigs had been the
most vociferous critics of British fiscal policy. Catherine Macaulay's
conjunction of the huge and destructive debt, the standing army,
placemen and pensioners, septennial Parliaments, an overweaning
executive, and supporting it all, heavy, ruinous, grievous taxes, captured perfectly the American perception of the faults of the society
from which they were breaking away.[29] Americans had no trouble accepting, then, the prevailing view that Britain's growing public debt
augured impending national bankruptcy and ruin. Indeed, it is this
view which provides the background for understanding how Americans came to see every step as the unfolding of a conspiracy against
their liberties. The decision to tax the colonies in the aftermath of
the Seven Years' War convinced Americans that they were about to
be bled dry by imperial authorities seeking to relieve the tax burden
on the British populace. It was a central premise of American revolutionary ideology that England, oppressed by debts and drained by

[28]J. R. Pole, *Political Representation in England and the Origins of the
American Republic* (Berkeley, 1971), xiv.

[29]Bernard Bailyn, *Ideological Origins of the American Revolution* (Cambridge, 1967); Catherine Macaulay, *Observations on a Pamphlet Entitled,
"Thoughts on the Present Discontents"* (London, 1770), 14–16.

taxes, had, in order to keep up the vices of the court, turned her eyes on the property and liberty of the colonists, as "they considered her as a fallow field from which a large income might be drawn"; or, as Tom Paine argued, in her covetousness, Britain now regarded Americans as mere "mines of tributary wealth." Britain was about to sink under the weight of its heavy debt, Boston minister Charles Chauncy wrote Richard Price in 1774; but while it hastened to ruin, Americans were resolved never to submit to tyranny.[30]

The irony of the 1780s is that Americans who had launched a Revolution in an effort to escape the depredations of the British fiscal state should in that time have come to see British public finance as a worthy model for emulation in the aftermath of the financial wreckage left by fiat paper money finance of the war. A central feature of the nationalist campaign for a stronger national government during the 1780s was an effort to expose the nation to the teachings of political economists on the importance of capital supplies and monetary stability for economic development. To that end nationalist leaders like Robert Morris and Alexander Hamilton promoted the theories of James Steuart that a funded debt could circulate as capital, promoting the economic development of the nation. The nationalists' foes in the early 1780s were entirely untutored in matters of political economy, and were soundly trounced in the polemical battles over national and state economic policy.

If they were determined to resist the prospect of paying down the British debt, Americans' sanguine expectations that independence could be obtained quickly and cheaply proved false. Staggering sums were spent. The annual expense to Congress alone in the most intense years of fighting was over $20 million specie value; and totaled over $85 million by the war's end. The cost of the war to both state

---

[30]As, e.g. Anon., *Four Letters on Interesting Subjects* (Philadelphia, 1776), 5, in Thomas Paine, *Complete Writings*, Philip S. Foner, ed., 2 vols. (New York, 1945), I, 144, 172.

and national American governments has been estimated at between $101 and $135 million: roughly one-fifth of the nation's wealth.[31] The cost of the war overwhelmed the century-old colonial expedient of paying for war by paper-money emissions; the flood of paper emitted led to depreciation so severe that the currency virtually ceased to circulate. By 1780 the collapse of the nation's finances, grave problems of army supply, and the subsequent doubts about America's ability to continue the war, all contributed to the ascendancy of nationalists— among others, Robert Morris, James Wilson, Gouverneur Morris, and Alexander Hamilton—within the Continental Congress and many of the state governments. These men effected a transformation in American political economy.[32] As Hamilton declared to Robert Mor-

[31]E. James Ferguson, *The Power of the Purse: A History of American Public Finance, 1776–1790* (Chapel Hill, 1961), 28; Charles J. Bullock, *The Finances of the United States from 1775 to 1789* (Madison, Wis., 1895), 180–81; Ralph V. Harlow, "Aspects of Revolutionary Finance, 1775–83," *American Historical Review*, 35 (1930), 67–68; estimate of colonial *per capita* free white wealth (1774) from John J. McCusker and Russell R. Menard, *The Economy of British America, 1607–1789* (Chapel Hill, 1985), 61.

[32]Webster, January 8, 1780, in *Political Essays on the Nature and Operation of Money, Public Finances, and Other Subjects* . . . (Philadelphia, 1791), 51; E. James Ferguson, "The Nationalists of 1781–1783 and the Economic Interpretation of the Constitution," *Journal of American History*, 56 (1969), 241–45; Merrill Jensen, "The Ideal of a National Government during the American Revolution," *Political Science Quarterly*, 58, No. 3 (1943), 356–79, and Jensen, *The New Nation: A History of the United States during the Confederation, 1781–1789* (New York, 1950), 3–27, 43–53; Forrest McDonald, *E Pluribus Unum: The Formation of the American Republic, 1776–1790* (Indianapolis, 1979), 27–53; Ferguson, *The Power of the Purse*, 109–14; E. Wayne Carp, *To Starve the Army at Pleasure: Continental Army Administration and American Political Culture, 1775–1783* (Chapel Hill, 1984), 191–99, 204–5; H. James Henderson, *Party Politics in the Continental Congress* (New York, 1974), 248–54; Douglas M. Arnold, *A Republican Revolution: Ideology and Politics in Pennsylvania, 1776–1790* (New York, 1989), *passim*.

ris, "Tis by introducing order into our finances—by restoring public credit—not by gaining battles, that we are finally to gain our object." While some nationalists perceived the need for a stronger state as the short-term requirement of war with Britain, most hoped to create in the western hemisphere a mighty empire on the model of the great European nation states, and desired a government up to the task of making America, in the words of Robert Morris, a nation of "Power, Consequence, and Grandeur."[33]

Among the nationalists' ranks were men who, by commercial and scholarly backgrounds, were endowed with financial expertise unmatched in America. As a group, the nationalists were notably interested in the new science of political economy, and took pains to adorn their writings with citations of the preeminent European authorities. Men like Robert Morris and Pelatiah Webster instilled public confidence because of their extensive mercantile expertise and also because for years they had insisted that policies such as price controls and the absence of national taxes were ruinous; events now seemed to have vindicated their position. As historian Albert Bolles noted, "[t]ried by facts, [controls were] a total failure in achieving the end proposed by its authors, and ultimately had not a defender." Despite their enthusiasm for strong government, the nationalists were also distinguished by a deep distaste for government intrusion into business affairs and prices and by a belief that "natural" economic mechanisms could restore the disruptions left by war.[34] Restoring unhampered markets was a key part of the nationalist program for na-

[33]Hamilton to Morris, April 30, 1781, E. James Ferguson et al., eds., The Papers of Robert Morris, 1781–1784, 9 vols. (Pittsburgh, 1973–1999), I, 32; Morris Circular to the Governors, July 25, 1781, ibid., 381.

[34]Albert S. Bolles, The Financial History of the United States, 2 vols. (New York, 1883 and 1886), I, 172–73; Hamilton, "Continentalist," in Harold C. Syrett, ed., The Papers of Alexander Hamilton, 27 vols. (New York, 1963–1987), III, 76–79, 99–100.

tional financial reconstruction. The shortages which plagued the army would vanish once price controls were eliminated, Robert Morris, wrote, while commerce "should be perfectly free" since rewards to the industrious and enterprising would result in plenty, and the means to purchase abroad whatever the army required.[35]

The key objective of the nationalist program, however, was to restore the nation's credit; the very size of the British public debt served as a commendation of its credit-worthiness. Thus the British financial Behemoth which only years before was being denounced as the embodiment of folly and corruption was now offered as the model for the rehabilitation of bankrupt America. British financial might, and her consequent good credit with Dutch bankers, Robert Morris declared, was the one reason the war continued. Britain could hold half the world at bay, Morris marveled, because "she draws strength from the Bowels of Domestic Credit." British credit, and the Bank of England paper which circulated on the strength of that credit, Hamilton agreed, "is a striking example of how far [note issue] may be carried when supported by public authority and private influence." It was only due to the "vast fabric of paper credit" created by the Bank

[35]*Pennsylvania Packet*, August 10, 1779; John Witherspoon to William Churchill Houston, January 27, 1778, in Edmund C. Burnett, ed., *Letters of Members of the Continental Congress*, 8 vols. (Washington, D.C., 1921–1936), III, 57; Gouverneur Morris, *Letters of Appreciation* (Philadelphia, 1780; reprinted 1784), 8; Robert Morris to George Washington, July 2, 1781, Ferguson *et al.*, eds., *Papers of Robert Morris*, I, 213–15; Clarence L. Ver Steeg, *Robert Morris, Revolutionary Financier, with an Analysis of his Earlier Career* (Philadelphia, 1954), 38. On popular opposition to price control, see Eric Foner, *Tom Paine and Revolutionary America* (Oxford, 1976), 151–53, 169–73; Cathy Matson, "American Political Economy in the Constitutional Decade," in R. C. Simmons and A. E. Dick Howard, eds., *The U.S. Constitution: The First 200 Years* (Manchester, 1989), n. 12; Richard B. Morris, *Government and Labor in Early America* (New York, 1st ed., 1946, rev. ed., 1975), 98–99, 102, 111, 117.

of England, gushed Hamilton, that Britain was able to wage its many wars. With the help of paper "raised on a visionary basis" England "has done, and is doing wonders." Thus, as Robert Morris bluntly put it, "Admiring we should endeavor to imitate."[36]

The fullest exposition of the nationalists' plans was Superintendent of Finance Morris' July 1782 *Report to Congress on Public Credit*, written in close collaboration with his aide Gouverneur Morris. It staked out a congressional claim to revenues for the payment of national debts, and was designed with care: couched in language to disarm American radical Whig suspicion of central government finance, it also employed the language of political economy to portray government finance as an instrument for the regeneration of private enterprise. Thus, the report argued that for a wise and honest government, public loans were preferable to taxes, since it was a well-known fact that the profit to farmers on their loans was double the rate of interest, and government borrowing would produce the same net gain for the entire community. Indeed, since the average rate of profit was double the interest rate—as Adam Smith claimed—every public loan increased the aggregate public wealth sufficiently to discharge the interest.[37] The report also preemptively addressed the

---

[36]Cf. John Witherspoon, Speech, August 5, 1782, in Burnett, ed., *Letters of Members of the Continental Congress*, VI, 419; Witherspoon to Governor William Livingston of New Jersey, December 16, 1780, *ibid.*, V, 488; Robert Morris, Circular to the Governors, February 9, 1782, Ferguson *et al.*, eds., *Papers of Robert Morris*, IV, 192, 194–96; Robert Morris to President of Congress John Hanson, February 11, 1782, *ibid.*, 208; Alexander Hamilton to Unknown, December 1779 and to James Duane, September 3, 1780, Syrett, ed., *Papers of Hamilton*, II, 245, 249, 414; Robert Morris to Governor George Clinton of New York and Governor William Greene of Rhode Island, December 11 and 29, 1781, Ferguson *et al.*, eds., *Papers of Robert Morris*, III, 369–71, 465–66.

[37]Robert Morris, "Report to the President of Congress on Public Credit," July 29, 1782, in Ferguson *et al.*, *Papers of Robert Morris*, VI, 56–

arguments—developed over the century in British debates—that funding diverted capital from established channels; reduced loanable funds for private borrowers; and increased the rate of interest through competition for loanable funds. Rather than take such risks, according to the report, the country should seek the unalloyed advantages of foreign loans: a lightened tax load and government stability.[38] Foreigners wouldn't lend money without the assurance of certain repayment; therefore the first step in reconstructing the nation's credit was to render justice to the public creditors by funding the public debt. Moreover, funding would restore funds to the industrious and enterprising creditors, and by "distributing Property into those Hands which could render it most productive, the Revenue should be increased, while the original Stock continued the Same." It would provide an instrument of credit for the mercantile community—as Hume had argued—and create an improved climate of trust and confidence, allowing paper to circulate again domestically, freeing up specie for trade.[39]

The grand financial machine sketched in the Report was destined to remain a mere blueprint, for Morris failed to grasp that prospects for public approval for extensive national taxation had deteriorated over the previous year. By 1782, the economy was in sharp contraction; moreover, the victory at Yorktown made the prospects of peace soon all but certain. The window of opportunity for the nationalists' ambitions slammed down hard.[40]

72; cf. Smith, *Wealth of Nations,* 97. See especially the editorial "Introduction" by Ferguson *et al.,* eds., *Papers of Robert Morris,* VI, 36–56.

[38]Ferguson *et al.,* eds., *Papers of Robert Morris,* VI, 56–72.

[39]*Ibid.*; quote, 63; David Hume, "Of Public Credit," in *Essays,* 353. See also Gouverneur Morris (1785) in Jared Sparks, ed., *The Life of Gouverneur Morris, with Selections from His Correspondence and Miscellaneous Papers,* 3 vols. (Boston, 1832), III, 452.

[40]Ver Steeg, *Robert Morris,* 113–15, 153–56; Ferguson, *Power of the Purse,* 154–55; Ferguson *et al.,* eds., *Papers of Robert Morris,* IV, 29; Jackson

The economic contraction only intensified in the postwar years, and public demands for economic reform—far from taking the form of replicating the British taxing, banking, and funding system—usually took the form of enthusiasm for new currency emissions to stimulate the economy and make tax-paying easier. The catastrophe of wartime inflation guaranteed that no one denied the potential dangers of a paper currency; paper proponents argued instead that with proper backing—land mortgages—the problem of depreciation would be avoided. Taking a page out of James Steuart's treatise *Political Oeconomy*, paper money proponents claimed that paper secured by real estate collateral allowed the "melting down of land" so that the real wealth of the nation might circulate, filling the deficiency of specie caused by a negative balance of trade.[41] Nevertheless, the land-backed money did depreciate, and to the nationalists the ill-fated experiments augured a post-Revolution society incapable of restoring stability; state experiments with paper, according to Forrest McDonald, were widely regarded by contemporaries as proof that "an eighteenth-century form of bolshevism had swept New England, and threatened to engulf the entire country."[42] "We are fast verging on anarchy & confusion,"

Turner Main, *The Antifederalists: Critics of the Constitution, 1781–1788* (Chapel Hill, 1961), 99; Max M. Mintz, *Gouverneur Morris and the American Revolution* (Norman, Okla., 1970), 157.

[41]See Joseph Dorfman, *The Economic Mind in American Civilization*, 5 vols. (New York, 1946–1959), I, 257–59; John Witherspoon, *Essay on Money as a Medium of Commerce* (Philadelphia, 1786), 25–26, 28, 46–49, *passim*; "Philadelphiensis," *Freeman's Journal* (Philadelphia), January 19, 1785, March 2, 1785. See also William Barton, *The True Interest of the United States, and Particularly of Pennsylvania, Considered* . . . (Philadelphia, 1786), 3–5; cf. Dorfman, *The Economic Mind*, I, 267.

[42]Louis M. Hacker, *The Course of American Economic Growth and Development* (New York, 1970), 49–50; Ferguson, *Power of the Purse*, 243–44; McDonald, *E Pluribus Unum*, 211–17, quote on 217.

Washington wrote to James Madison; economic distress had induced in "a considerable part of the people" a desire for the leveling of property; annihilation of public and private debts; and unfunded paper money. "What stronger evidence can be given of the want of energy in our government than these disorders?" he wrote. "If there exists not a power to check them, what security has a man of life, liberty, or property?"[43] For the nationalists the decade was indeed a critical period, and they saw their struggles to secure greater national power as a struggle for national survival.

III

The epic tale of the campaign which culminated in the Constitution and the efflorescence of the political theory from the years 1787–1789 tends to blind us to the more prosaic rhetoric of the previous years' campaign for national revenue and centralized power.[44] Because political economy dominated so much nationalist propaganda, their efforts during the 1780s were instrumental in promoting its prestige in America, and in popularizing theories of some of its most distinguished exponents. By their efforts the notion of the rational and beneficent nature of economic law became widely held, and interference with the natural economic order became suspect. Political economy was a powerful instrument of persuasion because it was science; but more importantly, it was the science of the legislator, which

[43]Washington to Madison, November 5, 1786, in Robert A. Rutland, ed., IX (Chicago, 1975), 161–62. See also Henry Lee to George Washington, September 8, 1786, and Charles Pettit to Benjamin Franklin, October 18, 1786, in Burnett, ed., *Letters from Members of the Continental Congress,* VIII, 463, 487.

[44]Cf. Jack N. Rakove, "From One Agenda to Another: The Condition of American Federalism, 1783–1787," in Jack P. Greene, ed., *The American Revolution: Its Character and Limits* (New York, 1987), 81, 92, *passim.*

"proposes to enrich both the people and the sovereign."[45] The nationalists' political economy offered a solution to the economic crisis of the 1780s: it promised to enrich the people by enriching the sovereign. If America would but imitate the "wise policy of Great Britain, in making an artificial medium of circulation, by funding their debts," wrote contemporary historian David Ramsay, the public debt would thereby become "a public blessing" by increasing the nation's capital.[46]

One of the most striking attributes of the nationalists' writing is frequent citation of authorities in political economy. "I make no apology for the number and length of the quotations here used," wrote James Wilson in a tract on the Bank of North America, "They are from writers of great information, profound judgment, and unquestioned candor . . . and should carry with them the greatest weight and influence; for the sentiments, which they contain and inculcate, must be considered as resulting from general principles and facts, and not as calculated for any partial purposes in this commonwealth."[47] The free-market theories with which nationalists had contested price control during the war were now directed against interventions such as paper money and debtor protection laws. Naturally enough they soon turned to the foremost proponent of "the natural system of liberty,"

[45]Smith, *Wealth of Nations*, 397.

[46]David Ramsay, *The History of the American Revolution* (1789), ed. by Lester H. Cohen, 2 vols. (Indianapolis, 1990), II, 652–53. See also Matthew M'Connell, *An Essay on the Domestic Debts of the United States of America . . .* (Philadelphia, 1787), iv; Pelatiah Webster, "Strictures on the Produce of the Taxes of Great Britain," August 4, 1785, in *Political Essays*, 468–70; "A Native Citizen and Servant of the State" (Alexander Contee Hanson), *Political Scheme and Calculations. Addressed to the Citizens of Maryland* (Annapolis, 1784), 1–25.

[47]James Wilson, "Considerations on the Bank of North America," in Robert G. McCloskey, ed., *The Works of James Wilson*, 2 vols. (Cambridge, Mass., 1967), II, 838.

Adam Smith. The nationalists popularized *The Wealth of Nations* in America, and established Smith as the foremost authority on political economy. In so doing they provided an illustration of the unintended consequences of human actions which would have undoubtedly delighted Smith, for by popularizing Smith, the nationalists gave the opponents of the arch-nationalist Alexander Hamilton one of their most potent weapons for attacking his financial program.

Smith originally appears as just one of many authorities cited by Americans, and the earliest citations of the book are mere adornment. Their tendency to mine sources made the book attractive to the nationalists, as it was a compendium of information on the history of trade, banking, and money; more importantly, it offered tailor-made attacks on unsecured paper money and the folly of government interference with free contract. The staunchly nationalist *New Haven Gazette*, for example, as part of its editorial campaign against the paper-money rage, ran a front-page extract from Smith, consisting of several pages on the dangers of unbacked paper currency, soon followed by another lengthy extract in which he explained and denigrated complaints about the scarcity of money. A week later several more pages from *Wealth of Nations* followed, detailing the natural progress of opulence and ridiculing the doctrine of balance of trade; still later, it ran a long passage on the "natural system of liberty." *The Gazette* continued to publish extracts from the book over the course of the year, and into the next.[48]

Perhaps the clearest illustration of the transformation of American political economy at the hands of the nationalists emerges from the debates over the Bank of North America. That contest pitted

---

[48]Cf. *New Haven Gazette and Connecticut Magazine*, July 13, 1786 (cf. *Wealth of Nations*, 308–11); July 20, 1786 (cf. *Wealth of Nations*, 403–9); July 27, 1786 (cf. *Wealth of Nations*, 356–60); November 2, 1786 (cf. *Wealth of Nations*, 649–51). See also issues of November 9, 1786, February 7 and 10, 1788.

Bank partisans in Pennsylvania's Republican Party—such nationalist figures as Robert Morris and James Wilson—against their Constitutionalist Party rivals over the issue of the revocation of the Bank's state charter, and creation of a rival land bank.[49]

Although the political economy of banking was a subsidiary issue, it still figured prominently in the debate. The Bank's foes charged that it facilitated specie outflow at a time of negative balance of trade. (James Steuart's analysis of the balance of trade—and the role of land-bank paper in relieving credit shortages caused by a negative trade balance—was for this reason almost tailor-made for land-bank advocates, and he was cited heavily.)[50] The Bank's defenders reacted to such arguments by summoning the free-market, anti-statist, republican rhetoric which had served the nationalists so well in the debates over price control and monetary policy during the Revolution. As part of their attack on the dangers of paper money, Smith's observations on banking and money were widely circulated in Philadelphia. He appeared as an authority in pro-bank pamphlets and newspaper columns, as well as speeches on the assembly floor. Since

[49]See generally Bray Hammond, *Banks and Politics in America: From the Revolution to the Civil War* (Princeton, 1957), 53–64; and McDonald, *E Pluribus Unum*, 87–116; and Foner, *Tom Paine and Revolutionary America*, 192–204.

[50]John Whitehill, in Mathew Carey, ed., *Debates and Proceedings of the General Assembly of Pennsylvania on the Memorials Praying a Repeal or Suspension of the Law Annuling the Charter of the Bank* (Philadelphia, 1786), 61; Gouverneur Morris, *Remarks on the Bank of North America* (Philadelphia, 1786), 440, 444; Pelatiah Webster, *An Essay on Credit, In which the Doctrine of Banks Is Considered, and some Remarks are made on the Present State of the Bank of North-America* (Philadelphia, 1786), 18; Anon., *Cool Thoughts on the Subject of the Bank, Addressed to the Honorable the Representatives of the Freemen of the Commonwealth of Pennsylvania in General Assembly* (Philadelphia, 1786), 7–16; "Philadelphiensis," *Freeman's Journal* (Philadelphia), March 2, 1785.

their opponents so often invoked the importance of the state's balance of trade, the Bank's defenders relied heavily upon Smith's authority in attacking the doctrine. They ridiculed it as "the metaphysics of commerce, which few understand, and which serve no other purpose than to disturb the imagination" and advised their opponents to quit "the dark lanterhorn of Sir James Steuart for the clear and bright lamp of Smith."[51]

The Bank's opponents were clearly outclassed. "Some of the arguments on the question [of the balance of trade] have been so much refined," BNA foe, John Smilie told the Assembly, "as to be above the comprehension of us country people." Although some might say that "the balance of trade was mere speculation," he still stoutly maintained that—even though he was not much acquainted with trade— there was "some such thing as a balance of trade—and that it is greatly against the country at present." That kind of argument was not effective with men of learning, who took the science of political economy seriously, if only as an influence on the judgments of others. Thus when James Monroe wrote to Jefferson in 1785 about the prospects of a bill before the Continental Congress to favor American shipping, he worried that the opinion of Smith in the *Wealth of Nations*, "that the balance of trade is a chimera in pursuit of which G.B. hath exposed herself to great injury," would cause the measure to come into disfavor. When, in a few years' time, men gathered at Philadelphia to revolutionize the structure of American politics with a new Constitution, the dramatically enhanced powers of that government to collect taxes, pay debts, borrow money, and issue currency had been prepared by more than the new science of politics; the science of political economy had prepared the way as well.[52]

---

[51]Carey, ed., *Debates*, 26, 101–2; "Artemon," *Pennsylvania Gazette*, March 16, 1785.

[52]John Smilie, in Carey, ed., *Debates*, 107; Monroe to Jefferson, June 16, 1785, in Julian P. Boyd et al., eds., *The Papers of Thomas Jefferson*

IV

Alexander Hamilton was the nation's first Secretary of the Treasury under the new government created by the Constitutions written in the Philadelphia summer of 1787. When he introduced his plans for the transformation of the American economy—based on assumption of state debts, a funding system, new revenues, a national bank, and the encouragement of national manufactures by the creation of new capital instruments and government corporate charters—the opposition which would quickly coalesce into the Jefferson Republican party began. The Republican critique of Federalist fiscal policy was not an agrarian response to capitalism, or a civic humanist critique of market relations. It was predicated upon the notion of a natural economic order, and the conviction that Hamilton's policies were destructive of capital, disruptive of economic growth, and subversive of a free and prosperous society. Republicans articulated the most modern and up-to-date principles of the political economy of the day in opposition to Hamilton's fiscal and economic heterodoxies; thus the economic orthodoxy cultivated by the nationalists during the Revolution became a weapon directed against nationalism's very apotheosis.

Hamilton's financial program was ideologically charged because finance was the mainspring of government, and the growing perception during the 1790s—that Hamilton sought the replication of British financial policies in America—carried with it the chilling conclusion that an imitation of all the worst corruptions of the British state would likewise be fastened upon the republic. Throughout the 1780s the practices which underlay the solidarity and strength of British public credit had been repeatedly urged upon Americans by Hamilton's allies as exemplary. Even when the abuses of British funding were conceded, its supposed fundamentals—heavy taxation guar-

(Princeton, 1950–), VIII, 208. See also Mary Schweitzer, "State-Issued Currency and the Ratification of the U.S. Constitution," *Journal of Economic History*, XLIX (June 1989), 311–22.

anteeing regular payments to creditors and a sinking fund to reduce the capital of the debt—were held up for imitation.[53]

The curious irony is that, although Hamilton was chastised for his slavish imitation of the "English financial system," what most distinguished his program was its *departures* from British fiscal orthodoxy of the 1780s. While most contemporary Britons were terrified by the size and growth of their national debt, Hamilton retained all the self-possession and confidence of his ability to manipulate the debt to national advantage which Walpole—who, perhaps not so coincidentally, confronted a national debt of roughly comparable size—had displayed a half century earlier.

This becomes clearer when one contrasts the foundation document for American financial reconstruction—his first "Report on Public Credit"—with the suggestions offered by the merchant William Bingham in response to Hamilton's request for advice. Bingham commended British practices as the very model of fiscal responsibility, as attested by the confidence of its creditors. Bingham wanted to replicate such confidence at home, and therefore strongly supported funding the debt: i.e., mortgaging certain taxes for the payment of public creditors. But nothing could be more destructive of confidence, Bingham wrote, than popular schemes to force creditors to accept a reduction in their rate of interest from 6% to 5%. Explained Bingham, if the government "takes advantage of the Distresses of the Times & a general Want of Confidence, in order to pay a debt which it had justly contracted, at a reduced value, it can never be expected that it will make new Loans on advantageous terms." The key to revived credit, he insisted, was assiduous attention to redemption of the capital of the debt. "Every Operation of Finance," he wrote, "ought to be directed to the wise pursuit of gradually redeeming the capital," since the shining example of British finance proved that its enlarged

---

[53]Cf. Anon., A *View of the Principles, Operations and Probable Effects of Funding System of Pennsylvania* . . . (Philadelphia, 1788), 6–8.

sinking fund "operated like a Charm . . . [once it began] annually extinguishing so large a portion of the capital, public Credit revived, and all the Train of Advantages that result from it, accompanied it."[54]

Hamilton's Report, by contrast, was a puzzling mirror-image of Bingham's program. Despite Hamilton's adamant insistence that public credit depended above all on "good faith [and] the punctual performance of contracts," and his repudiation of a unilateral reduction in the rate of interest paid to the nation's creditors as destructive of public credit, his funding proposal was predicated on just such a reduction—from 6% down to 4%—on the new securities which would replace old Continental securities.[55] The Congressional debt of over $54 million would be funded—taxes earmarked specifically for their repayment—but Hamilton also proposed that the federal government should assume the debts of the states, which he fixed at about $25 million; and without an interest reduction, revenues would be insufficient to cover annual interest charges. He rejected calls to scale down the debt and to discriminate between original creditors and speculators. A sinking fund of $100,000 would be established; but as a concession to the creditors for the interest reduction, their securities—and the debt—would be virtually irredeemable.[56]

Hamilton's abandonment of financial orthodoxy was apparent to all. "It is truly laughable," wrote "A Farmer," "to hear the Secretary and some members of Congress talk of supporting public credit, and yet offer only *four* per cent on all certificates." One aggrieved creditor acidly noted that Hamilton's measures were "so much at variance with the principles he has stated as the source from which they are derived that, to me, they appear as incompatible as the doctrine of transubstantiation and common sense." Despite the bewildering va-

---

[54]Bingham to Hamilton, November 25, 1789, Syrett, ed., *Papers of Hamilton*, V, 538–57; quotes on 543–44, 546, 547–48.

[55]Hamilton, "Report on Public Credit," *ibid.*, VI, 68.

[56]*Ibid.*, 66–110. Cf. Ferguson, *Power of the Purse*, 292–96.

riety of terms offered to the creditors, he noted, there was no disguising the plain fact that theirs was merely a Hobson's choice of a forced reduction in the rate of interest.[57] Creditors were outraged that Hamilton had violated the long-established practice of British financiers of letting the market set the interest rate. "Government may as well attempt to arrest the planets in their orbits," one creditor protested, "as to controul the market rate of interest, by the intervention of laws"; yet Hamilton was striking out a third of the interest due on securities by a stroke of his pen, in the face of clear evidence that the market rate of interest was likely to persist at or above 6% for years to come.[58]

Hamilton's interest reduction only made sense because assumption of state debts was impossible without it. In proposing the assumption, Hamilton blandly explained that assumption would require no greater resources than if the public debt was paid partly by the states and partly by the federal government. This was, of course, a truism; but he knew all too well that assumption would increase the *federal* debt quite beyond the capacities of the *federal* revenues. Assumption so increased the size of the debt that it alarmed even Gouverneur Morris, who wrote Hamilton that he was going to far, too fast.[59] Yet even though assumption required lopping-off a third of the interest contractually due to creditors, for Hamilton its allure lay in the fact that the revenues for state debt repayment would be in *his* hands, and that *all* the

[57]"A Farmer," *Pennsylvania Gazette*, January 30, February 17, 1790; "S. T.," "Remarks on the Report of the Secretary of the Treasury," *Pennsylvania Packet*, February 8, 9, 1790; "A Friend to the Public," *Remarks on the Report of the Treasury Secretary* (New York, 1790), 17–18, 23–24.

[58]Anon., *Fallacy Detected by the Evidence of Facts . . .* (Philadelphia, 1790), 10–20, 23–24, 25, *passim*.

[59]Joseph Charles, *The Origins of the American Party System* (Williamsburg, Va., 1956), 24; Hamilton, "Report on Public Credit" (1790), Syrett, ed., *Papers of Hamilton*, VI, 90–96.

creditors would be bound by their self-interest to the national government. If "all the public creditors receive their dues from one source" Hamilton wrote, "their interest will be the same. And having the same interests, they will unite in the support of the fiscal arrangements of the government." The key to creating support of government was to promote an active and constant interest in its support.[60]

This reason for Hamilton's financial apostasy was equally clear to contemporaries: assumption was a ploy to increase the debt's size to make it permanent, and justify more federal taxes. "The Secretary's people scarce disguise their design," Pennsylvania's self-described representative of the Republican party, Senator William Maclay, disgustedly wrote in his diary, "which is to create a mass of debts which will justify them in seizing all the sources of government, thus annihilating the state legislatures and creating an empire on the basis of consolidation." He complained that they were only interested in squeezing from Americans a sum equal to the royal revenues of England, and had therefore totally reversed the normal principles of ways and means: instead of searching for objects of taxation in response to great expenditure, they searched for a "plausible pretext for extending the arm of taxation, and ways and means to expend the collected treasures." Had Hamilton not deliberately swollen the public debt by thirty million through his assumption of the state debts, "Sidney" charged, he would have found that the impost alone would have easily discharged the debt. It was precisely for that reason assumption had taken place; the debt had to be increased to justify the "magnificent and ponded Fiscal fabric" and ample range of authority of Hamilton's design.[61]

---

[60]*Ibid.*, 78–80; cf. Hamilton Speech, June 18, 1787, in Adrienne Koch, ed., *Notes of Debates in the Federal Convention of 1787 Reported by James Madison* (Athens, Ohio, 1966), 130–31.

[61]William Maclay, *Sketches of Debate in the First Senate of the United States in 1789–90–91*, George W. Harris, ed. (Harrisburg, Pa., 1880), 202,

The protests against Hamilton's policies were largely motivated by an anxiety that Hamilton's real objective was a permanent and growing debt which would allow Treasury and the executive to aggrandize wealth and power, and create on American soil a duplicate of the corrupt polity of the British court; and statements by Hamilton and his supporters only inflamed such suspicions. Federalists openly denied that the debt was a national burden to be lifted as rapidly as possible, and consistently portrayed the debt as beneficial. One of Hamilton's correspondents candidly advised him that nothing would so effectively strengthen the executive as the collection of taxes, hence "the impolicy of paying the principal of the national debts" which served as a "gentle compulsion to the to citizens of a country to pay that homage and respect which is really necessary to its existence." Hamilton insisted that the debt was an economic boon, and invoked Gale's thesis that the only evils of public debt arose from fluctuating value: a funded debt, Hamilton argued, would stabilize its value and trade at par; thus, it would become a net addition to the capital stock of the country. Former Antifederalist Elbridge Gerry of Massachusetts declared to the U.S. House of Representatives that since a funded debt enlarged the capital of a nation, its increase would be beneficial. "Great Britain increased her national debt to an astonishing degree," he said, yet while all Europe waited for her to sink beneath her burden, she emerged stronger and more prosperous than ever, because her debt "furnished the means for the expansion of her commerce and manufactures." Fisher Ames pursued this argument

284; "Sidney," part 3, *Dunlap's American Daily Advertiser*, May 14, 1792. See also Thomas Jefferson to George Washington, September 9, 1792, and "The Anas," in Merrill D. Peterson, ed., *Thomas Jefferson: Writings* (New York, 1984), 997, 679; John Taylor, *Examination of the Late Proceedings in Congress Respecting the Official Conduct of the Secretary* (Richmond, 1793); "Caius," *Dunlap's American Daily Advertiser*, January 21, 1790; *New York Journal*, September 7, 1790.

with language borrowed from James Steuart: a funded debt, he claimed, increased capital because it allowed the circulation of both the debt's principal and interest income, and it therefore enabled the nation's "very land and houses to circulate."[62]

Federalists also promoted the British court Whig doctrine that—in the words of the quasi-official *Gazette of the United States*—a "national debt attaches many citizens to the government who, by their numbers, wealth, and influence, contribute more perhaps to its preservation than a body of soldiers." Massachusetts Federalist Christopher Gore wrote to his colleague Rufus King that funding the debt "would be very favorable to many of the most influential men of the Commonwealth, and engage them most warmly to promote the operations of this government;" while Elbridge Gerry argued before the U.S. House that the stockholders of the Bank of the United States would be powerful supporters of the government.[63]

Such declarations confirmed the Jeffersonian Republicans' fears that Hamilton's administration of the Treasury was directed at cementing, rather than discharging, the debt; and a national debt was to Republicans an unalloyed curse. Pennsylvania Congressman Albert Gallatin (future Treasury Secretary) summed up the Republican view when he declared in 1795 that "there is no object of so great importance to the U.S. as the extinction of the curse of the country, the Public Debt."[64] The Republican anxiety about a perpetual debt

[62]James Jarvis to Hamilton, February 10, 1790, Syrett, ed., *Papers of Hamilton*, VI, 253–61; "Report on Public Credit," *ibid.*, 70–71; Elbridge Gerry, *Annals of Congress*, I, 1137; Fisher Ames, *ibid.*, II, 1483.

[63]"Tablet," *Gazette of the United States*, April 24, 1790; Gerry, February 7, 1791, *Annals of Congress*, II; Oliver Wolcott to Oliver Wolcott, Sr., March 27, 1790, quoted in Charles, *Origins of the American Party System*, 29.

[64]Thomas Jefferson to George Washington, September 9, 1792, in Peterson, ed., *Writings*, 997; see also *ibid.*, 679; Taylor, *Examination of the Late Proceedings*; Albert Gallatin, *Annals of Congress* (4th Congress, 1st sess.),

reflected the conventional wisdom of the era. Similar anxiety was responsible for Pitt's adoption of Price's plans for a rehabilitated sinking fund; yet Hamilton also diverged from orthodoxy in his design for America's sinking fund. Its meager size plainly bespoke a lack of zeal to liquidate the debt's capital, and its operation clearly eschewed the miracles of compound interest for the progressive and rapid elimination of the principal of the debt. Believing, as Hamilton did, that men are governed less by realities than by sounds and appearances, he rather expected that the mere fact of the fund's existence— rather than the sums actually retired by the fund—would send a soothing message to creditors and increase the government's ability to sell its bonds. Hamilton's sinking fund—like Walpole's—was intended merely as an instrument for managing revenue and for controlling the price of government securities by the fund's sales or purchases of government stock. "A principal object with me," Hamilton confided to one of his sinking fund agents, "is to keep the Stock from falling too low;" he therefore urged that purchases should not be made below "the prescribed [price] limits;" and advised him ("in great confidence") that stock purchases should aim at aiding "those gentlemen who support the funds," i.e., the bulls in the market.[65]

Hamilton's heterodox political economy only served to inflame the fears of nascent Republicans that his fiscal program bespoke insidious motives which had little to do with restoring the nation's credit. Simultaneous with the publication of Hamilton's first Report

340. See also "Caius," *Dunlap's American Daily Advertiser*, January 21, 1790; "Mercator," *ibid.*, September 3, 1792; "Republican," *ibid.*, February 18, 1792; "Brutus," *National Gazette*, March 15, 19, 1792.

[65]Hamilton to William Seton, August 16, 1791, Syrett, ed., *Papers of Hamilton*, IX, 71–72. Cf. Donald F. Swanson, *The Origins of Hamilton's Fiscal Policies* (Gainesville, Fla., 1963), 59–64, 69–72, esp. 76–80, 83–84; Forrest McDonald, *Alexander Hamilton: A Biography* (New York, 1979), 154–65, 170–71.

on Public Credit, a series of newspaper essays by "The Observer" in its defense began to appear.[66] "The Observer" was immediately attacked for promulgating theories which were contrary to the soundest principles of political economy. To claim that a funded debt was a blessing because it augmented the circulating capital, one essayist retorted, was to ignore the testimony of Hume that paper substitutes invariably drove out specie and raised the price of labor and commodities, as well as the clear statement in his "Essay on Public Credit" of funding's deleterious effects on the nation's industry. "Besides Hume, I might introduce Smith on the *Wealth of Nations*, Price, and several other writers," he concluded. "Now I demand of the Observer to show what writer, either on government or finance, has ever introduced these fanciful doctrines; if no writers agrees with him, it rests, of course upon his own authority; and if that authority be contrary to reason, his simple efforts will avail him but little."[67]

The Republicans held that substantial rewards to investors offered by government finance, far from being a social benefit, actually distorted natural capital flows and crowded-out private, productive investment. Private capital markets were starved by funding, Robert Livingston explained. Merchants would not—contra Hume—put their trading stock into government securities, because stock profits arose from the kind of careful buying and selling which was incompatible with trading stock liquidity; therefore anything they invested in government stock would be money that would otherwise have been invested in private loans or invested in land: private credit would be beggared by the public.[68] In 1792 Jefferson warned (following a Bank of the United States declaration of a 10% dividend) that since the

---

[66]See "The Observer," beginning January 8, 1790, and running for twenty numbers to the end of March 1790 in the *Pennsylvania Packet*.
[67]"An Independent Observer," *New York Daily Gazette*, March 1, 1790.
[68]Anon., *Considerations on the Nature of a Funded Debt* . . . , 10–11.

actual yield on capital investment was 26% per annum, "Agriculture, commerce and everything useful must be neglected when the useless employment of money is so much more lucrative."[69] Funding, amplified "A Farmer," would check the flow of wealth into agriculture; farmers would find it virtually impossible to borrow money to improve their lands, "for who will lend money to an individual for 6 per cent, when government securities will yield 8 and 12 percent?"[70]

Two major anti-Hamilton—soon-to-be Republican—propagandists, George Logan and William Findley, both wrote pamphlets which drew heavily upon the authority of Smith and other classical authorities attacking Hamilton's program for its violations of natural economic law, distortions of natural capital flow, and misunderstandings of the relationship between capital and circulating media. The debt would never serve as real money or as an addition to the nation's capital stock. Instead, the expansion of the debt by the assumption of state debts was merely a ploy to increase the tax powers of the federal government, in order to fund an expansion of government-privileged creditors who would be the basis of a new aristocracy, and the recreation a British-model balanced government of artificial ranks and privileges. The sinking fund would never retire the debt, as it was only intended to keep up the value of stocks. The corruption inherent in control of so great sum of money and resources as the

[69]Jefferson, quoted in A. J. Nock, Mr. *Jefferson* (Delevan, Wis., 1983), 117–18.

[70]*Pennsylvania Gazette,* February 3, 10, 1790. Another writer claimed funding "would check . . . commerce, manufactures, agriculture, and improvements, both public and private . . . [f]or who would employ their money in either of these ways, who could, without risk or labor, receive 24 or 30 per cent on his capital by purchasing . . . certificates?" ("A Citizen of Philadelphia," *Pennsylvania Gazette,* February 3, 1790.) Cf. Gouverneur Morris, "Observations on the Finances of the United States in 1789," in Sparks, ed., *Life of Morris,* III, 471–72.

national debt mandated a speedy retirement of the debt, even at the cost, in the short term, of a heavy tax burden.[71]

The man who would become the first Republican Treasury Secretary, Albert Gallatin, was a keen student of Smith's political economy.[72] He denied absolutely that a national debt, any more than an individual's indebtedness, was a contribution to wealth, welfare, or prosperity; for Gallatin, the debt was merely a burden to be relieved as quickly as possible. His first exercise in constructing a financial policy (a 1791 proposal for the reconstruction of Pennsylvania's state debts) was a strikingly Smithian prescription: full performance of the contractual obligations to the creditors, along with substantial and inviolable revenues to pay the interest and redeem the principal.[73] He led the effort to overturn the corporate charter of the city of Philadelphia—in order to break the monopoly it granted to the city's merchants and retailers—by attacking "privileges granted to one class of citizens as an infringement on the rights of others," and

---

[71]George Logan, *Letters to the Yeomanry of the United States . . . on Public Revenue* (Philadelphia, 1791); George Logan, *Five Letters, Addressed to the Yeomanry of the United States: Containing Some Observations on the Dangerous Scheme of Governor Duer and Mr. Secretary Hamilton, To Establish National Manufactories* (Philadelphia, 1792); George Logan, *Letters Addressed to the Yeomanry of the United States Containing Some Observations on Funding and Bank Systems* (Philadelphia, 1793), *passim*; William Findley, *A Review of the Revenue System . . .* (Philadelphia, 1794), 9–17, 18, 20, 29–31, 125, 33–34, 34–36, 98, 128–29, 52–53, 43, 47–48.

[72]Cf. Virgle G. Wilhite, *Founders of American Economic Thought and Policy* (New York, 1958), 351, 356, 360–61, 381.

[73]Cf. Raymond Walters, Jr., "The Making of a Financier: Albert Gallatin in the Pennsylvania Assembly," *Pennsylvania Magazine of History and Biography* (July 1946), 260–63; Raymond Walters, Jr., *Albert Gallatin: Jeffersonian Financier and Diplomat* (New York, 1957), 41–44; Edwin G. Burrows, *Albert Gallatin and the Political Economy of Republicanism, 1761–1800* (New York, 1986), 423–30.

summoning Adam Smith's authority in opposition to the folly of restrictions on trade, when self-interest could better regulate trade than
any rules drafted by the legislature.[74]

Gallatin's *Sketch of the Finances of the United States*[75] was a metic-
ulous dissection and assessment of Federalist fiscal policy after six
years of operation, deeply rooted in both the political economy of
Adam Smith and the analysis of a century of dissenting Whiggery. He
drew heavily on Smith's teachings on public finance at almost every
section of the report.[76] His analysis of the economic effects of funding
was a gloss on the corresponding section of *Wealth of Nations*. Public
spending was unproductive, he wrote, although necessary; the destruction of capital was the unavoidable evil which all public spending entailed, whether paid for with taxes or borrowing; taxes were
preferable to loans because they more often fell on expense; loans
always consumed capital. He paraphrased Smith's dismissal of the
doctrine that a funded debt increased the capital of a society, and
insisted its extinction "will in no shape whatever impoverish the
country."[77]

By the end of the decade, then—due in no small part to the nationalists' assiduous efforts to promote the authority of the science of
political economy—the nascent Republican opposition to the Hamilton financial program could take the Secretary to task for departing
from the orthodox teachings of masters like Hume and Smith by
claiming that public debt could be beneficial, and showing too little
zeal for its rapid elimination. At the very time when Britain was mak-

[74]"Report of the Debates in the Pennsylvania Legislature," *Dunlap's
American Daily Advertiser*, January 7, 18, 1792.

[75]Albert Gallatin, *Sketch of the Finances of the United States* (New York,
1796), 12–15, 28–49, 67. Burrows' account in *Gallatin*, 440–51, is a useful
precis.

[76]Gallatin, *Sketch*, 12–15.

[77]*Ibid.*, 123–33; cf. *Wealth of Nations*, 877–81.

ing stringent efforts to reduce its public debt, the American political faction vilified for emulating the corrupt practices of British finance was pursuing policies quite out of step with orthodox British economic and political thinking, by an opposition which beat them with a stick of their own devising.

Voting "Rites":

The Implications of Deference in Virginia Electioneering Ritual, 1780–1820

Andrew W. Robertson

The American Revolution may have transformed political institutions but it did not transform political rhetoric and ritual. As J. R. Pole has observed, people "imagine themselves to be governed" by rhetorical forms "belonging to the past."[1] Electioneering ritual in the South likewise adhered to a traditional Anglo-American form for at least a generation after America's institutional ties with Britain were broken. This essay, part of a larger study of early republican elections and electioneering, examines electioneering rituals in Virginia. Virginia remained, in Ronald Formisano's words, a "deferential-participant" political culture. The term has a paradoxical ring to it; but the tension between its elements has not been fully explored. From the Revolution onwards "deferential-participant" politics in America was an unstable amalgam; even in tradition-bound Virginia it gradually gave way to a different form of politics.

This essay examines the tensions within Virginia's political culture, focusing on electioneering rituals. Although historians have devoted much attention to defining and describing Virginia's habits of deference and patterns of electioneering, they have paid surprisingly

[1] J. R. Pole, *Political Representation in England and the Origins of the American Republic* (London, 1966), 526.

little recent attention to the connections and interactions between the two and what this tells us about Virginia politics and society in the early republic. Electioneering lies at the very heart of the American deferential order because it is the point of contact between the few and the many. By examining electioneering historians can learn much about deference and about politics in the late eighteenth century. Electioneering tells us that Virginians continued to imagine themselves governed by deferential forms until some time after the turn of the nineteenth century. Electioneering also tells us that a deferential political culture which relied on personal ties and the oral transmission of information gradually gave way to a new political culture, which mobilized voters on abstract issues and disseminated information in print. The print medium gave readers an opportunity to reflect on issues, individually and in private. Private reading eventually transformed public discourse and public ritual.

In defining deference within an American context, Formisano borrowed conceptually from Pole.[2] In "Historians and the Problem of Early American Democracy," first published in the *American Historical Review* in 1962, Jack Pole identified a paradox at the center of eighteenth-century American politics. Drawing upon his work on voter turnout in the early republic, Pole concurred with Robert E. Brown that adult white male participation in late eighteenth-century elections was widespread.[3] Pole disagreed with Brown, however, about

[2]Ronald P. Formisano, "Deferential-Participant Politics: The Early Republic's Political Culture, 1789–1824," *American Political Science Review*, LXVIII (1974): 483–84. Formisano appropriated the term "deferential-participant" from political scientists Gabriel Almond and Sydney Verba. See *The Civic Culture: Political Attitudes and Democracy in Five Nations* (Boston, 1965), 455; and Walter Bagehot, *The English Constitution* (London, 1872).

[3]Pole, "Historians and the Problem of Early American Democracy," reprinted in *Paths to the American Past* (New York, 1979), 223–49; Robert E. Brown, *Middle-Class Democracy and the Revolution in Massachusetts*,

the implications of extensive participation. Many freeholders—perhaps a majority of adult white males—may have voted; only a favored few, sifted from the ranks of the gentry, could stand for office. "How," asked Pole, "are we to explain the paradox of popular consent to a scheme of government which systematically excluded the common people from the more responsible positions of political power?" Pole observed that in "a society of deference and dignity, it was possible for the broad mass of the people to consent to a scheme of government in which their own share was limited." Because at least some of those excluded from government expected one day to be included themselves, they might concur in their own exclusion. Deference did not seem to Pole "a very secure cement to the union of social orders. Yet to those who live under its sway it can be almost irresistible."[4]

Pole relied on Walter Bagehot's classic formulation of Victorian deference in *The English Constitution*, applying it to colonial and early national America. Pole's consideration of deference was certainly suggestive, and he elaborated on it in *Political Representation in England and the Origins of the American Republic*.[5] The task of further defining American deference he left to other historians. Pole had launched a cottage industry among early American historians who are still arguing over deference's decline and death. And deference in America has proved, even in death, a slippery designation: to paraphrase Twain, rumors of deference's demise have been greatly exaggerated. Joyce Appleby has called deference the "quark" term in

1691–1780 (Ithaca, N.Y., 1955), 401–8. Pole points out that the suffrage in Virginia "was often exercised by persons to whom it did not belong as a right under the law." *Political Representation*, 146; see also Robert E. Brown and B. Katherine Brown, *Virginia 1705–1786: Democracy or Aristocracy?* (East Lansing, Mich., 1964).

[4]*Ibid.*, 249.

[5]*Ibid.*, 227. See *Political Representation*, 146.

eighteenth-century history: like the subatomic particle, we can only infer its existence from observing its effects. Like quarks, deference appears to have different properties depending on the observer: Pole, Formisano, Jack Greene, Gordon Wood and J. G. A. Pocock have provided very different perspectives on deference and have contributed to our understanding of deference in a larger context.

Jack Greene offers a corrective to the stereotypical view of deference in "Society, Ideology and Politics: An Analysis of the Political Culture of Mid-Eighteenth Century Virginia," first published in 1976. The traditional view of Virginia, "dominated by a small body of privileged aristocrats who ruled by overawing and closely controlling the rest of society derives, one suspects, less from the society itself than from the romantic writings of later historians," says Greene. "Enjoined by the election law to choose 'Two of the most fit and able Men' among them for their representatives, the freeholders regularly returned the same men whom the leading gentry also found most suitable."[6]

In *Blackwell's Encyclopedia of the American Revolution*, Pole and Greene elaborate on the paradoxical effects of a deferential political order. According to Pole and Greene, men of the lower and middling classes, by consistently voting for their social superiors, lent legitimacy to the social and economic order. Without challenges from below to their exercise of power, "members of the colonial elite frequently felt free to compete openly among themselves, and in the pro-

---

[6]Jack P. Greene, "Society, Ideology and Politics: An Analysis of the Political Culture of Mid-Eighteenth Century Virginia," reprinted in *Negotiated Authorities: Essays in Colonial Political and Constitutional History* (Charlottesville, Va., 1994), 265, 271. T. H. Breen sees challenges "to the hegemony of the great Tidewater planters" becoming increasingly common before the Revolution because of the planters' increasingly precarious economic position. See Breen, *Tobacco Culture: The Mentality of the Great Tidewater Planters on the Eve of Revolution* (Princeton, 1985), 160.

cess to encourage political mobilization among members of the community." And confident of their continued ability to lead, the elite "were prepared to challenge British plans for reorganizing the empire during the late colonial period."[7] While Pole and Greene have emphasized the political ramifications of deference, Gordon Wood has characterized its social and economic underpinnings. In *The Radicalism of the American Revolution* Wood describes the mechanics of deference as "not a mere habit of mind." Since "much of the economy was organized into webs of private relationships," deference had "real economic and social force behind it."[8]

J. G. A. Pocock formulates a definition of political deference that describes the way in which private relationships operated in the political sphere. He defines deference as "the voluntary acceptance of a leadership elite by persons not belonging to that elite, but sufficiently free as political actors to render deference not only a voluntary but also a political act." Pocock says that the elite "owe their authority less to their own superiority than to the acknowledgment— it would be proper to call it election—of their inferiors." He draws upon the important functional distinction in politics between "debate" and "result" that Harrington makes in *Oceana*. For Pocock, deference provides an institutional balance between the few and the many. According to Pocock, it was the responsibility of the few "to conceive and initiate policies, to articulate the differences between them, to argue the cases for and against each one." When the debate of the few was at an end, however, the many would render a verdict on the former's conduct.

While all these descriptions consider deference from a political perspective, historians have more recently begun to consider defer-

[7]Jack P. Greene and J. R. Pole, eds., *The Blackwell Encyclopedia of the American Revolution* (Cambridge, Mass., 1991), 35.

[8]Gordon S. Wood, *The Radicalism of the American Revolution* (New York, 1992), 63–64.

ential behavior from an ethnographic perspective. Historians have
paid much attention recently to the social and economic manifestations of deference in manor houses and meeting houses, in church
and in court, but they have paid less attention to electioneering.[9]
Like church and court, the other important community venues Rhys
Isaac describes from an ethnographic perspective in *The Transformation of Virginia, 1740–1790*, the polling place reinforced the deferential order even after the Revolution.[10]

Polling days in colonial Virginia were relatively rare occasions.
Elections to the House of Burgesses frequently occurred only once
every seven years.[11] In the 1790s, however, Virginians often took to
the polls once or twice a year: once in February or March for congressional elections; once in April for the assembly; every four years
in November for presidential electors. Virginians may have found
the duty inconvenient but they were required to discharge their
suffrage anyway. "An act for the election of representatives" passed
in 1788 made voting mandatory.[12] Freeholders who met the prop-

---

[9]Rhys Isaac, *The Transformation of Virginia, 1740–1790* (Chapel Hill,
1982); Breen, *Tobacco Culture*; Allan Kulikoff, *Tobacco and Slaves: The
Development of Southern Cultures in the Chesapeake, 1680–1800* (Chapel
Hill, 1986); Jan Lewis, *The Pursuit of Happiness: Family and Values in Jefferson's Virginia* (Cambridge, 1983). For a study of Virginia electioneering
that builds on newer perspectives, see Daniel P. Jordan, *Political Leadership
in Jefferson's Virginia* (Charlottesville, Va., 1983), esp. 102–32; for an analysis of similar electioneering practices in New York in the 1790s, see Alan
Taylor, " 'The Art of Hook & Snivey': Political Culture in Upstate New
York during the 1790s," *Journal of American History*, 74 (1993): 1371–96.

[10]Isaac, *Transformation of Virginia*, 88–114.

[11]After an act of 1769, see Pole, *Political Representation*, 145.

[12]"An act for the election of representatives pursuant to the constitution of government of the United States." See Chilton Williamson,
American Suffrage from Property to Democracy, 1760–1860 (Princeton,
1960), 112–14; Jordan, *Political Leadership*, 133.

erty qualifications would walk, ride or row from all corners of the constituency and voice their preferences. Voice is the operative word: Virginia electors announced their choices *viva voce* until after the Civil War.

Polling took place over the course of several days, and occasioned a festival atmosphere. Like Sabbath days and court days, polling days were opportunities for socializing and for spectacle. Political spectacle, like its liturgical and legal variants, self-consciously aimed at illumination, intimidation and entertainment. In all three arenas, the gentry—their entrances and exits, their mannerisms and dress, their retinue and equipage—offered the most entertaining visual spectacle for the audience. And, as in court, aural attention focused on the gentleman gladiators who would do battle with words in a contested election, pleading their cause before the eyes and ears of freeholders, wives, children, slaves, drunkards and strangers who gathered around the hustings.

The hustings, like the altar and the bench, was a raised platform on which the attention of the community focused, reinforcing hierarchical norms.[13] The traditional forms of communication from the hustings also sustained deference: candidates, like vicars and judges, delivered long-winded recitations orally, alluding frequently to classical texts, written in a recondite language. In the colonial Church, Anglican priests read from the already antiquated language of the King James Bible and the Book of Common Prayer. In colonial courts lawyers and judges made arcane references, in English and Latin, to procedure and to statutes, precedents and commentaries. On the hustings, candidates frequently made vivid allusions to Plutarch or Livy; they often made learned references to the Venetian or

---

[13]Later on, a table or perhaps a tree stump (thus "stump speech") would constitute the focal point around which the electioneering ritual centered. See Charles S. Sydnor, *Gentlemen Freeholders: Political Practices in Washington's Virginia* (Chapel Hill, 1952), 20.

Roman republics and they sprinkled their delivery with quotations in Latin and Greek. The priest, the justices of the peace and the high sheriff presided over these occasions and lent a well-practiced air of decorum to the procedure. In electioneering, as in the liturgy and the law, the effect was simultaneously illuminating and intimidating for the audience.

An election could be intimidating for a gentleman candidate. Like horse racing, cock fighting, or gambling at cards, electioneering was a somewhat more sober variation of what Isaac has called "deep play": that is, a form of high-risk gambling in a society that greatly esteemed risk.[14] In a society in which reputation itself rested on an external display of honor, a gentleman's subjecting himself to the whims of electors was a high risk enterprise: the taunts and insults of an unruly crowd could permanently damage his reputation.[15] Losing an election might cost not only a seat in the legislature but lucrative opportunities at the bar. Humiliation at the polls wounded some gentlemen so deeply they departed entirely. Men as different as James Madison and Henry St. George Tucker spent considerable time worrying about humiliation at the polls.[16] As Jack Greene observes, candidates were "always at the mercy of 'the humours of a

[14]Isaac, *Transformation of Virginia*, 119.

[15]Peter Burke, *The Historical Anthropology of Early Modern Italy: Essays on Perception and Communication* (Cambridge, 1987), 13–14, 223.

[16]Madison had to overcome "an extreme distaste to steps having an electioneering appearance," when he considered running for the first Congress. Madison to Henry Lee, November 30, 1788, in Robert A. Rutland and Charles F. Hobson, eds., *The Papers of James Madison*, vol. 11 (Charlottesville, Va., 1977), 372. Tucker wrote to his father, "Please to take notice I am no *electionerer*." Henry St. George Tucker to St. George Tucker, March 1, 1807, *Gentlemen Freeholders*, 45, and Jordan *Political Leadership*, 103.

fickle crowd.' Only the most secure candidate did not find it neces-sary to 'lower' himself a little to gain election."[17]

Electioneering was more than just a variation on other eighteenth-century social rituals, however. In one key respect poll-ing departed from the common features it shared with church and court. The whole electioneering cycle, from beginning to end, called for two reciprocal and complementary forms of deference to be dis-played, one by the voters to their social superiors and the other by the would-be representatives to their masters, the freeholders. Def-erence, in other words, was a two-way street.

"Courting" the voters involved a kind of status inversion, with deference displayed by the candidate in letters to the freeholders; as well as in "spouting," and "treating" (i.e., speaking and providing refreshment).[18] In *The Candidates*, Robert Munford's satire of a Vir-ginia election in the 1770s, Wou'dbe observes that "in order to se-cure a seat in our august senate, 'tis necessary a man should either be a slave or a fool; a slave to the people, for the privilege of serving them, and a fool himself, for thus begging a troublesome and expen-sive employment." Colonel Landon Carter of Virginia, never a champion of the common folk, confided to his diary in 1776 that his son Robert Wormeley Carter had been defeated for the Virginia con-stitutional convention even though he had "kissed the arses of the people, and very servilely accomodated himself to others."[19]

The very word "courting" itself is instructive in thinking about electioneering ritual because it draws a parallel with another ritual

[17]Jack P. Greene, *Political Life in the Eighteenth Century* (Williamsburg, 1986), 27; also Greene, "Society, Ideology and Politics," 271.

[18]Peter Shaw, *American Patriots and the Rituals of Revolution* (Cam-bridge, Mass., 1981), 204–26.

[19]*The Diary of Colonel Landon Carter of Sabine Hall, 1752–1778*, ed. Jack P. Greene, 2 vols. (Charlottesville, Va., 1965), II, 1009.

involving transposed deference. In many traditional societies, courtship involves an extended display of flattery, humility and protestations of worthy conduct on the part of the suitor, who will, if successful, exercise considerable authority over his intended. In a traditional society, a woman and her family have only the determinative power of refusal. If she would marry wisely, a woman must confer her consent on a worthy suitor. The greater the authority the suitor will exercise after the wedding ceremony, the greater his need to persuade his intended bride by an elaborate display of words and gestures, that he will worthily exercise that authority. A similar dynamic applied in eighteenth-century politics: the greater the authority a candidate might wield after being elected, the more he had to flatter and cajole the freeholders. Since a typical burgess might serve a seven-year term, he generally needed a great deal of persuasion, flattery and perhaps some subtle forms of bribery to secure voters' consent.

Electioneering was predicated on the congruence of personal, rather than political, interests between candidates and electors. In "courting" the electors through written letters and by "spouting" and "treating," the candidates appealed to personal ties. As with most other forms of deferential behavior, an inverted form of deference was an acknowledgment of personal dependence. St. George Tucker wrote to William Wirt that in former times the "Rich rode in Coaches, or Chariots, or on fine horses, but they never failed to pull off their hats to a poor man whom they met."[20] In a world of very formalized and explicit status hierarchies, where honor, standing and credit depended upon personal ties, the tenant deferred to his landlord, the artisan to the merchant, and the large landowner acknowledged his dependence on the good will of his neighbors. As T. H. Breen observes, large planters dared not risk the antagonism of the small planters, since "these were the men, after all, who

---

[20]St. George Tucker to William Wirt, September 25, 1815, *William & Mary Quarterly*, 1st ser., 22 (1914), 252.

voted in local elections."[21] Similarly the legislator declared his dependence on his constituents, in the uniformly recognizable rituals of deferential behavior. In *The Candidates*, Wou'dbe referred to this behavior as "the grimace and compliments."[22] As Daniel Jordan notes, "perhaps a politician's having to address the freeholders constituted a psychological deference to them in the tradition of 'treating.' Candidates stood socially above the average voters, but the requirement for a public appeal to them helped minimize class differences and established a proper democratic image for gentry office seekers." As Pole has observed of New England, social deference "was compatible with a very vigorous notion of one's own importance."[23]

Before the polling, candidates and their friends published printed appeals, most often in letter form, in local newspapers. These "letters" addressed the freeholders in obsequious terms, seeking from the voters the "honour of representing them." Candidates for election would "respectfully request," "beseech," "entreat" or even "humbly beg" their constituents to vote for them. Contestants might make explicit reference to a reward constituents would receive for the "honor of their suffrages." This usually took the form of "treating" with refreshment. Candidates generally avoided proclaiming what their conduct would be once elected to office: or, as one candidate declared, "I do not mean to make a parade of what I will do."[24] The letter usually concluded with the candidate noting he was "pleased to have the honor" of being his constituents' "obedient servant." Such solicitations indicated that moral criteria were important to voters in determining whether a candidate deserved the honor of acting as legislative representative. They were signed by the

[21]Breen, *Tobacco Culture*, 101.

[22]Robert Munford, *The Candidates*, Act I, scene i, Wou'dbe's address to Sir John Toddy, in *William and Mary Quarterly*, 3d ser., 5 (1948), 231.

[23]Jordan, *Political Leadership*, 116; Pole, *Political Representation*, 46.

[24]*Aurora and General Advertiser*, September 24, 1796.

candidate himself or by his "friends," who might praise the candidate for his "honesty," "independence," "integrity" and "fidelity."[25]

While printed letters often stressed a candidate's moral qualities, "spouting" or "stumping" showed off his oratorical abilities. Contestants often appeared in person before the electors and delivered extemporaneous speeches. In addressing a crowd, a candidate had to steer a stylistic course between obvious flattery and transparent condescension. An aspirant for office usually addressed his listeners as "Gentlemen," often making grateful allusions to "the partiality shewn me" in previous elections for "the honor of your suffrages." Great pains were taken to insure that this exercise in reversed deference roles was enacted without transparent hypocrisy. The ritual thus insured that political honors were reserved only for those with persuasive abilities.

At the hustings candidates courted the freeholders collectively in their speeches; they wooed them individually in casual conversation. "Treating," the custom of providing free food and drink as a reward for the electors at the candidate's expense, furnished opportunities for personal contact between the candidate and the voters. Although treating was prohibited by law in colonial times and again in 1788, the law was honored more in the breach than in the observance until well into the nineteenth century.[26] As Edmund Pendleton put it in 1783,

> In a neighbouring County (as I am told) three Candidates have emploied as many Months in canvassing, not only from house to house, but at frequent and expensive treats; a species of bribery the more dangerous, since it is masqued, and appears not in its plain shape as a piece of proffered gold would. In our County, a new declaring Candidate at the last

[25]Taylor, " 'Art of Hook & Snivey,' " 1381–86.
[26]Sydnor, *Gentlemen Freeholders*, 55–59.

Court, made a sacrifice of much wine, bottles and glasses to the fortunate Deities.[27]

In King William County in 1769 one critical observer noted that at an election, "the merits of a Candidate are always measured by the number of his treats; his constituents assembled, eat upon him, and lend their applause, not to his integrity or sense, but the quantities of his beef and brandy."[28]

Treating made broad allowances for merriment and dissipation and sometimes even melee and riot. Electioneering had much in common with festival days in early modern Europe: elections were a liminal period in which the hierarchical order was symbolically overturned and then reaffirmed.[29] Elections, like festivals, could prove tumultuous and even violent. As Nathaniel Beverly Tucker wrote to his father in 1807, "There are violent contests every where that I have been, to the great annoyance of old John Barleycorn, who suffers greatly in the fray."[30] Close contests might generate insults, intimidation and crowd violence. Candidates and their "friends," might assault or humiliate an opposing candidate, cursing him, beating him or threatening him with tar and feathers. Duels occasionally provided a bloody climax to a fiercely contested poll.[31]

---

[27]Edmund Pendleton to Richard Henry Lee, March 14, 1783 in *The Letters and Papers of Edmund Pendleton, 1734–1803*, ed. David John Mays, 2 vols. (Charlottesville, Va., 1967), II, 477.

[28]Reid, "Religion of the Bible and the Religion of K[ing] W[illiam] County Compared," in Richard Beale Davis, ed., *The Colonial Virginia Satirist: Mid-Eighteenth Century Commentaries on Politics, Religion and Society* (Philadelphia, 1967), quoted in Greene, "Society, Ideology and Politics," 271.

[29]Victor Turner, *The Ritual Process: Structure and Anti-Structure* (Chicago, 1969), esp. 166–203; Natalie Zemon Davis, *Structure and Culture in Early Modern France* (Stanford, Calif., 1975), 97–123.

[30]Nathaniel Beverly Tucker to St. George Tucker, April 25, 1807; Sydnor, *Gentlemen Freeholders*, 57.

[31]Jordan, *Political Leadership*, 131–32.

In *The Candidates* Sir John Toddy was a veteran of many years of "swilling the planters with bumbo": treating the electors to free rum. Munford has a good ear for the dialogue, perhaps because he was himself a burgess from Mecklenburg County.[32]

SIR JOHN. Gentlemen and ladies, your servant, hah! my old friend Prize, how goes it? how does your wife and children do?

SARAH. At your service, sir. (*Making a low courtsey.*)

PRIZE. How the devil come he to know me so well, and never spoke to me before in his life? (*aside.*)

GUZZLE. (*whispering Sir John*) Dick Stern.

SIR JOHN. Hah! Mr. Stern, I'm proud to see you; I hope your family are well; how many children? does the good woman keep to the old stroke?

CATHERINE. Yes, an't please your honour, I hope my lady's well, with your honour.

SIR JOHN. At your service, madam.

GUZZLE. (*whispering Sir John*) Roger Twist.

SIR JOHN. Hah! Mr. Roger Twist! your servant, sir. I hope your wife and children are well.

TWIST. There's my wife. I have no children, at your service.

SIR JOHN. A pretty girl: why Roger, i[f] you don't do better, you must call an old fellow to your assistance.

TWIST. I have enough to assist me without applying to you, sir.

SIR JOHN. No offence, I hope, sir; excuse my freedom.[33]

Occasionally in politics, life imitates art. Another Munford, in this case George Wythe Munford, offered this account of a real Vir-

---

[32]Greene, "Society, Ideology and Politics," 271.
[33]Munford, *The Candidates*, Act II, scene i, 241–42.

ginia election, the congressional contest between John Marshall and John Clopton in 1799.

Liquor in abundance was on the court green for the friends of either party. A barrel of whiskey for all, with the head knocked in, and the majority took it straight. Independent of the political excitement, the liquor added fuel to the flame. Fights became common, and every now and then there would be a knock-down and drag-out affray to quell which required all the power of the county justices.

. . . The candidates, as was then the custom, were seated on the justice's bench, and it was usual, when a vote was cast, for the candidate in question to return thanks. Sometimes, "I thank you, sir." Sometimes, "May you live a thousand years," etc. There were several noisy, impudent fellows, who made comments on the voters as they came up—sometimes amusing, sometimes insulting; and then the partisans of each would make a welkin ring with their exhilarating huzzas and animated retorts. . . .

There were shoutings and hurrahs perfectly deafening. Men were shaking fists at each other, rolling up their sleeves, cursing and swearing, with angry and furious denunciations. Some became wild with agitation. . . . One fellow growled out an imprecation, and another replied, "You sir, ought to have your mouth smashed for your impudence." . . .

"Mr. Blair," said the sheriff, "who do you vote for?" "John Marshall," said he. Mr. Marshall replied, "your vote is appreciated, Mr. Blair." . . . "Who do you vote for, Mr. Buchanan?" "For John Clopton," said the good man. Mr. Clopton said, "Mr. Buchanan, I shall treasure that vote in my memory. It will be regarded as a feather in my cap for ever." The shouts were astounding. Hurrah for Marshall! Hurrah for Clopton![34]

[34]George Wythe Munford, *The Two Parsons; Cupid's Sports; the Dream; and the Jewels of Virginia* (Richmond, 1884), 208–10.

This account of a Virginia congressional contest has been quoted at length by Charles Sydnor and commented upon by many serious scholars describing traditional forms of electioneering. Yet there is more to this election than one would gather from reading Sydnor. This election was very close and it offers evidence of strenuous party competition and was not decided entirely on the basis of personality. As one can see from reading the original Munford account, a hint of competitive nineteenth century party politics appears in this contest.

> The candidates were John Marshall, who had been minister to France and secretary of state under Mr. Adams, and John Clopton, an eminent member of the bar; each the exponent of the principles of his party. Their success or defeat involved what each party believed the wellbeing and future prosperity of the country. It was believed the contest would be very close. The parties were drilled to move together in a body; and the leaders and their business committees were never surpassed in activity and systematic arrangement for bringing out every voter. Sick men were taken in their beds to the polls; the halt, the lame and the blind, were hunted up, and every mode of conveyance was mustered into service.[35]

In nearby Maryland partisanship was even more contentious. In the 1788 Baltimore assembly election, the unsuccessful candidate was Revolutionary war hero, Samuel Chase, later to become a Federalist justice of the United States Supreme Court. Chase's campaign partner, Alexander McMechen, also running for the assembly, "reportedly visited each of the taverns at [Fells] Point," the latter dressed "in the shabby tarred dress of a sailor." He treated the seamen to grog and urged them "to parade on Monday morning, in his and Mr. *Chase's* favour." At the designated hour, Chase and McMechen gathered their supporters at the Point and "marched from the Point to the

---

[35]*Ibid.*, 210.

place of election, with a flag, a liberty cap, and a representation of a pilot-boat." Not to be outdone, their opponents "*paraded* through the town, with a body of sailors carrying a ship and pilot-boat with drums beating, fifes playing, and colours flying, followed by a large body of respectable characters, merchants and gentlemen, and a very large number of persons NOT entitled to vote; and the *whole body* took possession of the polls." The reaction by one observer in the *Maryland Journal* was not surprising.

> The *real* sense of the town cannot be determined by the election, as it cannot be ascertained in whose favour the number of LEGAL votes would have been, if the election had been conducted in a proper and legal manner.—If this election can be supported, this town can no longer boast of the greatest privilege of freeman—THE FREEDOM OF ELECTION.[36]

Party politics, with its issues, symbols, parades, mass mobilization and crowd violence had intruded on the traditional political culture of the Chesapeake. As the Baltimore observer noted of the 1788 election, if such politics were "permitted in this town, the like" would "soon be practiced in the counties." Baltimore later witnessed the worst outbreak of early republican mob violence in the attack on the *Federal Republican* in the summer of 1812.

Urban Baltimore was certainly not Tidewater Virginia but the Old Dominion was in for many a rude interruption of its decorous politics. The congressional election of 1799 was the most closely contested of all the Virginia polls in the early republic. In that year, moreover, and in every subsequent election, issues—real and imagined— intruded on the web of personal relationships that constituted the foundation of Virginia politics. In June of 1799, a popular meeting

[36]Baltimore *Maryland Journal*, October 14, 1788. See also Charles G. Steffen, *The Mechanics of Baltimore: Workers and Politics in the Age of Revolution 1763–1812* (Urbana, 1984), 89–97.

convened in Southside Prince George County and drafted an address that opposed paper money, demanded court reform, and asked for revision of the law on British debts. As Norman Risjord observes of this meeting, "Popular meetings of this sort had appeared in the early days of the Revolution, and George Mason occasionally used them to vent his political views. But as an instrument of political pressure the device was comparatively new."[37]

The Embargo provided another important issue around which parties could rally. In Jefferson County in 1808, a gathering of Federal Republicans met at Charles Town to offer resolutions before their congressional nominations.

> *Resolved,* That in the present awful and perilous crisis of public affairs, and at a moment so replete with individual calamity and distress, it beho[o]ves the friends of liberty and the constitution to adopt such measures as are best calculated to produce a redress of exciting grievances, and to contribute to . . . prosperity and peace.
>
> *Resolved,* That as one important mean of promoting these inestimable objects, it is expedient that the Federal Republicans of this district should unite in the support of a fit and suitable character to represent the district in Congress.[38]

What was unusual about these resolutions was their order of priority. Political issues seized precedence over personality, at a time when in western Virginia Federalists recognized the opportunities for capitalizing on an unpopular policy.[39] As "A Federal Voter" put it in August of 1808:

[37]Norman K. Risjord, *Chesapeake Politics, 1781–1800* (New York, 1978), 219.

[38]Charles Town *Farmer's Repository*, September 16, 1808.

[39]David Hackett Fischer, *The Revolution of American Conservatism: The Federalist Party in the Era of Jeffersonian Democracy* (New York, 1965), 64.

We have no time to lose—the present is a precious and glorious time for our electioneering campaign—and you should take the lead.—You can, you may, nay, you must send many good bits from your presses. Keep the embargo, the *dum*-bargo sounding in the ears of the farmers . . . this is a precious morsel, and cannot be too often printed and reprinted—the affair of the Chesapeake . . . The purchase of the French province of Louisiana—the probable insurrection in the democratic state of Vermont . . . It is not enough for you to usher these precious morsels from your presses, we must sound them aloud by our own voices in all places—we must engage some *choice spirits* (and we can get plenty of them) to be unceasingly sounding these dear, dear scraps of *News*, at court times, vendues, in the streets, lanes and allies, as well as in taverns— this will be rare sport.[40]

"A Federal Voter" described more than an expedient opportunity, however. A member of a minority party in an overwhelmingly Republican state, he attested to the growing importance of written information and external information in gaining votes for Federalists. Both parties were building a sense of community by means of the printed word. In New England and the Middle States, the web of relationships between editors, correspondents and readers grew and thickened, beginning in the seaboard cities and steadily moving west.[41] In Virginia the number of newspapers nearly tripled from 1790 to 1800, growing from nine to twenty-six. The editors of these newspapers corresponded with one another, copied one another, lauded and attacked one another and formed alliances with the postmasters.

[40]Charles Town *Farmer's Repository*, August 5, 1808.

[41]The number of newspapers publishing in the states north of the Potomac was 72 in 1790, 170 in 1800, 267 in 1810 and 333 in 1820. See Alfred McClung Lee, *The Daily Newspaper in America* (New York, 1937), 711.

This print community, launched out of fierce partisanship, helped by the very intensity of its focus to create a national "imagined community," to use Benedict Anderson's term; and in this way fostered a growing sense of nationalism.[42]

In the years between 1790 and 1835 these editors created an extended print community that rivaled, and in the North overturned, the older deferential-participant communities. At the same time, the newspapers themselves, in their use of emphatic typography and iconography, mimicked the emphasis, the cadence and the spontaneity of the older forms of "stump" oratory. In this way the print community paid homage to the vitality of the deferential community. But printed forms of information generated a different kind of response on the part of the readers than the older forms of oral delivery. Newspapers, party broadsides and other printed communications provided an independent arena for posting information about political assemblies, mobilization efforts and issues. Print provided the means for political reflection on the part of the individual and coherence on the part of the group. An individual, reading in isolation, could form his opinion more independently of his superiors and with less pressure or distraction from his peers.

In Virginia, however, the older political culture based on personal relations endured throughout the early republic. This was due in part to the limited extent of literacy in Virginia. The restrictions on suffrage

[42]Benedict Anderson says that "the printer-journalist was essentially a North-American phenomenon. Since the main problem facing the printer-journalist was reaching readers, there developed an alliance with the postmaster so intimate that often each became the other. Hence, the printer's office emerged as the key to North-American communications and community political life." Anderson, *Imagined Communities: Reflections on the Origin and Spread of Nationalism* (London, 1991), 62. See also Richard D. Brown, *Knowledge Is Power: The Diffusion of Information in Early America* (New York, 1989).

undoubtedly precluded the successful mass mobilization that occurred in Northern States and in neighboring states like North Carolina and Tennessee. Another reason for the persistence of a traditional political culture was voice voting, which reinforced the importance of personal relationships between candidate and voters.

By the end of the first decade of the nineteenth century, a kind of stalemate existed between two political cultures; between the friends of the "good old way" and the activists of the new. The old ways in combination with the new opened opportunities for some ambitious candidates: some observers found it hard to judge which was worse. "A Freeholder" complained in 1813 that John Clopton's opponent had "taken great pains to secure his election to Congress; barbecues and fish-fries have been given to get the people together," and, the latter went on in an injured tone, "a hand bill has been put out & sent all over the district *against* Mr. Clopton."[43] As "A Friend to the Good Old Way" remarked ironically in the election of 1807:

New notions, new practices, and new men, are starting up every day; so that it appears as if good old fashioned patriotism would be rooted out of the earth. I never expected to live to see the day when the salutary influence of Whiskey Treats, and Barbecues, in the cause of Virtue and civil liberty, would be doubted and sneered at.[44]

What are we to make of these accounts of election ritual? In essence the second and third decades of the nineteenth century marked a collision between two forms of "imagined communities."[45] As Pole has observed, the older deference community persisted because "people imagine themselves to be governed" by forms belonging to the past. Freeholders continued to follow the forms of deferential partic-

[43]Richmond *Enquirer*, April 6, 1813.
[44]Richmond *Virginia Argus*, March 27, 1807.
[45]Anderson, *Imagined Communities*, 62.

ipant politics in Virginia partly because of external constraints, but also partly because reciprocal expressions of deference apparently did nothing to contradict what Jordan calls "a proper democratic image" in the minds of the voters for "gentry office seekers." At the same time, a more active participatory political culture intruded into Virginia, introducing a different kind of "imagined community" created around partisanship, policies and ardent nationalism. Unlike the Middle States, which succumbed entirely to the new partisanship, Virginia contained both of these conflicting political cultures in an uneasy coexistence. Virginians saw no reason to reject the call of nationalism their statesmen had played so large a part in creating. On the other hand, neither did they see any reason to abandon the process of selection that brought forward these same statesmen. The crowning achievement of eighteenth-century Virginia's political culture was its capacity, in the midst of all the fawning, fighting and posturing, to select distinguished men for office. In the words of Robert Munford, "E'en then, Virginians could much virtue boast."[46]

---

[46]Munford, *The Candidates*, Prologue, 230.

E Pluribus Unum:

The Ideological Imperative in Revolutionary America

Joyce Appleby

In 1809 during the last month he spent in the White House, Thomas Jefferson received a letter from the Westward Mill Library Society of New Brunswick County, Virginia, inviting his patronage. "Our society," the secretary reported "is composed of farmers, mechanics, Justices of the Peace, ministers of the Gospel—Military Officers, Lawyers, School masters—merchants—postmasters, one member of the Assembly & one member of Congress. Our present president Wm E. Bradnax," the secretary continued, is "a substantial & respectable farmer and the Librarian James Wyche one of Mr. Grangers many Deputies." He then gave the names of the six directors for the year, 1809, and closed his letter with an arresting question: "Query will such an heterogeneous body ever firmly ... coalesce?"[1] Here in microcosm is the macrocosmic problem of the American people, what I have called the ideological imperative of

This paper was originally given at All Souls College, Oxford, October 3, 1990.

[1] John Wyche to Thomas Jefferson, March 19, 1809, Bixby Collection, Missouri Historical Society, St. Louis. See also my *Inheriting the Revolution: The First Generation of Americans* (Cambridge, Mass., 2000).

E Pluribus Unum, the intensely felt need to create a union from the seemingly disparate groups that formed their country.

We are often told about Americans' pride in their unique heritage, but before they were transmogrified into a single heritage, the conspicuous differences among the people of the United States caused much uneasiness. Americans knew that the ideal of a commonwealth was one king, one church and one tongue, and certainly colonial leaders had striven to achieve that organic unity. The Revolution offered patriots the rhetorical opportunity to treat America's social diversity as a summons to a new kind of nationhood, but old sensibilities lingered on. What a successful War for Independence could not supply were the shared sentiments, symbols, and social explanations necessary for an integrative national identity. Much of the bombast about America's unique calling to nurture freedom for the entire human race should be heard as rather noisy whistling in the dark or, more accurately, whistling through the graveyard of republics.

Will such a heterogeneous body ever firmly coalesce? Coming from a local group within a rural community, the question makes salient what Americans confronted when they thought about union. Our preoccupation with political history has encouraged the view that national integration was largely a matter of muting the autonomous tendencies of thirteen once-sovereign states or of working out compromises among antagonistic sections of the United States. Indeed that political agenda did exist, but creating a common identity involved different challenges from the project of integrating governmental institutions. The Westward Mill Library Society presents the situation in its most mundane form: could a people split into a dozen religious denominations, shedding the social forms that separated mechanics from militia majors, divided between native-born and naturalized citizens unify? And if so, on which and whose terms? Could Americans will themselves into a national culture as they had willed themselves into a War for Independence?

The familiarity with which these strangers addressed their president shows how easily Americans had sloughed off the skin of monarchical forms, abandoning entirely the formality which earlier marked petitions to royal officials. Jefferson, highly attuned to the politics of social forms, invited this familiarity by answering the door of the White House himself, receiving callers in his lounging robe, and establishing the protocol for presidential dinner parties as "nearest to the door goes in first."

The Baptists and Methodists are the only religious affiliations mentioned in the letter, giving us a clue that this is a relatively new community, outside Tidewater Virginia where the Episcopalians retained some vestiges of their old colonial prestige. It also reflects the remarkable success of the evangelizing sects which in a quarter of a century had displaced in popularity the once-dominant Congregational, Anglican and Presbyterian churches. The conviviality which the Baptist deacon and Methodist elder were sharing in the Westward Mill Library Society indicates as well the dampening down of competitive revivalism. After two generations of religious upheaval, Virginians were learning to live with denominationalism, that peculiar American *via media* between the churchly and sectarian traditions of Christendom.

The secretary's sweeping reference to a membership of farmers, mechanics, merchants, magistrates, lawyers, militia officers and school masters should probably not be taken literally, but it does announce an endorsement of egalitarian sociability. The mingling of designations—planter, assemblyman, naturalized citizen, church elder—indicates also that there were many ways to earn acceptance in this rural community.

The purpose of the society is noteworthy. Each member paid 2 shillings a year to create a fund for book purchases. Such a pooling of purchasing power meant that the militia major, the Baptist deacon, and the member of congress felt that they shared enough intellectual interests to benefit from a group collection. It also presumed a fairly easy access to printed material. Publishing in the United States was in fact booming, stimulated in part by enterprising publishers who had laid networks of book salesmen across the country-side. Reading had become a necessity of life; it had also become the most important activity in nation-building.[2]

This document does not explain, but it does epitomize the qualities in American life which gave shape to a new national identity. There is first of all this exercise of initiative. A group of undistinguished men form an association for personal goals but unselfconsciously take on the responsibility for thinking about social cohesion. Matters of state—that jealously guarded preserve of gentlemen, magistrates and ministers—had been breached. The line between the public and private was being blurred. Americans were fashioning a new civil society, broadly inclusive and voluntarily organized, at a time when governments elsewhere still had the power to define the areas of public concern.

The mingling of Baptists and Methodists with legislators and militia officers is also surprising. It is not just the respectability accorded sectarians so recently despised as evangelizing zealots, but also the presumed compatibility of all of their reading tastes. Both sides of an earlier cultural divide had moved to the common ground of mutual accommodation. Venerable demarcations between the saved and the damned, the learned and the vulgar, the authorized and the unauthorized, had dissolved into a freemasonry of the tolerant and the self-improving. The intellectual ambitions which were once the hallmark of the free-thinker were now embraced by Baptists and Methodists who had earlier viewed with deep suspicion those who displayed book learning. They had all become people of the book, but the book was likely now to be David Ramsay's *History*

---

[2]William J. Gilmore-Lehne, *Reading Becomes a Necessity of Life* (Nashville, Knoxville, 1789); Rosalind Remer, *Printers and Men of Capital: Philadelphia Book Publishers in the New Republic* (Philadelphia, 1996); and Richard John, *Spreading the News: The American Postal System from Franklin to Morse* (Cambridge, 1995).

of the American Revolution or Jedediah Morse's *American Geography.* This softening of older lines of differentiation helped make possible the budding of a new, American identity.

And finally this library society in rural Virginia was using the market in a way that strengthened the commercial linkages between country and city, no mean consideration in a society so predominantly agricultural. Modernization as measured by literacy, social mobility, enhanced wealth and political forms ran well ahead of industrialization in the United States, a fact of considerable importance considering the hierarchical order imposed in factories. By pooling their money to buy books, these library societies—and there were hundreds of them all over the country—were not only stimulating the economy, they were also registering social demands with their consuming tastes. The market thus acted as an amplifier of the imagination of ordinary consumers acting without reference to authority or majority vote. Growing in its reach and density, the market enhanced the range of choice in the same decades that choice itself became a signifier of American distinctiveness.

Twenty years earlier the thirteen independent states represented a hodgepodge from which to form a nation. Only retrospectively can we assign to their similarities more prominence than their differences. The commonalities that did exist among them—those of language, law and institutional history—all pointed in the wrong direction, backwards to the past, towards an association with England whose utility as a contemptible oppressor could not easily be done without.

There was one common and inspiring document—the Declaration of Independence, but its self-evident truths that all men were created equal proved more divisive than conciliating as the prolonged debates in the various state constitutional conventions demonstrated. Because many Americans took natural rights literally they began agitating for repeal of the state laws which created property in human beings. Their success marked the first abolitionist movement in which one by one the Northern States abolished slavery, and as they did so turning the surveyors' boundary between Pennsylvania and Maryland, the Mason-Dixon line, into a potent symbol of difference and a boundary of contested statuses.

If the nation, as a whole, did not have natural cohering forces, the three regions which composed the United States did, and they—New England, the mid-Atlantic States and the Southern States—had generated very different meanings of the Revolution during the fighting of the War for Independence.

Examining voting behavior in the Continental Congress, James Henderson detected the presence of strong voting blocs centering on regions.[3] That is, delegates from the three regions voted together and were able to attract enough other votes to lead the Congress at differing stages of the Revolution. Looking at this schematically we can see three distinct forms of republicanism emerging during the fighting of the war as each regional bloc came in for its period of national leadership as its region became the theater of military operations.

The war began in Massachusetts, and New Englanders composed the first voting bloc that dominated the Continental Congress. They folded events into the Puritan story of fall and redemption. The American Revolution appeared to them as an opportunity to recover lost grace. Throwing off the yoke of tyranny was also an opportune occasion for throwing off the luxury and corruption of the tyrant and making way for a new Christian Sparta.

We could call theirs Regenerative Republicanism with its fusion of natural-law doctrine and Biblical imperatives. Virtue was a political not a private value, measured by material sacrifice and individual commitment to the common good. Revolutionary themes appeared in New England that were both radical and conservative—the acceptance of an established leadership of the virtuous existing alongside

---

[3]H. James Henderson, "The Structure of Politics in the Continental Congress," in Stephen G. Kurtz and James H. Hutson, eds., *Essays on the American Revolution* (Chapel Hill, 1973).

insistence upon strict accountability. Accustomed to participating in town meetings, ordinary New Englanders knew how to castigate their social superiors. High and low spoke the language of sin-prone man and divine anger. They also mixed their righteousness with a tough, practical discipline exemplified in hard work and sound investments which often struck others as hypocritical.

The New Englanders' vision of the American Revolution as an opportunity for regeneration found little appeal outside the confines of the old Puritan colonies. When fighting moved away from Massachusetts early in the war the region became almost as insulated from outside influence as it had been before.

With military engagements concentrated in New York, New Jersey and Pennsylvania, the burden of fighting and paying for the war passed to these states. The response of their congressional delegates was a tough, practical one—we could call theirs a pragmatic republicanism. Already distinguished by their ethnic and religious pluralism, the mid-Atlantic States had a tradition of tolerance championed in New Jersey and Pennsylvania by the original Quaker settlers. Their leaders demonstrated their modernity and sophistication by guiding Congress towards workable policies. Convinced of the need for a more efficient central government, they restructured the workings of Congress, taking power away from congressional committees and giving it to executive departments. They also made ingenious fiscal arrangements that kept the Union afloat. Mid-Atlantic leaders revealed less civic virtue and more shrewdness at manipulating men's interests. While directing continental affairs, mid-Atlantic delegates tried to amend the Articles of Confederation, but were unable to secure the unanimous vote necessary for altering the Articles. Mid-Atlantic delegates, like New Englanders before them, failed to convert their voting bloc into a national party. When the war turned southward the ideological initiative went with it.

Southerners controlled Congress during those last years of the fighting, the ones that laid waste the countryside of Virginia and North and South Carolina. Once the war ended the Southern voting bloc continued to dominate the Confederation Congress, its delegates taking the initiative in articulating peacetime policies for a continental nation. Their goals reflected the Tidewater gentry's long-standing zeal for westward expansion. Only now, under Jefferson's guidance, the landowners' program for speculative investments was turned into a republican vision of a society of free and independent farm families.

Jefferson got Congress to extinguish old colonial land claims and create a national domain, the one tangible asset the United States took away from the war. His prototype for the Northwest Ordinance banned slavery from the area above the Ohio River. (Though it is worth indicating the power of national mythology to point out that the Southwest Ordinance ignored in all American history texts permitted the Southern spread of slavery.) We might call this Southern program expansive republicanism, playing off the double meaning of the actual westward movement and the effusive declarations about an empire for liberty.

Perhaps because they were the last to grapple with the general problems of governing the United States from the center, Southern leaders, specifically Virginians, led the campaign for reforming the Articles of Confederation. They prodded the other states into attending a constitutional convention in Philadelphia in 1787. They provided the plan which set the constitutional convention on the path toward an entirely novel frame of government. And their statesmen presided as presidents for thirty-two of the first thirty-six years under the Constitution.[4]

---

[4]Henderson, "The Structure of Politics in the Continental Congress," 190–91, n. 37, remarks that "Historians have not fully appreciated the extent to which the Convention was a Virginia production," noting that a canvass of letters written among political leaders in the years before the Convention reveals that only three letters relevant to the constitutional movement were sent to Alexander Hamilton compared to 74 sent to Madison.

The case for a reconstructed national government was not built on sympathies but rather upon reasoned arguments about defensive strategies against foreign powers and interstate cooperation for trading purposes. Despite the openness of the ratification process with its specially-elected conventions in the states, the 1500 some delegates represented an extension of the revolutionary elite. They earned their offices in free elections while retaining the political mores of a closed ruling body. Theirs was a nationalism of practical wisdom. Outside their circles of political conversation, there were few shared assumptions operating at the intimate level of human experience and a paucity of positive symbols easily recognized from one end of the Atlantic shelf to the other. Once the Constitution had been ratified, the United States had an institutional roof without walls, as one contemporary described it.[5] It was a nation without a national ideology, save the shared understandings of its leaders. Indeed the founding fathers offered a neocolonial answer to the problem of unity, direction from the center exercised by officials deliberately holding themselves aloof from the people.

The success of establishing this new and more powerful federal government did stimulate enthusiasm for America's special destiny. The return of prosperity after a post-revolutionary depression also strengthened confidence in the republican experiment, but the working out of the content of American identity did not take place until the mid-1790s.

At that critical juncture a domestic movement converged with a momentous tidal shift in European politics. Finally convinced of the elitist intentions of the government he was serving as secretary of state, Jefferson in league with James Madison set out to alert a

---

[5]John M. Murrin, "A Roof without Walls: The Dilemma of American National Identity," in Richard Beeman et al., eds., Beyond Confederation: Origins of the Constitution and American National Identity (Chapel Hill, 1987), 333.

largely inert political community of voters about the undemocratic tendencies of the Washington administration. This effort coincided with receipt of the news of the execution of Louis XVI. Quite unexpectedly the proclamation of the French Republic called forth a new cohort of American radicals, most of them too young to have engaged in the protests against the British. They took up the French cause as their own, finding in the destructive fury of 1793 a confirmation of the portentousness of the moment.

The French Revolution opened the way for a new group of dissidents to interpret their own Revolution as the initial act in a historic drama of liberation. The French embrace of newness itself suggested that the novelties of American society were harbingers of things to come rather than egregious examples of raw provincialism. Long uprooted from the European past, Americans could plant themselves in the imaginative soil of a visionary future. The rhetoric of Republican France roused political passions in America at the very time that Federalists were congratulating themselves upon achieving stability through the workings of an energetic central government. The hoped-for deference from ordinary voters dissolved into a round of public demonstrations in support of French military victories. Political clubs formed in flagrant imitation of the Jacobins, and Republican newspapers were founded for the sole purpose of attacking the government.

Federalists responded by condemning France. The muted praise for British institutions that had always existed in their circles was made public and the example of Great Britain was advanced as a model for the United States to emulate. The Federalists' defense of conservative wisdom was forthright. They made it clear that democracy stopped on election day, defending the decorum, formality, even the secrecy of the Washington administration as necessary for effective governing. Although they endorsed meritocracy and sponsored mobility, they stressed those qualifications for public office rarely possessed by ordinary men. Vulgar, ignorant, insolent, unruly, frenzied and envious were the adjectives hurled at the aspiring unmeritorious citizens who claimed new rights as part of their revolutionary legacy.

In an unusually probing analysis of the social basis for elite power, the new radicals—who called themselves Republicans— treated the Federalist rhetoric as a psychological ploy to undermine ordinary men's confidence in themselves. British radicals, fleeing prosecution under the Sedition Law of 1792, contributed to the inflammatory polemics of the day. Beginning with the outrage expressed for Washington's Neutrality policy, denunciatory attacks on Federalist leadership continued unabated until the election of Jefferson in 1800. As Andrew Robertson has detailed, the passionate rhetorical battles of the 1790s popularized politics as they established a populist variant of older campaign traditions.[6]

America after 1789 entered into a period of great commercial prosperity—in part a consequence of its role as a neutral carrier for the belligerent nations of Europe. This prosperity promoted the construction of roads, the extension of postal services and the founding of newspapers in country towns. A dense new communication network vastly increased the resonance of partisan disputes. The control over information and opinions once exercised by an elite had been wrested away by articulate critics of the elite. Male literacy outside the South approached the 90% figure with female literacy following the same upward climb. The tactical advantages that accrued to an upper class small enough for concerted action were now overpowered by the mobilization of popular majorities through print campaigns.

This dramatic reversal of expectations precipitated a divisive controversy about popular political participation itself. Thus disputes about specific issues brought to light even more profound disagreements about the nature of democratic governance. The Jeffersonian

---

[6]Andrew Robertson, *The Language of Democracy: Political Rhetoric in the United States and Britain, 1790–1900* (Ithaca, N.Y., 1995), 30–35.

Republicans argued for the literal meaning of such terms as popular sovereignty and public servant. They predicted the government intimidation that materialized in the Alien and Sedition Acts of 1798. As the Philadelphia Democratic Society announced: "It has ever been a favorite and important pursuit with aristocracy to stifle free inquiry, to envelop its proceedings in mystery, and as much as possible to impede the progress of political knowledge."[7]

Federalists fought back. Believing in a conspiracy of incendiaries and trouble-makers, George Washington used his considerable influence to plead for the repudiation of the Republican clubs which he dismissively called "certain self-created societies." Even with congressional support, the gambit didn't work. The radicals defended private associations as exemplifying the first principle of social life. What after all, asked one, was the United States itself but "a great self-created society."[8] If much of this sounds like the London Corresponding Society it is worth considering the difference in outcomes. Thomas Jefferson won the presidency on his second attempt in a campaign which sharply defined the choices between gentry rule and popular power; ordinary Englishmen waited another half century for the vote.

Jefferson's policies more than fulfilled the Republicans' expectations. He let noxious Federalist laws lapse, decreased the size of government, reduced taxes, established land offices in the West, and paid off the Revolutionary debt which justified the fiscal policies through which Federalists had intended to direct economic growth. Most significantly he weeded out from the civil service all those with pronounced Federalist sympathies, including army officers down to the rank of captain. Thus twelve years after the ratification of the

[7]Joyce Appleby, *Capitalism and a New Social Order: The Republican Vision of the 1790s* (New York, 1984), 65–66.

[8]January 21 and 28, 1795, Philadelphia *Independent Gazetteer* as quoted in Appleby, *Capitalism and a New Social Order*, 67–68.

Constitution, the national elite, established with such high hopes for a stabilizing center, was gone and with it that union of social and political power essential to a ruling class.[9] Meanwhile the westward movement of families away from the Eastern center of authority and refinement—which Federalists had so feared—began in earnest. Land sales went from 67,751 acres in 1800 to 497,939 acres in 1801. The expansive republic had arrived.

In retrospect one can see that the French Revolution liberated Americans from their Eurocentric orientation, but it was a socially specific liberation. The spirit of high Federalism had flourished in America's major cities and throughout New England. The Federalists' defeat at the polls predisposed Federalist families to withdraw from national politics and leave the issue of nationalism for others to define. Deeply offended by the crass self-assertion of common folk, they turned their educated refinement into an end in itself, strengthening their ties with the English world that shared their values.

Indeed the rambunctious politics of the 1790s brought disillusionment to a number of cultural nationalists like Noah Webster, Charles Brockden Brown, Samuel Latham Mitchill, and David Ramsay. They had expected the free institutions of America to promote literature, science and scholarship; their nationalist fervor had been nourished by fantasies of American greatness in areas marked out by the high civilization of metropolitan Europe. For them the outburst of revolutionary passion from uneducated men had proved the conservatives right: when the pot boils the scum rises. The political rejection of the Federalists reflected more than a change of personnel; it was the defeat of a venerable conception of authority. Ruminating about these political changes and the paucity of achievement in the arts and scientists, Federalists became America's

[9]Nobel Cunningham, *The Process of Government under Jefferson* (Princeton, 1978).

first cultural critics. Their laments, however, were those of a spurned elite dispossessed of its admiring following. Responsibility for defining American character passed down the social ladder.

Those who were liberated from America's traditional orientation to Europe were the undistinguished men and women who sought affirmation of their tastes and values in the celebration of what was distinctively American: its institutional permissiveness, its pervasive practicality, its reforming zeal, above all its expanded scope for action for ordinary people.

In the decades that followed Jefferson's election the meaning of a democratic political order became manifest. People did not just want to vote; they wanted to experience full social participation—gathering in quasi-public meetings, debating matters of policy, mobilizing fellow citizens, and forming groups based on the affinities of conviction. The single most striking feature of social life in the years following the Republican victory was the spontaneous generation of thousands of voluntary associations, a phenomenon that reached its per capita peak in the mid-1820s tapering off to numbers high enough to guarantee the United States its lasting reputation as a nation of joiners.

Societies to build circulating libraries like the Westward Mill Library abounded. The zeal for self-improvement also found outlets in debating and study clubs, a particular favorite among young adults. Fire societies multiplied with the growth of cities along with other mutual benefit associations. Almost all religious denominations had auxiliaries. Women were unusually active in this new associational life as the principal organizers for the provision of charity and relief from suffering. Every town had its Female Domestic Missionary Society and its Home for Friendless Women.

The formation of new voluntary associations was only limited by the reigning social imagination. There was even an Association of American Patriots for the Purpose of Forming a National Character, started in 1808. The most common impulse promoting voluntary clubs was the urge to reform society—often prompted by a religious

revival. First and most enduringly there was the temperance movement, then reform of prisons and hospitals, sabbatarianism, later nativism and most productive of reforming zeal—the antislavery
movement. There were literally hundreds of antislavery societies,
many flourishing in the South. These multifarious voluntary associations revealed an efficiency in mobilizing recruits and in circulating
information that far exceeded anything done by public authority.[10]

Where the educated elite had wished to establish national
identity upon the basis of America's distinctive contributions to established realms of achievement, the reformers and revivalists were
expressing a different sense of nationhood. For them the United
States represented a new kind of social existence where personal ful-
fillment came through public initiatives. The activists' optimism
about concerted efforts to eliminate slavery, correct the treatment of
the insane and criminal, reorganize charity, and raise the tone of
public morals became a part of American character. Solidarity in this
highly mobile society would be fashioned from the outpouring of energy devoted to social betterment.

It's a significant feature of these voluntary associations that the
members invariably wrote constitutions. Occasionally that was the
only thing that they did and they often published their constitutions
as well. The Westward Mill Library Society had a printed constitution which the secretary sent to Jefferson. This passion for specifying
group objectives and rules of conduct in a written document represented more than a mimicry of state and federal constitution-writing.
It familiarized ordinary men and women with the forms of political
construction. More subtly, it was a way of denying the special place of
government. Where Federalists had used awe as an arm of authority,
Republicans promoted competence.

---

[10]See Frank W. Crow, "The Age of Promise: Societies for Social and
Economic Improvement in the United States, 1783–1815" (unpubl. Ph.D.
diss., University of Wisconsin, 1952).

What needs to be put into this picture of bootstrap moral reform is the darker side of American freedom in the half century after Independence. The decline of traditional ordering mechanisms was accompanied by deteriorating standards of personal behavior. Those who weren't reformers needed reforming. More liquor was drunk per capita in this generation than ever before or since. Not only drinking, but gambling and ritualized violence figured prominently in public life.[11] Mobs formed easily. The lightly-governed, newly-settled communities in the West had their urban equivalent in the older cities where the decadal doubling of population created entirely new neighborhoods. Moving up usually involved moving out, so the churning population of post-revolutionary America contained a disproportionate number of young men, always a group at risk in matters of social order. Geographic mobility offered cover to those fleeing from family and creditors. Real social problems fueled reforming engines as they added combustible material to the evangelical fires that were burning across the American landscape.

More profound than the toppling of upper-class political leadership was the transformation of American religion. Radical religious revivals reshaped the character of American Protestantism in the first generation after the Revolution. Like the actualization of popular sovereignty in national politics, this surge of vital religion overpowered both the leaders and the forms of leadership in America's established churches. The "mushroom candidates" ridiculed by Federalists had their analogues in the backwoods preachers who took religion to the unchurched. A cohort of youthful, uneducated, revivalist ministers nurtured the people's spiritual longings while spreading

---

[11]William A. Rohrbaugh, *The Alcoholic Republic: An American Tradition* (New York, 1979) and Joyce Appleby, "New Cultural Heroes in the Early National Period," in Thomas Haskell and Richard F. Teichgraebner III, eds., *The Culture of the Market: Historical Essays* (Cambridge, 1993), 181–82.

lessons about individual empowerment that echoed the Republicans' political message.[12]

Self-conscious outsiders, the circuit riders and itinerants were hostile to orthodox belief. They scrutinized established religious doctrine for evidence of upper-class prejudice. New Christian denominations proliferated, most of them carrying the rallying cry of "No creed but the Bible." Spurning the genteel religious routines of the learned clergy, the revivalists innovated with new techniques to bring sinners to Christ and, once won, left them with confidence in their own ability to discover Christian doctrine unaided. In their sermons, the radical preachers attacked hierarchical ecclesiastical structures as well as the Calvinists' preoccupation with damnation. Here was another form of liberation for ordinary Americans. They responded by deserting the Congregational, Presbyterian and Episcopal churches and flocking to the evangelizers, particularly the Baptists and Methodists. The number of preachers per capita went from 1 in 1500 at the time of the Revolution to 1 in 500 thirty years later. By the 1830s the Freewill Baptists alone equaled the number of Episcopalians, the Antimission Baptists outnumbering the Roman Catholics and Lutherans combined.

Despite the well-advertised religious skepticism of Jefferson, most revivalist congregations supported him because of his famous—or notorious—opposition to both precedent and privilege. Merging their social and religious goals, the evangelical leaders fought their battles against the established religions in the language of politics. An aristocracy of Calvinist clergy, they said, was trying to control the soul of the nation and crush the simple congregational freedom of ordinary worshipers. Often ardent Jeffersonians, the revival leaders made self-reliance the base of liberty and worked to undermine people's dependence upon authorities, be they in the pulpit, the legis-

[12]Nathan Hatch, *The Democratization of Christianity* (New Haven, 1989).

lative hall or the surgery. In their many successes they revealed not only the power of their preaching but the brilliance of their organizing skills as well. Francis Asbury, the founding bishop of the American Methodist Church, estimated in 1811 that over 3 million Americans attended camp meetings—more than a quarter of the total population. Alarmed at the success of these self-taught preachers, the old guard Calvanist leaders did organize, but they ended up adopting the revivalists' techniques and completing the transformation of American Protestantism.[13]

Like Jeffersonian Republicans in their campaign against Federalists, revivalists used printed material to maintain their organizational networks. Reform journalism flourished alongside and often within the magazines and pamphlets the evangelicals used to build their mass movements. Printed sermons, song books, denominational journals—all relied upon and strengthened the national communications system. A skeleton at the time of the ratification of the Constitution and the return of prosperity in 1789, it fleshed out quickly. While the population was doubling in the next twenty years, the number of post offices increased thirty fold, going from 75 to 2,300; the number of miles of post roads grew twenty-one fold from 1,875 to 44,000. Fifty years earlier there had only been private libraries and they usually in the control of gentlemen who took seriously their responsibility to screen the reading material of the *hoi polloi*. Now the wide diffusion of learning forced people to be the arbiters of the sources of information and opinion. As one dejected Federalist noted, "knowledge has induced the laity to think and act for themselves."[14]

[13]These developments can be followed in Edwin Gaustad, *Historical Atlas of America* (New York, 1962) and *A Religious History of America* (rev. ed., New York, 1974).

[14]David Daggett, *Fourth of July Address* (New Haven, 1787), as quoted in Richard D. Brown, *Knowledge Is Power: The Diffusion of Information in Early America* (New York, 1989), 80.

Voluntary associations distributed thousands of tracts. The number of newspapers and books produced and sold in the United States
took similar quantum leaps. The 96 weeklies and biweeklies of 1790
had grown by 1810 to 376 papers—many of them dailies. In that
year Americans bought 22 million newspapers annually, the largest
aggregate circulation of any country of the world. And America's
population was less than eight million with a mean age of 16 and a
20% enslaved group forbidden to read.[15]

The social implications of a commercially-articulated reading
universe did not escape notice. As early as 1803 Samuel Miller complained that the booksellers had replaced the aristocrats as "the great
patrons of literature." "The spirit of trade," he went on to explain,
"leads men to write in accommodation to the public taste, however
depraved." A leader in the Presbyterian stronghold of Princeton,
Miller no doubt included the flourishing revivalist congregations
among the depraved. Less captiously, the French *philosophe,* Pierre
Samuel Dupont, noted that a large portion of the American public
read the Bible, but all of the nation, he said, "assiduously peruses the
newspapers. The fathers read them aloud to their children while the
mothers are preparing the breakfast."[16]

The juxtaposition here of the Bible and the newspapers should
not be taken as a conventional differentiation of religious and secular reading publics, for it was exactly their convergence which created a new identity for the nation. We can see this in the language
they employed. The preachers' zeal for empowering ordinary men
frequently gave a Lockean cast to religious exhortations while the
expectation of a morally-elevated society encouraged all reformers to

[15]Robertson, *The Language of Democracy,* 37–38.

[16]Brown, *Knowledge Is Power,* 81; Howard B. Rock, *Artisans of the
New Republic: The Tradesmen of New York City in the Age of Jefferson* (New
York, 1979), 36–37; and Appleby, *Capitalism and a New Social Order,*
76–77.

use a millenarian vocabulary. Radicals in both religion and politics supported the constitutional separation of church and state—"the wall of separation" was the phrase Jefferson coined when he refused to proclaim a national day of thanksgiving. Similarly popular religious and political leaders inspired their adherents to form and join voluntary organizations. Every revival left a cluster of new missionary and charitable societies in its wake just as every reform campaign—be it temperance, sabbitarianism, antislavery or nativism—led inexorably to the mobilization of voters.

The unexpected eruption of confrontational politics, the sweeping success of religious revivals, and the extended reach of communications—developments which historians quite naturally treat discretely—were in reality highly interactive. Their effect was cumulative. They focused upon the same people—literate, undistinguished men and women open to the idea of dismantling the traditional hierarchical order. Never firmly transplanted to America, that order was politicized in the 1790s, its benign intentions impugned, its eternal verities mocked, its most trusted handmaidens—church and state—democratized.

The model citizen of deferential politics—the man who respects what has already been established—was replaced by the assertive individual who bends every effort to make his own way, both socially and intellectually and reads his own reform as a sign of the possibilities for society at large. We can see in the experience of being wooed by the proselytizing organizations of the early republic how that self-reliant personality was fostered. Simultaneously appealed to as voters, candidates for salvation, prospective club members and subscribers to publications, ordinary men acquired a sense of self-worth. Their individuality was promoted by repeated calls to form personal judgments, choose goals and make their own decisions. The once uncontested membership in a family network or inherited community was replaced by selective belonging with its sociability of shared beliefs, its adhesion of like-mindedness. Encouraged to act in the public realm, those who joined the new political clubs, the revivalist denominations and the reform associations ended up restructuring American society.

Elite families did not cease to exercise extraordinary influence in public life. Rather it was the case that the respect given to lineage, education and the civilized display of wealth—what we might call the social capital of gentlemen—depreciated while the common stock rose. Like Barton Stone's Christian movement which set out to unite America's faithful in one church and ended up spawning yet another new denomination, upper-class efforts to uplift the common folk through sponsored societies only added to the proliferation of voluntary associations.

In blocking gentry social control in the decades after the ratification of the Constitution these popular initiatives I have described did not produce a coherent body of democratic thought so much as a *modus operandi*. Americans had created a highly developed political society independent of the state and frequently in opposition to established social authorities. Local in their origins, the multiplying Protestant denominations and voluntary associations built national networks. As early as 1814, that most institution-proof of all sects, the Baptists, had brought representatives of their 2633 congregations into a national organization. But despite the commonalities shared by religious and political activists and the national reach of their organizational skills, their efforts did not unify the nation. The like-minded organized, but their associations only advertised the fullness of the "pluribus" which was seeking unity. Indeed Americans had created so many identities from religious denominations, political preferences and social aspirations that all hope of unity based on uniformity vanished. Only the method for expressing the diverse social impulses offered common ground for national identity.

Commitment to the free circulation of information, spontaneous social action and individual empowerment stood in for the goals they were designed to attain. Without the cutting edge of well-defined ends, the means themselves were sharpened into tools for excluding the non-conforming: first the unredeemably dissolute—the targets of reform that remained unreformed—then the Catholic immigrants who resisted the behavioral norms of associated Americans and finally the South, that section of the Union that had originally promoted Expansive Republicanism not expecting that the ideological imperative of "E Pluribus Unum" would produce a popular, reformist public spiritedness totally inimicable to its peculiar institutions. A heightened sense of group participation among democratic activists and moral reformers revealed a contradiction in the spirit of E Pluribus Unum; the social action at the heart of American national identity generated both solidarity and exclusion even as social boundaries were redrawn to include the previously excluded.

PART THREE

The Outcome:
A National Political Culture at Work

Republicanism, Radicalism and Sectionalism:

Land Reform and the Languages of American Working Men, 1820–1860

Lawrence Goldman

In the 1960s and 1970s our understanding of the American Revolution was deepened and expanded by the work of many scholars interested in political ideas and political ideology who paid close attention to what the revolutionary generation said and wrote. The focus of attention was on the careful recreation of the colonists' political outlook and on the provenance of their ideas in British political culture of the seventeenth and eighteenth centuries. Jack Pole's study of political representation takes its place in this corpus; indeed, it occupies a very prominent position as the work of a scholar steeped in the history of early modern English political thought and practice, who was able to demonstrate the working-out of aspects of the Whig tradition in the colonies.[1] We are the richer for that generation's careful identification of the elements of

This essay was originally presented at Sidney Sussex College, Cambridge, May 27, 1995, and stresses workingmen's languages in the land-reform movement. Compare, for example, to Jamie L. Bronstein, *Land Reform and Working Class Experience in Britain and the United States, 1800–1862* (Stanford, Calif., 1999).

[1] J. R. Pole, *Political Representation in England and the Origins of the American Revolution* (London, 1966).

an American version of republican thought, which explains why the Revolution occurred and why it took its distinctive course. Latterly, and inevitably, historical attention has changed to a consideration of the implications of this revolutionary republicanism for subsequent American history. To Jack Pole's credit, he was in the forefront of this re-evaluation: having helped to establish a new understanding of American colonial and revolutionary political thought, his most ambitious book on *The Pursuit of Equality* attempted to work out the implications of a central component of republican ideology, captured in the first sentence of the preamble to the Declaration of Independence. In a book remarkable for its range and subtlety, Pole examined the meaning of equality for Americans as it has affected relations between races, genders, and classes. It was a *tour d'horizon* that showed what might be built on the reassessment of the ideas of the Revolution.[2]

Pole recognized that the "rhetoric of American independence," incorporating a commitment to the equality of men, was a potent weapon that movements of the underprivileged have used ever since, justifying their claims in terms of the founding ideals of the republic. "Equality," he wrote, "had entered into the language of justice." That language could be used to express any number of political and social demands, while equality in itself, though its meanings were many and often contested, could be used as a standard by which to assess the laws and judgments of the republic. Many of the great themes and struggles in American history have been the product of the pursuit of equality in this sense—as a goal to aim for. But Pole also understood that the introduction of "an egalitarian rhetoric to an unequal society" might serve to compound that inequality, beguiling the unequal into an acceptance of their inferiority. The message was so attractive, and came from such revered sources, that

[2] J. R. Pole, *The Pursuit of Equality in American History* (Berkeley, 1978).

few questioned this founding national myth. Equality, in other words, was double-edged, confirming and denying simultaneously.

Perhaps no group of historians has been so keen to work through the implications of these insights than those interested in the development of an American working class in the nineteenth century. For republicanism seemed to offer an explanation for many of the apparently troubling aspects of ordinary Americans' political and social behavior, notably their "failure" when compared with Europeans, to establish a coherent and powerful labor movement that might have protected and represented them. To all the other explanations for the absence of a national working-class movement that have been debated since Werner Sombart first posed the question in 1905, could now be added a compelling analysis based upon the very values that formed America in the late eighteenth century and which proved so attractive to American workers, however delusive that attraction.[3]

But the complex nature of "equality," and the ambiguous ideological legacy of the Revolution, which Pole analyzed nearly twenty years ago, has led these historians into contradiction. On the one side are those who have used American fidelity to the republican tradition to explain the failure to develop alternative social identities, and any wide-ranging critique of the distribution of rewards and property in the United States—who have emphasized, in other words, that the rhetoric of equality encouraged an acceptance of the *status quo*. And on the other, are those who have found in republicanism an ideology of working-class resistance amounting to a complete denial of the economic order of nineteenth-century America.[4]

[3]Werner Sombart, *Warum gibt es in den Vereinigten Staaten keinen Sozialismus?* (Tübingen, 1906) (*Why is there no Socialism in the United States*, first English ed., New York, 1976).

[4]Leon Fink, "Looking Backward: Reflections on Workers' Culture and Certain Conceptual Dilemmas Within Labor History" in J. Carroll

Rather than inhibiting workers, republicanism promoted and enno-
bled their struggles. In both cases, the simplest references to revolutionary heroes and ideas are often taken as evidence of republicanism
at work, whether in furtherance or obstruction of working-class interests. The difficulties are evident in Paul Krause's wonderful evoca-
tion of the world and work of the Homestead steel workers of the
late-nineteenth century, who were inspired to resistance, in Krause's
view, by their own blend of civic humanism—"the ideas of common good, virtue and independence" as he puts it. But Krause can
see as well that these workers were opposed by a rival reading of
republicanism—that of Andrew Carnegie and Henry Clay Frick,
no less—emphasizing "the sanctity of property and the virtue of accumulation," and in which "natural rights" translated into "the right
to limitless appropriation." Thus the Homestead dispute and other
labor struggles of the period are presented by him as "a contest over
the meaning of republicanism in modern America."[5]

How can this contradiction be resolved? It cannot. Republicanism had these two opposed meanings, and many more as well. It has
proved so flexible and malleable down the generations that almost
anything may be legitimated by it.[6] Moreover, the fascination with
republican ideology, especially as expressed by American workers,
has blinded us to other contexts which defined nineteenth-century
Americans, and to other languages which they used to describe their
place and justify their actions. The study to follow will not ignore

Moody and Alice Kessler-Harris, eds., *Perspectives on American Labor History: The Problems of Synthesis* (DeKalb, Ill., 1989), 12.

[5]Paul Krause, *The Battle for Homestead, 1880–1892: Politics, Culture
and Steel* (Pittsburgh, 1992). For a helpful review of this book, see Sean
Wilentz, "A Triumph of the Gilded Age," *New York Review of Books*,
October 22, 1992.

[6]Daniel T. Rodgers, "Republicanism: The Career of a Concept," *Journal of American History*, 79, 1 (June 1992) 11–38.

the place of republican ideology in explaining the campaigns of Northern workingmen from the 1820s to the 1860s for the free grant of homesteads on the public domain for urban workers, but it will contend that republicanism was but one of three languages used by them, and must be balanced by consideration of at least two other discourses: an Anglo-American language of radicalism, and the sectional discourse on slavery that came to dominate mid-nineteenth-century politics and social theory. Equally, the study that follows will take a skeptical view of the conclusions that may be drawn from the use of specific, identifiable political languages like republicanism. Too often, historians working in this area have accepted without demur that the language employed is a straightforward reflection of the consciousness and outlook of the historical actors under scrutiny: that those who repeated wise republican saws must have been true republicans. They have forgotten that politics is about strategy, and that language may be used to persuade, to camouflage and to obfuscate, as well as to reflect—that language, in short, is an instrument as well as a mirror. Dan Rodgers, critical of the manner in which contemporary historians have approached the analysis of republican discourse, has called for "a more strategic sense of language than the ideational and linguistic structures for which republicanism's inventors and borrowers often yearned." It will be argued below that some radical working men of the 1830s and 1840s had such a "strategic sense of language" and employed it to good effect.[7]

I

The National Reform Association, formed out of earlier radical movements in New York in 1844, and active for about a decade thereafter, has found a small, though not very important niche in the history of the American labor movement. It was founded in large

[7]*Ibid.*, 38.

part by British radicals in the United States, which makes possible a comparative approach to the history of American radicalism in this period. It campaigned for the free grant of homesteads of 160 acres, carved out of the public domain in the West, to be distributed to settlers from the Eastern cities, which gives it a place in that complex of issues concerning land, expansion and the Western territories which was so central to the years preceding the Civil War.

It took its place in a succession of artisans' movements that were thrown up in response to economic changes in the Northeast in the first half of the nineteenth century. Traditional rural communities were de-stabilized by the commercialization of agriculture, the pressure of growing population on land resources, and the consequent decay of household production, forcing people off the land and into the cities. Here, traditional craft production was in competition with an emergent factory system, and fighting rearguard actions against mechanization, the dilution of craft skills and the imposition of new labor disciplines. Opposition to the changes of the market revolution took many shapes: in this formative period we are dealing with a hybrid—neither solely a movement of organized labor closely associated with issues of the workplace, nor just a succession of reformist causes sponsored by philanthropists and publicists, but a combination of the two. The term "labor movement," as used by John R. Commons and his associates in the early years of the century when this history was first investigated systematically, described a progression of organizations and issues held together by the continuity of personnel—by groups and individuals moving from one form of resistance to another. Broadly, a unique political movement in the late 1820s and early 1830s, led by the Working Men's parties of New York and Philadelphia, and held together by the New England Association of Farmers, Mechanics and Other Working Men, gave way to a trade union movement in the mid-1830s. Trade unions were formed in at least thirteen Northeastern cities, and from 1834–1837 the movement was led by the first attempt at a National Trades' Union. But the financial panic of 1837 destroyed these early efforts at workingmen's organization, and the 1840s witnessed a change in direction: the pursuit of reformist panaceas like associationism, the communitarian movement following the doctrines of Charles Fourier; the "Protective Unions" of consumers' and producers' cooperatives, founded in 1850–1851; and land reform as preached by the National Reform Association. The Ten Hours Movement, led by the New England Workingmen's Association dates from the late 1840s, and was followed in the mid-1850s by a revival of a trade union movement with limited ambitions centered on the workplace—"pure and simple" unionism as it was known.[8]

Among the ideas entertained by these movements, from the 1820s to the 1850s, was that of land reform. In one form, though it was evanescent and evoked little support, land reform meant the equalization of all real and private property and the abolition of inheritance in areas already settled. This was advocated by Thomas Skidmore, briefly leader of the New York Working Men's Party in late 1829, in his tract of the same year, *The Rights of Man to Property!*[9] But far more durable and persuasive were those schemes that sought to open Western lands to the settlement of Eastern artisans. In Oc-

[8]John R. Commons *et al.*, *History of Labor in the United States*, 4 vols. (New York, 1926–1935), I; John R. Commons *et al.*, eds., *Documentary History of American Industrial Society*, 11 vols. (Cleveland, 1910–1911), V–VIII, 1820–1860. Philip S. Foner, *History of the Labor Movement in the United States* (New York, 1947), I.

[9]Thomas Skidmore, *The Rights of Man to Property! Being a Proposition to make it Equal Among Adults of the Present Generation; and to Provide for Its Equal Transmission to Every Individual of Each Succeeding Generation, on Arriving at the Age of Maturity* (New York, 1829). For a discussion of Skidmore's ideas and his role in New York artisan politics, see Sean Wilentz, *Chants Democratic: New York City and the Rise of the American Working Class, 1788–1850* (New York and Oxford, 1984), 183–216, and Pole, *The Pursuit of Equality*, 126–30.

tober 1828, the *Mechanics' Free Press* of Philadelphia, the first labor paper published in America for any considerable period, and the first for which any file has been preserved, petitioned Congress to place "all the public lands, without delay of sales, within the reach of the people at large."[10] The suggestion was repeated in a resolution condemning the prevailing system of disposal for public land—which invariably became the object of speculation rather than settlement—at the first convention of the National Trades' Union in 1834.[11] Land reform was a radical option in the early years of the movement, therefore, especially after 1832 and Andrew Jackson's declaration that the public domain should cease to be used as a source of revenue and be turned over to individual settlers instead, but it jostled for position in the radicals' agenda with attacks on the Bank of the United States and "monopoly" in general, and particularly with schemes for educational reform.

That it was briefly influential in radical circles in the mid- and late-1840s was the work of George Henry Evans, described by Commons as "the thinker of the workingmen's party" and the archetypal Anglo-American radical of the era.[12] Evans had been born in 1805 into a moderately prosperous family of metal craftsmen turned manufacturers from Tenbury, Worcestershire.[13] He emigrated in 1820 with his father and brother, Frederick William Evans, later a member of the Owenite community at Massilon, Ohio, and eventually an elder of the American Shakers, in response to the economic depres-

---

[10]*Mechanics Free Press*, October 1828, p. 1, cited in Commons *et al.*, eds., *Documentary History*, V, 430.

[11]John R. Commons, "Horace Greeley and the Working Class Origins of the Republican Party," *Political Science Quarterly*, 24 (1909), 479.

[12]*Ibid.*, 478.

[13]Newman Jeffrey, "The Social Origins of George Henry Evans, Working Man's Advocate" (unpublished M.A. thesis, Wayne State University, 1960), *passim*.

sion in Britain after the Napoleonic wars.[14] He settled initially in Binghampton, New York, already home to two of his uncles. He was apprenticed as a printer in Ithaca in 1821 and moved to New York in 1827 where he set up in business and became writer and printer for George Houston's free thought journal, *The Correspondent*. Houston, a friend of Richard Carlile when in Britain, had been imprisoned in Newgate on a charge of blasphemy for having published a translation of d'Holbach's *L'Histoire de Jésus Christ*.[15] With an "infidel" background, Evans became involved with the notorious "Free Enquirers" around Robert Dale Owen and Frances Wright who came to New York in 1829 after the dissolution of the Owenite community in New Harmony, Indiana.[16] He was also associated with the New York Working Men's party and its later reincarnation in 1836–1837 as the Loco-Foco party, publishing at this time the first series of the famous radical newspaper, the *Working Man's Advocate*.

After 1837 and the collapse of radical organizations, ill health prompted Evans to leave the city, and he farmed in New Jersey. From this period dates his renewed interest in land reform. He apparently became convinced that industrial action would not suffice. In 1835, after the failure of a shoemakers' strike in Newark, he had contended

[14]Frederick William Evans, *Autobiography of a Shaker* (New York, 1869). It was claimed by Norman Ware in 1924 that Evans' father was "a disciple of Thomas Spence," the English advocate of land nationalization in the late-eighteenth century, but Jeffrey's research has uncovered no evidence to support this. Ware probably confused George Evans with two of Spence's most devoted followers, Thomas Evans, Sr. who in 1821 wrote a *Life of Mr. Thomas Spence*, and Thomas Evans, Jr. See Jeffrey, *The Social Origins of George Henry Evans*, 149–51 and Norman Ware, *The Industrial Worker 1840–1860* (New York, 1924), 181.

[15]Frank Thistlethwaite, *The Anglo-American Connection in the Early Nineteenth Century* (Philadelphia, 1959), 60; Wilentz, *Chants Democratic*, 154.

[16]Wilentz, *Chants Democratic*, 182.

that mechanics "must look to something more radical than turnouts to give them a just remuneration for their labor."[17] And in 1844 he was unequivocal:

> Not only do I think that trade associations are not the remedy for the oppressions of the working man, but I doubt whether they would be a remedy at all. They have been tried repeatedly and almost universally failed, except when they have degenerated into mere partnerships. And why? Simply because associations of landless men can no more keep up the price of their labor than can individuals. They must put their labor in the market when hunger pinches, and sell it for what it will bring.[18]

That said, Evans and his fellows remained sympathetic to trade unionism, and the *Working Man's Advocate* was full of appreciative references to the specifically industrial organizations of American workers.[19] Drawn back by the labor revival in New York in 1844, he formed there the National Reform Association, and led the Eastern workingmen's demand for homesteads until his death in 1856.[20] Essentially a publicist, editing a series of newspapers including the *Working Man's Advocate* (1829–1836 and 1844–1845), the *Daily Sentinel* (1830–1834), *The Man* (1834–1835), *The Radical* in the early 1840s, and *Young America* between 1845 and 1849, Evans faded from prominence in the early 1850s. By then his cause had been taken up by other and more influential editors, notably Horace Greeley of the *New York Tribune* who was an enthusiastic supporter of the National

---

[17] *The Man* (New York), May 21, 1835.

[18] *Working Man's Advocate*, November 23, 1884.

[19] Wilentz, *Chants Democratic* 341–43.

[20] For an affectionate contemporary portrait of Evans, see Frederick W. Byrdsall, *History of the Loco-Foco or Equal Rights Party* (New York, 1842), 14–15. On the land-reform movement in New York in the 1840s, see Wilentz, *Chants Democratic*, 335–43.

Reform Association after 1844, and who first declared himself in favor of free homesteads in the West in January 1846.[21]

Many more of those who joined the National Reform Association had a past history of radical politics. John Commerford, active in the land reform movement into the 1860s, had been president of the General Trades' Union of New York in 1835 and editor of its paper, *The Union*. John Windt, secretary and then treasurer of National Reform, had been prominent in the Loco-Foco party.[22] John Ferral, the organizer of land reform in Pennsylvania in the 1840s, had organized the short-lived Trades' Union of Pennsylvania in 1833 and had been president of the National Trades' Union in 1835.[23] James Pyne was a former English Chartist.[24] And Thomas Ainge Devyr, "physical force" Chartist from Ireland, had been involved in the so-called "Anti-Rent War" on the Van Rensselaer estates of the lower Hudson Valley in the early 1840s before his natural migration from one land-reforming cause to another.[25]

[21]*Young America*, January 31, 1846; Roy M. Robbins, *Our Landed Heritage: The Public Domain 1776–1936* (Princeton, 1942), 102. Daniel Walker Howe, *The Political Culture of the American Whigs* (Chicago, 1979), 195; Eric Foner, *Free Soil, Free Labor, Free Men: The Political Ideology of the Republican Party Before the Civil War* (New York, 1970), 27–28.

[22]Commons *et al.*, eds., *History of Labor in the United States*, I, 527 (Henry E. Hoagland).

[23]*Ibid.*, V, 325–26.

[24]Wilentz, *Chants Democratic*, 340.

[25]From 1839, tenants on the Van Rensselaer estates had obstructed attempts to collect arrears of rent and had protested at the refusal to convert their leaseholds into freeholds, except for unreasonably high payments. They organized to resist the payment of rent, to resist the fines then imposed and to get the legislature at Albany to alter or abolish the old "patron system" of land tenure. Cooperation between the Anti-Renters and National Reform was sporadic from the mid-1840s until the 1850s. See Henry Christman, *Tin Horns and Calico* (New York, 1945).

As Greeley, who himself converted from one panacea, Associationism, to another, "land for the landless," explained in the *Tribune*, "the new party styled National Reformers" was "composed of like materials and in good part of the same men with the old Working Men's party."[26] Evans called National Reform "a second edition, revised and corrected" of the New York workingmen's movement of 1829–1830.[27]

The members of the first central committee of National Reform consisted of four printers, two cordwainers, one chair-maker, one carpenter, one blacksmith, one bookbinder, one clothier, one picture-framer and a sole machinist—the leaders of the movement were from the ranks of endangered, skilled artisans threatened by mechanization and the factory. In the first month of its existence, therefore, the Association appointed a committee to analyze the causes of immizeration in the East: "to inquire into the causes which produce in this republic a depression of labor and a social degredation of the laborer, very similar to that which prevails under the detestable governments of Europe."[28] It concluded that

> First, we find in our cities and factory stations, an increasing population, the great majority of whom depend for their subsistence on Mechanical Labor: and secondly, we find the new-born power of machinery throwing itself into the labor market with the most astounding effects—withering up all the human competition with the sudden decisiveness that leaves no hope for the future.[29]

The machine could not be beaten; so it had to be escaped. "We may wrestle with the machine as the toilers of England wrestle, till

[26]*New York Weekly Tribune*, November 29, 1845.
[27]*Working Man's Advocate*, June 8, 1844.
[28]*Working Man's Advocate*, March 13, 1844.
[29]*Ibid.*, July 6, 1844.

myriads of us perish in the unequal strife." Instead, "our refuge is upon the soil, in all its freshness and fertility—our heritage is on the Public Domain, in all its boundless wealth and infinite variety." National Reform's precise aims were three: the free grant of the public lands, held by the federal government, to the landless settler who was to become an owner-occupier; the limitation of the quantity of such land that an individual could own to 160 acres to prevent the hated "monopoly of the soil," and the exemption of homesteads from execution for debt. The land was to be given free on the condition that the settling family remain *in situ* for five years. The Association believed that agricultural labor on the land was morally superior to work for wages in cities. It was also aware that by drawing-off the surplus labor in the East, the bargaining position of the operatives and artisans who remained, and who faced the competition of mechanization, would be improved. In this way land reform could be presented as a complete solution for labor, both for those who went West and those who stayed behind.

The Association came into being in the early spring of 1844, originally as the National Reform Union. It met in Croton Hall in the Bowery. Its first forays into the New York streets met with the derision of the conservative press. But within a year it had five local ward organizations in the city and there were communicating groups not only in twelve counties in New York state but in several other Northern states as well. In January 1846, *Young America* reported land reform groups in Ohio, Pennsylvania, Kentucky, New Jersey, New York, Connecticut, Illinois, Wisconsin and Virginia, and noted the support of labor journals, among them the Lynn, Massachusetts, *Awl* and *True Workingman*, and the Lowell *Voice of Industry*.[30] By 1847 Greeley's *Tribune* knew of at least fifty journals that endorsed land reform, and by the early 1850s Frederick William Evans estimated that over 600

---

[30]Helene S. Zahler, *Eastern Workingmen and the National Land Policy 1829–1862* (New York, 1941), 45–46.

newspapers (out of about 2,000 such publications at this time) were favorable.[31] Seven years later, a reporter from Cincinnati writing in the *New York Daily Tribune* explained that for eighteen months he had "travelled in Ohio, Michigan, Illinois and Indiana . . . advocating Land Reform and Free Schools, and have held about 350 meetings. In no place have I succeeded in calling out any opposition, though the plainest challenge has been given."[32]

In 1845 the National Reform Association linked with the New England Working Men's Association to call a national convention under the name of the Industrial Congress, which met annually until 1856 and provided the movement with contacts to the rest of organized labor, notably through the attendance at the congresses of delegates from "industrial councils"—organizations of local labor associations in the Eastern cities.[33] The first meeting of the congress, held in New York in October 1845, drew a distinguished company including L. W. Ryckman of Brook Farm, Albert Brisbane, Fourier's American disciple, Horace Greeley, and Gerrit Smith, the abolitionist.[34] Subsequent congresses were held in Boston (1846), New York, Philadelphia, Cincinnati, Chicago, Albany, Washington, Wilmington, Trenton, Cleveland and New York (1856). The Industrial Congress was the only effort at an organization of labor wider than the local craft in the 1840s and 1850s and so makes the history of National Reform into something more than the story of isolated radicals and a single issue.

The political focus of the movement, indeed, led National Reform to the heart of national debate, as we shall see. With a slogan of

[31]Evans, *Autobiography of a Shaker*, 18.

[32]L. A. Hine in the *New York Daily Tribune*, March 4, 1853, in Commons *et al.*, eds., *Documentary History*, VIII, 60–61.

[33]Joseph G. Rayback, *Free Soil. The Election of 1848* (Lexington, Ky., 1970), 220.

[34]Commons *et al.*, eds., *Documentary History*, VIII, 21–25.

"Vote Yourself a Farm," land reform was not the preserve of visionaries, but sought to use the democratic process for its own ends. As Evans explained in the *Working Man's Advocate* in December 1844, "Since legislation controls land distribution, the poor must wield their power as a class in politics. With universal suffrage, the equal right to land could be carried by the vote." One Fourierite had written at about the same time, "Look to yourselves, not to politicians, look to the plan of God and not your own."[35] According to Brisbane, "if we can, with a knowledge of true social principles, organize one township rightly, we can, by organizing others like it, and by spreading and rendering them universal, establish a true Social and Political Order."[36] But National Reform had no patience with utopianism and change by an example in the wilderness. Evans believed "that the one great error of our system was political, and that, like men who understand their business, we should begin by removing that error."[37]

The essential tactic, therefore, based on Evans' analysis of the failure of independent workingmen's politics in the 1830s, was to promise to deliver votes for any candidate for elective office who would support the cause of land reform.[38] According to one land reformer, Lewis Masquerier, long after the movement had disappeared, "After pursuing this policy for five years, the principles of the reform party began to be adopted into political platforms and at last resulted in the present Homestead Law."[39] To give an example, when in mid-

[35]*The Phalanx* August 10, 1844, 229, cited in Commons *et al.*, eds., *Documentary History*, VII, 331.

[36]Albert Brisbane, *A Concise Exposition of the Doctrine of Association* (New York, 1840), 73–74.

[37]*Working Man's Advocate*, April 20, 1844.

[38]See *Working Man's Advocate*, March 18, 1844, and *Young America*, September 23, 1848.

[39]Lewis Masquerier, *Sociology: Or The Reconstruction of Society* (New York, 1877), 94.

July 1848, Martin Van Buren, in a letter to Alvan E. Bovay, the chairman of the executive committee of the Industrial Congress, hinted that he was not unsympathetic to National Reform, the prospect of influence sent representatives to the Buffalo convention of the Free Soil Party some weeks later. In the end, however, land reform votes in the presidential election actually went to the candidate of the abolitionist Liberty Party, Gerrit Smith, who had ensured that his party's platform looked to the day "when the land will be no more bought and sold; and when the right of every human being to land, light, air and water will be universally acknowledged to be as perfect and absolute as his right to his body."[40] This formulation exemplifies also the success of National Reform in shaping the language in which land reform was discussed. Galusha Grow, Representative from Pennsylvania, and the so-called "Father of the Homestead Law," consistently used an argument based on natural rights as a justification. But according to Commons, his first great speech on the issue in 1852, published by him as *Man's Right to the Soil* "was merely an oratorical transcript from the *Working Men's Advocate*."[41]

II

What *was* the language of land reform? First, and unsurprisingly, it was the language of American revolutionary republicanism. Property and its distribution had always been central themes in the republican tradition, and were so for the Founding Fathers. A society of landholders was held by them to be superior in a moral sense to any other form of social organization. George Washington, according to popular legend and the pages of the *Working Man's Advocate*, was loath

[40]Ralph Volney Harlow, *Gerrit Smith. Philanthropist and Reformer* (New York, 1939), 253; Commons et al., eds., *Documentary History*, VIII, 21; *Proceedings of the National Liberty Convention*, 9, 25.

[41]Commons, "Horace Greeley and the Working Class Origins of the Republican Party," 484.

to leave the cultivation of his estates at Mount Vernon to take up the presidency.[42] According to Jefferson, of course, "those who labor in the earth are the chosen people of God."[43] But Jefferson went further:

> Wherever there are in any country uncultivated lands and unemployed poor, it is clear that the laws of property have been so far extended as to violate natural right. The earth is given as a common stock for men to labor and live in . . . it is not too soon to provide by every possible means that as few as possible shall be without a little portion of land. The small landholders are the most precious part of the State.[44]

Writing to Madison from Paris in 1787, Jefferson "remarked that gross inequalities of property could cause society to lose its stability, thus provoking revolution."[45] Five years later Madison could suggest enactments to prevent "the inequality of property" and to even out its distribution in the new republic.[46] And even more conservative Fathers, like John Adams, who feared to give a place in politics to the propertyless, saw the need for a broad distribution of land and wealth, and recognized their own obligation so to fashion the legal and institutional framework of society to make it possible for men of industry and virtue to join the ranks of full, participating citizens by acquiring property. The Founding Fathers, though they occasionally mused on the need to restrain great concentrations of wealth and land, actually put their faith for the future in making land available to as many as possible who would work for it.[47] But what was to hap-

---

[42]*Working Man's Advocate*, November 30, 1844.

[43]Thomas Jefferson, *Notes on the State of Virginia* (1784, Harper Torchbook ed., 1964), XIX, 157.

[44]Thomas Jefferson, *Writings* (Monticello ed., Washington, D.C., 1904), XIX, 187.

[45]Pole, *The Pursuit of Equality*, 122.

[46]*Ibid.*, 122.

[47]*Ibid.*, 42–48.

pen, when, by the 1830s, this process of acquisition was becoming more difficult, and was not the automatic reward for thrift and hard work?

For American radicals who faced this situation, the solution was clear: use the arguments and language of the Founders to make a case for land reform. As the *Working Man's Advocate* explained, land reform would "establish a principle more in accordance with our republican theory." It would "increase the number of freeholders and decrease the anti-republican dependence of those who might not become freeholders."[48] The American political tradition, as understood by them, was grounded on a society of small property holders; virtuous political association was intimately connected with a mass of independent landowners. In the words of one Chicago newspaper in 1848, "We are a republic. If we desire to continue so, let us pass the public lands into the hands of the people."[49] Radicals claimed consistency with the founding ideals of this republic: they were the true conservatives, seeking to return the republic from a brave new world of wage labor and tenancy on the land, to an older and fairer past. This variant of republicanism, looking back to the Revolution, evoked a pre-lapserian age of social equality before the degeneration of the early nineteenth century. It functioned as a social myth in ways similar to the idea of a Saxon community of individual freemen held to have been rudely destroyed by the "Norman yoke" of exploitation and inequality at the Conquest. Indeed, comparisons with Britain were the stock-in-trade of this republican language, for in that degraded society of monarchy and jobbery, "capital, monopolizing Land and Machinery, takes all the profit of Labor to itself." But in this country, wrote Greeley, "things have come to no such pass as yet, thanks to our Republican institutions and to the Republican spirit which

[48]*Working Man's Advocate*, November 30, 1844.
[49]*The Chicago Democrat*, quoted in the *New York Tribune*, February 19, 1848.

generally pervaded and directed the first settlers on these shores."[50] And in America, "the enjoyment of inviolable Homes shall be commensurate with the existence of Republican Freedom."[51]

In this specifically republican discourse, land reform was justified in terms of inherent "natural rights." In brief, man's right to life was held to be the source of all other rights, so that the right "to be" implied the right to use the materials of nature necessary for being— light, air, water, soil and so forth—and thus the right to land as the source of these necessities. As Evans put it, "If a man has a right on the earth, he has a right to land enough to raise a habitation on. If he has a right to live, he has a right to land enough for his subsistence."[52] Or, as his brother, Frederick William, explained, "The right to be and the right to land each included the other: we held that they were identical: and hence we waged a fierce and implacable war against all forms of property accumulation that owed their origin to land monopoly, speculation or usury."[53] An effective argument for land reform could have played upon the savings to public funds should the public lands be thrown open to the urban indigent and those in receipt of charity. Early in the campaign Evans reported that "thirty years ago the number of paupers in the whole United States was estimated at 29,166 or 1 in 300. The pauperism of New York City amounts *now* to 51,600 or 1 in 7 of the population."[54] Yet a utilitarian argument was rejected, with Evans contending that "while showing the economy of the plan, we wish it to be borne in mind that we advocate the measure on much stronger ground, on the ground of each man's nat-

[50]Horace Greeley, "The Emancipation of Labour" in *idem, Hints Toward Reforms* (1850, New York 1857 ed.), 22.

[51]Greeley, "Homestead Exemption" in *ibid.*, 325.

[52]*The Radical*, No. 1, February 2, 1841.

[53]Evans, *Autobiography of a Shaker*, 7.

[54]*Working Man's Advocate*, July 6, 1844.

ural right to the use of a portion of the soil sufficient for his subsistence."[55] One of the National Reform Association's handbills had
termed the movement "a true American party, having for its guidance
the principles of the American Revolution." Hence the reliance on
"the rights of man."

In this republican discourse of rights, Jefferson, cited continually,
was patron to the movement. As Pole has noted, Jefferson's Declaration of Independence was the fundamental textual reference and
legitimator of all radical schemes, even when its assertions were held
to have been insufficient.[56] As Evans expressed it, "That equality
which is declared, by the great charter of our independence, to be the
birthright of all, is not realized."[57] Thomas Skidmore, contending that
"Mr. Jefferson speaks of the rights of men in terms which, when they
come to be investigated closely appear to be very defective and
equivocal," sought to change the Declaration to read that men "are
endowed by their creator with certain inalienable rights: and that
among these are life, liberty and property," because, as he explained,
"how they expected this 'pursuit' [i.e. 'the pursuit of happiness']
without property of any description, to be of any avail, or at any rate,
of avail equal to that which a fortunate possessor of an estate could
enjoy, it is not easy to conceive."[58] Despite such points, however,
Skidmore retained the original text and still situated his own "declaration" in the terms and form of the hallowed document.

Throughout the ante-bellum period, indeed, radical thinking
glossed, repeated and reworked the original document of 1776. This
was as true of the anti-slavery movement in the 1850s as of the land
reform movement somewhat earlier. The language of the Declaration
was employed to convince the skeptical that these movements were

[55]*Working Man's Advocate*, March 13, 1844.
[56]Pole, *The Pursuit of Equality*, 137.
[57]*Working Man's Advocate*, March 16, 1844.
[58]Skidmore, *The Rights of Man to Property!*, 58.

within the parameters of acceptable political discourse; the ideals of the Declaration could be contrasted with the degenerate actuality of America. According to Skidmore, "the declaration, that the creator had created such an equality, but the legislation of man had destroyed it, became at once the theory of our government on the one hand, and its practice on the other."[59] The point is illustrated in an extract from the autobiography of Frederick Willam Evans concerning his early association with the New York "Free Enquirers":

> We held the Constitution to be only a compromise between the first principles of the American government, as they were set forth in the Declaration of Independence, drawn up by Jefferson, and the then existing vested rights and property rights of all sorts, secular and religious; and we contended that the mutual, well-understood intention and design of the founders of the government was that, as soon as was possible, the Constitution should be amended, so as to conform more and more to the ideal pattern set forth in the declaration of rights inherent in humanity, it being only a question as to how long an acknowledged wrong should be permitted.[60]

Aside from the novel view this presents that in certain ways the Constitution was only an interim settlement, and one that represented (as historians from Beard onwards have contended, though in different ways) a "declension" in terms of political virtue from the idealism of the 1760s and 1770s, it is richly suggestive of the centrality of the Declaration to those groups seeking to return America to the true republican path in the nineteenth century. As late as 1877, one old land reformer, Masquerier, published his *Reconstruction of Society* in which he announced not only a new Declaration of Independence by which the signatories "have superseded and annulled the present

---

[59]*Ibid.*, 62.
[60]Evans, *Autobiography of a Shaker*, 16.

form of society, government and property" but also a "Model Constitution: Being an Attempt to Declare the Thorough Principles of Social and Political Science: A New Form and Society and Government, and Adapted to any State or Nation."[61] America was to be reborn, but in this process the mechanism of its initial foundation was still held adequate to the task of aligning practice with republican theory.

III

Land reform, in this linguistic context, is simply another of many nineteenth-century movements that campaigned within a republican ideological framework. But could all of these movements have meant the same things when appealing to this common heritage? Could that heritage have really been so capacious and flexible as to have encompassed such diversity? And did all believe with equal conviction in the slogans and language they employed? Or were the terms employed just because this was a universal social language that all understood and respected, and because of its hallowed coinage in the fires of independence and revolution? Would other social vocabularies, perhaps more accurate to the movements that generated them, though also perhaps, more obscure, have had the same effect? The questions need to be asked because we are in danger of losing the individuality of historical movements in current analyses of their language that go no further than a recognition of their common adherence to republican shibboleths. They must also be asked because many of the ideas associated with American republicanism in this period were not unique to that tradition. Republican ideology as understood and employed by workingmen asserted the equality of men; gave dignity to labor as cash nexus; was opposed to vested interests and social privilege; was conceived as conservative and defensive, embattled against

---

[61]Masquerier, *Sociology: Or the Reconstruction of Society*, 84.

the innovations of technology and market relations. But in each case, these ideas had their analogues in a different "language of radicalism," that had emerged in the late eighteenth century in Britain, and which had been taken with them by the many British emigrants who staffed and led the land reform and other labor movements of the Jacksonian period. Radicalism was different from, but conformable with republicanism—so conformable, indeed, that its voice in the language of American protest has, in recent years, fallen on deaf ears. To hear it again we must recreate an Anglo-American world of radical political protest.

This is not hard to achieve for there were many links—personal, institutional, ideological—tying radicalism together on both sides of the Atlantic. Thistlethwaite argued, with only a little exaggeration, that the American labor movement "may, in its early stages, be fairly treated as an extension of the British, taking its cue from situations which were already chronic in the older country, but were coming to be recognized as dangerous for the new."[62] Both labor movements had similar origins in the trade societies of the late eighteenth century; the first "unions of trades" were established in Manchester and Philadelphia in 1826 and 1827, respectively; and national associations were attempted in the 1830s—Owen's Grand National Consolidated Trade Union and the American National Trades' Union. British innovations and institutions were more secure, because the movement there was so much bigger and more broadly-based, but the institutional parallels are striking. In the 1840s meanwhile, National Reformers took up their cause just because they feared that a republic with vast resources of land might yet go the way of Lancashire. As Evans enjoined when he printed the report of the committee that investigated the immizeration of the American cities in 1844, "Read it Working Men, you that would escape the fate that overwhelms your brother men in Europe." And as Devyr explained in a concluding

[62]Thistlethwaite, *The Anglo-American Connection*, 56.

remark to a pamphlet he had written in Britain in 1836 and reissued on his arrival in America in 1842, "So long as the land can be easily purchased by the incoming emigrant, all shall go on well: but when it comes to be wanted for the 'Absolute Owners,' farewell to the plenty, and happiness and freedom of the New World, and welcome the rampant tyranny, the slavery and wretchedness of the Old."[63]

America was a fertile ground for social experimentation—Owenism, Fourerism and so on—as it was a new society which could be shaped the more easily because of its youth, and because it was vital to seize the opportunity to imprint a different mark upon her before she went the way of the Old World. In Robert Dale Owen's pamphlet of 1830, *Wealth and Misery*, the failure of industrial capitalism in Britain to secure an equitable distribution of the products of the new industries was used as a warning to the United States. The concern among British radicals—both those removed to America and those still in the British Isles—that America be prevented from developing in similar fashion to Britain, was caught by one, Robert MacFarlane, originally a Scots dyer, who, in the mid-1840s organized the Mechanics Mutual Protection Association in Philadelphia: "In our country the evil is but faintly discerned because we are young in manufactures. But Oh! I have seen enough of it to convince me of its future evils unless we stand between the living and the dead."[64] Wendell Phillips, writing in *The Liberator* in 1847 at a time when the state of the laboring classes in America had been made into an issue that abolitionists had to address, denied the progressive immizeration of Northeastern workers by arguing that "American questions" could

---

[63]Thomas Ainge Devyr, *Our Natural Rights* (1836, New York, 1877 ed.), 134.

[64]Clifton K. Yearley Jr., "Britons in American Labor: A History of the Influence of the United Kingdom Immigrants in American Labor, 1820–1914," *Johns Hopkins University Studies in Historical and Political Science*, LXXV, no. 1 (1957), 35.

not be viewed "through European spectacles." The "eloquent complaints against capital and monopoly which are well-grounded and well-applied there" could not be applied "to a state of society here where they have little meaning or application." But as Eric Foner has pointed out, Phillips "perhaps failed to appreciate fully the central importance of fear of 'Europeanization' as an ideological inspiration of the labor movement."[65] Though it must be said that when Phillips emerged from abolitionism in the 1870s, his trajectory took him towards the defense of the labor movement.

It would seem that many European emigré radicals realized without prompting that capitalism and industrialization were not narrowly national but "western" phenomena, and realized as well that their concept of America was being violated by the very evils they had sought to escape. And this European consciousness could find a home within a whig-republican tradition which had broken its association with "European corruption" in the late eighteenth century. That corruption was now material—sweatshops, powerlooms, factories—rather than moral and political, but it was easy for the radical mind to find intellectual sustenance and emotional solace in a tradition which held, in Jefferson's words, that "for the general operations of manufacture, let our workshops remain in Europe."[66] This is captured in Robert Dale Owen's address, delivered in Cincinnati in 1848, on *Labor: Its History and Prospects*. The future of the working classes was, he argued, "a world-wide subject" applicable "wherever man lives and labors." If it did not compel attention in the United States as yet, it undoubtedly soon would. "Is not the laborer here, as in Great Britain, a 'commodity,' bid for in the market, as

[65]Eric Foner, "Abolitionism and the Labor Movement in Antebellum America" in Christine Bolt and Seymour Drescher, eds., *Antislavery, Religion and Reform: Essays in Memory of Roger Anstey* (Hamden, Conn., 1980), 265.

[66]Jefferson, *Notes on the State of Virginia*, XIX, 158.

wheat or cotton is; of much value, if very scarce; commanding less wages as population gradually fills up the market for labor and appropriates the region of vacant land?"[67] Owen actually referred to the public lands as a "safety valve" that might prevent the operatives of Lowell, Lynn and Salem going the same way as "the oppressed laborers of Britain." Thus he drew attention to the importance of land reform: "When in the older states wages no longer furnish comfort, there is room and to spare, here, in the wide and ever-extending west."[68]

The difficulty of separating British and American influences on the workingmen's movement of this period are evident when we consider the provenance of Evans' ideas. As a printer, Evans issued one of Thomas Spence's tracts on the reform of British landholding, and published a complete edition of Thomas Paine's works in 1837. This included Paine's *Agrarian Justice* of 1796 in which he argued that each landed proprietor owed a "ground rent" to a common fund which would pay everyone, at age twenty-one, compensation "for the loss of his or her natural inheritance, by the introduction of a system of landed property." At the annual New York celebration of Paine's birthday in 1850, Evans toasted the "Author of *Common Sense* and *The Crisis:* His *Rights of Man* effective artillery for bearing down despotisms: His *Agrarian Justice* excellent material for building up democratic and social republics."[69] Yet he explicitly discounted the influence of Spence and Paine on his plans for land reform, asserting in November 1844 that it was Skidmore, an American precursor and a former colleague in the New York movement of 1829–1830, who first made him reflect on the issue of land ownership, even if their respective solutions, the leveling of private property, as opposed to the distribution of the pub-

[67]Robert Dale Owen, *Labor: Its History and Prospects* (Cincinnati, 1848), 62.

[68]*Ibid.*, 61.

[69]*The Boston Investigator*, February 13, 1850, quoted in Zahler, *Eastern Workingmen*, 52.

lic domain, were quite different.[70] And yet, as Edward Pessen has pointed out, Skidmore's intellectual precursors were all British: general denunciations of private property from the various Ricardian Socialists of the 1820s, Charles Hall, John Gray, John Francis Bray, William Thompson and Thomas Hodgskin, and attacks on private property in land specifically from Paine, Spence and William Ogilvie, author in 1781 of an *Essay on the Right of Property in Land*.[71] It is almost impossible to separate these two radical cultures, marked as they were by the confluence and reworking of ideas outside their original social and national contexts as they became the common property of a single radical tradition. By the time Evans was denying the direct impact of Paine and Spence, they had become part of American thought, and inspirations to an international, English-speaking radical movement.

The same point may be made by examining the personnel of the National Reform Association and other labor organizations. Three of the six founding members of the Association—Evans, Devyr and Windt—were British born, as were three other land reformers who were active in New York at this time—Benjamin Offen, James Pyne and Dr. Frederick Hollick. Influenced by the coverage of American affairs in Britain, some 600 or 700 active Chartists are estimated to have emigrated to the United States between the 1830s and 1850s. Of these, seventy or so have been traced as involved in the American labor movement.[72] Many turned to trade unionism. John C. Cluer in the 1840s was perhaps the best-known advocate of the ten-hours movement in New England. John Bates founded in the Pennsylvania anthracite fields in 1849 the first mineworkers union in the United

---

[70]*Working Man's Advocate*, November 16, 1844.

[71]Edward Pessen, "Thomas Skidmore: Agrarian Reformer in the Early American Labor Movement," *New York History*, 35 (July 1954), 286–87.

[72]Ray Boston, *British Chartists in America 1839–1900* (Manchester, 1971), 21.

States. In the late 1850s and 1860s, Charles Daniel Weaver in eastern Missouri and Thomas Lloyd in adjacent southwest Illinois created the first national mine union, the American Miners Association.[73] In relation to land reform, the most interesting of these ex-Chartists was Thomas Ainge Devyr. He had arrived in America in 1840 with a price on his head, accused of raising seventy armed men against the state in Newcastle, and after having made a spectacular escape from the militia at Liverpool docks. Coming from Ireland, where the reform on land tenure and usage was the most explosive of all issues, Devyr's tract of 1836 entitled *Our Natural Rights* set forth a solution to Irish poverty: the reduction of rents by three-quarters, the grant of perpetual leases, and the limitation and equalization of landholdings until all Irishmen held twenty acres. He was thus primed and ready for the cause he would adopt in New York. He believed that "every occupier of land has an inalienable right to the soil he cultivates" and, like Skidmore, he recognized no right of inheritance of property. Indeed, in Ireland in 1836 Devyr had called for the formation of a society of land reformers and the publication of a journal "advocating the principle of limited ownership" that almost seems to prefigure the National Reform Association itself.[74]

These Anglo-American radical linkages and lineages have grown in significance, and have become much easier to explain thanks to the work of Gareth Stedman Jones on the nature of radical protest, and Chartism in particular, in early industrial Britain. Dissatisfied with a traditional interpretation of the early English working class that has understood them as first and foremost anticapitalist in outlook, and as seeking redress for economic and social grievances, Stedman Jones has shown how the language of radicalism was preeminently political, and focused upon the corruptions of the ruling

[73]Yearley, "Britons in American Labor," 31–34.
[74]Thomas Ainge Devyr, *Our Natural Rights: A Pamphlet for the People. By One of Themselves* (Belfast, 1836, 2nd ed. Williamsburg, L.I., 1842).

class and its clients rather than the exploitation practiced by employers. Political exclusion rather than poverty inspired the movements of the new working classes up to 1850; the sinecurist was a more potent figure of derision than the factory master. Indeed, it was the nature of the state and its moral standing with the people that formed popular consciousness, rather than exploitation by unscrupulous masters.[75] Stedman Jones traces the origins of this radical tradition to the revolutions of the seventeenth century and the country party critique of ministerial corruption in the first half of the eighteenth century, both of which were sources for the "ideological origins of the American Revolution," of course. Subsequently, the radical tradition was itself influenced and consolidated by the example and ideas of the American rebellion and its English supporters.[76] But it did not expire as the factory system spread: it continued to shape working-class consciousness so that Chartism, pulling together the many strands of radical protest in the mid-1830s, has to be understood not as the first great mass movement of an industrial proletariat, but as the last and climactic act of a radicalism with pre-industrial roots.

As American historians have begun to realize, this reinterpretation, and its especial focus on the language of radicalism, has interesting implications for the United States.[77] An English working class movement focused on the conditions of its employment and its living standards, and in fundamental opposition to the economic system of the day, seemed unlike the radicals, utopians and republicans who peopled the working men's movements of the Jacksonian era.

[75]Gareth Stedman Jones, "Rethinking Chartism" in *idem*, *Languages of Class. Studies in English Working Class History 1832–1982* (Cambridge, 1983), 90–178.

[76]*Ibid.*, 102–3.

[77]Fink, "Looking Backward," 7; Sean Wilentz, "Against Exceptionalism: Class Consciousness and the American Labor Movement 1790–1920," *International Labor and Working Class History*, 26 (Fall 1984), 3–4.

Comparisons between a society where the factory system had taken root and one where it existed only in isolated places were difficult to make. The American artisanate, threatened to be sure, nevertheless looked very different from the British working class of the same period. Stedman Jones's work, by emphasizing radical ideology and radical aims—manhood suffrage, freedom from intrusive government, economic independence, an end to "old corruption"—makes British workers rather more like their American contemporaries, and makes American journeymen and artisans rather less exceptional than once they seemed.

If radicalism was not the property of any *class*, but "of the 'people' or 'nation' against the monopolizers of political representation and power," as Stedman Jones has contended, then it could be transferred more easily to a society where no identifiable working class of a British type could be said to have existed.[78] If the radical program envisaged "a more or less egalitarian society, populated exclusively by the industrious, and needing minimal government," it was conformable with the minimalist conceptions of the exercise of power and authority that characterized Americans of all description, then and now.[79] And if the "polarity" in radical thinking in Britain "was not that between 'working classes' and 'middle classes,' but between the working classes and the idle classes," then it was identical to the polarity that American workingmen recognized between the useful and useless, between workers and parasites.[80] "Why should Speculation and Scheming ride so jauntily in their carriages," asked Greeley, "splashing honest work as it trudges humbly and wearily by on foot?"[81] Indeed, nothing has more puzzled historians of the early American labor movement than such ambiguous moral distinctions, and their

[78]Stedman Jones, "Rethinking Chartism," 104.
[79]*Ibid.*, 168.
[80]*Ibid.*, 128.
[81]Greeley, "The Emancipation of Labor," 14.

blurring of the classical language of class, and in this matter Stedman Jones is especially helpful. For he shows that in the language of the Chartists, the real enemy was not "the emergence of an industrial capitalism" but "a process of financial plunder" of the state and the people by a parasitical class of "placemen, sinecurists and fundholders" who were living off the British taxes on consumption.[82] Indeed, Thomas Hodgskin and John Gray, among other radical theorists, acknowledged the creative role of masters in the productive enterprise and, in some respects, their identity of interest with their workers.[83]

In this context, the language and definitions of American radicals no longer sound aberrant. In the Jacksonian period the term "working man," synonymous with the performance of "useful toil," was employed to describe all save the rentier or speculator uninvolved in the process of production. As Commons has recognized, "the movement at first was not so much the modern alignment of wage-earner against employer, as the alignment of the producing classes against the non-producers."[84] At the third meeting of the New York Working Men's Party, it was not the employers who were given five minutes to leave before proceedings began, but "persons not living by some useful occupation, such as bankers, brokers, rich men, etc."[85] Small masters were to be found in all the various workingmen's parties and were accepted as valid contributors to the cause. The trades' union in Boston admitted masters to membership because "the boss is often brought back to journeywork by hard luck, and the journeyman may expect in his turn to become an employer, while both of them are invariably imposed upon and treated as if belonging to an inferior grade of society by those who live without laboring."[86] Evans con-

[82]Stedman Jones, "Rethinking Chartism," 171–73.
[83]*Ibid.*, 136–37.
[84]Commons *et al.*, eds., *Documentary History*, V, "Introduction," 24.
[85]*Working Man's Advocate* (first series), October 13, 1829.
[86]*The Man*, May 30, 1834 in Commons *et al.*, eds., *Documentary History*, V, 24.

tended in 1841 that only one man on the executive committee of the New York Working Men's Party in 1830 was not a "workingman"— he was a broker, in fact—and so included under the appellation five grocers, two merchant tailors, one oil merchant, one teacher and one farmer.[87] As he explained in 1845, "my definition of a Working Man has always been one who followed any useful occupation, mental or physical, for a livelihood."[88]

It was from Marx and Engels and their observations of British workers in the 1840s that historians derived their view of Chartism as a class movement of the proletariat.[89] Marx was wrong in this, as he was in his description of the National Reform Association "as a result of the proletarian movement" in America.[90] Writing in 1847, he believed that "As in England under the name of the Chartists, so in North America under the name of National Reformers, the workers have formed a political party whose battle slogans in no way include republic or principality, but rule of the working class against rule of the bourgeois class."[91] Marx was incorrect in his social and ideological analysis, but closer to the mark in the identity he wanted to establish between the two movements. Individual Chartists became land reformers in the United States, as we have seen. Meanwhile in England, after the failure of the first two Chartist petitions of 1839 and 1842, the Chartist Land Company was created and a Land Plan set in motion. Estates were purchased and each subscriber

[87]*The Radical*, No. 1, February 2, 1841.

[88]*Young America*, March 29, 1845.

[89]Stedman Jones, "Rethinking Chartism," 92.

[90]Karl Marx, "The Economics of the *Volks-Tribun* and Its Attitude Toward Young America" in *Circular Against Kriege*, May 1846, in Karl Marx, *On America and the Civil War*, The Karl Marx Library, Vol. II, ed. S. K. Padover (New York, 1972), 3.

[91]Karl Marx, "Moralizing Criticism and Criticizing Morality," *Deutsche-Brusseler Zeitung*, November 11, 1847 in Marx, *Marx on America and the Civil War*, 8.

given a few acres—two, three or four—to farm. Their rents were used to buy more land for more subscribers. In all, five communities were created, but financial difficulties, malpractice, and the hostility of the authorities led to the Plan's disbandment in 1851.[92] For both movements the ownership and use of the land offered a way forward. In 1837, the year in which the London Workingmen's Association framed the six points of the People's Charter, it protested against American workers allowing so much of their land to pass into the hands of "swindling bankers and grinding capitalists who seek to establish (as in our country) a monopoly of land which nature has bestowed in common upon her children."[93] Almost every issue of the *Working Man's Advocate* and *Young America* from 1844 cited the *Northern Star*, the famous Chartist weekly, generally under the title "News from the Rotten Monarchies," and did not ignore the Land Plan. The *Northern Star*, meanwhile, discussed the American land question some eight times in 1844 alone.[94] Chartism and National Reform were both predicated on the concept of inalienable rights. They both looked for an escape from exploitation and dependence: land, according to the rules of the National Land Company, was "a means of making them independent of the grinding capitalists."[95]

[92]Alice Mary Hadfield, *The Chartist Land Company* (Newton Abbot, 1971); Joy McAskill, "The Chartist Land Plan" in Asa Briggs, ed., *Chartist Studies* (London, 1959); W. H. G. Armytage, "The Chartist Land Colonies 1846–1848," *Agricultural History*, 32 (1958).

[93]William Lovett, *Life and Struggles of William Lovett in His Pursuit of Bread, Knowledge and Freedom* (1878, 1967 ed., London), 108.

[94]The *Northern Star* discussed the question of American land reform on April 20, 27; June 1, 22; July 6, 20; August 10; Sept. 4, 1844. The Chartist Land Plan was discussed twice in 1844 in the *Working Man's Advocate*, September 7 and November 30.

[95]"Rules and Regulations of the Chartist Land Co-operative Company," *Northern Star*, May 3, 1845, in David Jones, *Chartism and the Chartists* (London, 1975), Appendix 3, 201.

And the *New York Sun* termed the local land reformers "neither more nor less than the English Chartists transported to this country."[96]

The two movements are even alike in the treatment that their respective ideas about the land have been received from historians. Norman Ware described National Reform as "utopian" even though a Homestead Act was passed in 1862: "Evans wanted every man under his own vine and fig-tree. It was only when this transcendentalism failed that a realistic approach was made, an attempt to challenge the new order on its own ground."[97] Likewise, the Chartist Land Plan "has been damned as a hopelessly utopian venture, or as a diversion from the real political struggle of the Six Points."[98] Gammage, the first and perhaps the finest historian of the movement, called it a "great folly," the Webbs wrote of "an ignoble scramble for the ownership of small plots of land."[99] But as John Saville has argued and Dorothy Thompson echoed, the Land Plan was extraordinarily popular among humble followers of the movement and emerged from a series of vibrant debates about land and its use that preoccupied the radical movement in Britain in the 1830s and 1840s.[100] These concerned "the desirability of making allotments and cottage gardens available to agricultural laborers; the advantages and disadvantages of peasant holdings; the merits of spade husbandry compared with field cultivation; the

[96]Thomas Ainge Devyr, *The Odd Book of the Nineteenth Century, Or, "Chivalry" in Modern Days: A Personal Record of Reform — Chiefly Land Reform — For The Last Fifty Years,* 2 vols. (New York, 1882), II, 139.

[97]Ware, *The Industrial Worker,* xxvi.

[98]John Saville, "Introduction: R. G. Gammage and the Chartist Movement" in R. G. Gammage, *History of the Chartist Movement 1837–1854* (2nd ed., 1894, 1969 reprint, New York), 48.

[99]Gammage, *History of the Chartist Movement,* 249. Sidney and Beatrice Webb, *History of Trade Unionism* (London, 1894), 160.

[100]Saville, "Introduction," 47–62; Dorothy Thompson, *The Chartists. Popular Politics in the Industrial Revolution* (2nd ed., Aldershot, 1986), 300–306.

problems of land tenure, organization and rural social structure" and the relative advantages of individual proprietorship, as advocated by Feargus O'Connor, and land nationalization, as favored by Bronterre O'Brien and Harney.[101] Land was important because radicals and Chartists saw the expropriation of the land, sanctioned by the state and the political process through innumerable acts of enclosure in the seventeenth and eighteenth centuries, as the "ultimate source" of their condition.[102] Indeed, it confirmed their belief that only political action could alleviate this condition, because it had been caused by the corruption of political power. British wage laborers thus saw in the Land Plan "an escape from dependence"; domestic workers saw an alternative to "encroaching proletarianization."[103] The motives were akin to those that influenced supporters of land reform in the United States. O'Connor's attack on mechanization and the monopoly power it granted a few employers in the *Management of Small Farms* which he published in 1843, and his recognition that the cultivation of the land offered a physical escape from this for some, and the prospect of higher wages in the cities for others, all found their echo in the *Working Man's Advocate*.[104]

Reevaluation of the early movements of the working classes of Britain has thus narrowed the differences between them and their counterparts across the Atlantic. The hybrid nature of American organizations, mixing industrial struggles with reformism, and their ambiguous definitions of a "working man" no longer appear aberrant when compared with the working-class causes in Britain which owed more to the language of eighteenth-century radicalism than to the language of late nineteenth-century class. In both traditions, land and its use were central concerns: the United States might have had enor-

[101]Saville, "Introduction," 51.
[102]Stedman Jones, "Rethinking Chartism," 153.
[103]Saville, "Introduction," 60.
[104]Thompson, *The Chartists*, 302.

mous resources in the public domain, but the reasons why some urged settlement on it were not different from those that drove English radicals back to the land. America was exceptional in the sense that she had more land to distribute, and not in the sense that land offered a unique solution to the problems of her urban artisans and wage earners. Nor was a discourse on the political virtues of a landholding society unique to the republican tradition. Indeed, the complex roots of many American radical institutions of this period in ideas first articulated in Britain, the involvement of British-born workers in almost all of them, the parallel development of such organizations in both societies, and the development of a shared language through which to understand, criticize and change them, suggests how limited are approaches to the history of American labor in the nineteenth century which focus on "worker republicanism" alone. American workers *were* republicans; but they were also radicals in a tradition and discourse that linked them to their fellows across the Atlantic.

IV

They were also free. They were not slaves. And they came to understand themselves in terms of a third language also, or what Eric Foner has recently called "a master metaphor" that was "employed in social movements of all descriptions" but had particular relevance to the labor movement in America.[105] American workingmen appropriated a sectional rhetoric, called themselves "wage slaves," compared their situation with the supposedly paternal treatment of chattel slaves in the South, and contrasted middle-class moral detestation of slavery in the North with its tolerance of low wages, long hours and the loss of independence intrinsic in the contract for free labor. This was "a standard component of labor rhetoric in these years" and ran through

[105]Eric Foner, *Slavery and Freedom in Nineteenth-Century America* (Oxford, 1994), 2.

the gamut of organizations and campaigns.[106] Seth Luther's famous *Address to the Working Men of New England* in 1832 argued that Northern mill hands labored longer than Southern field hands.[107] Orestes Brownson contended in his essay on *The Laboring Classes* in 1840 that wage labor enabled employers "to retain all the advantages of the slave system without the expense, trouble and odium of being slaveholders."[108] The women of the Lowell mills referred to themselves during a strike as the "white slaves" of New England. Their journal, *The Voice of Industry*, claimed that they were "in fact nothing more nor less than slaves in every sense of the word."[109] These rhetorical devices—a specific political language being used instrumentally— were employed to urge that reform begin at home, in the cities of the Northeast rather than the fields of the South. By adopting and using the dominant political discourse of the day, the language of sectionalism and of freedom from bondage, land reformers and workingmen sought to publicize their case, draw attention to themselves, and find the contradictions in the argument of their opponents. The language of republicanism was employed by radicals to show that their causes fell within the ideological consensus from which the Union had emerged. So the language of sectionalism could be used to indicate more than one kind of exploitation. This did not mean that those who employed the "language of slavery" necessarily believed themselves to be akin to slaves; this was but a device to demonstrate the peculiar myopia of many abolitionists, and the all-too-common human tendency to seek to remedy distant abuses while ignoring those closer to home.

[106]Foner, "Abolitionism and the Labor Movement," 255–56.

[107]Seth Luther, *Address to the Workingmen of New England* (Boston, 1832), 25.

[108]Orestes Brownson, "The Laboring Classes" (1840) in W. Huggins, ed., *The Reform Impulse* (New York, 1972), 99–101.

[109]Foner, "Abolitionism and the Labor Movement," 256.

It was sometimes contended that the Northern working classes were hostile to abolitionists because they feared a glut of freedmen joining the labor market and driving down wages. But as Eric Foner has argued, we must distinguish their attitude to abolitionists and the threat of black competition from a more deeply-felt hostility to slavery which overtly "contradicted the central ideas and values of artisan radicalism—literacy, democracy, equality, independence."[110] Evans, for example, was a dedicated opponent of slavery. In New York, the only journal to publicly defend Nat Turner's rebellion was Evans' *Daily Sentinel*.[111] And as he explained later in 1844, "We have made 'the experiment' of speaking out against slavery. We believe the black has as good a right to be free as the white; that 'all men are created equal'; and I have frequently asserted this right, in print, years ago. I believe that all men have equal natural and political rights; and I harbor no prejudice against color."[112] Another National Reformer and labor leader, John Commerford, was a notable abolitionist. Yet by the 1840s some the most vociferous opponents of the labor movement were leading abolitionists. It was an antagonism founded on competing claims for the type of reform that should have primacy, and on tensions between the evangelicalism of many abolitionists and the free-thinking traditions of the artisanate. Again there was a parallel to this in Britain where attitudes to slavery were similarly mediated through class relations: a comparable hostility to the abolition of chattel slavery was expressed by a group of vocal British trade unionists and radicals in the 1850s and 1860s, who adopted this attitude in opposition to the anti-slavery sentiments of many of the leading British manufacturers of the day.[113] As Bronterre O'Brien ex-

[110]*Ibid.*, 257.

[111]*Daily Sentinel*, September 17, 1831.

[112]*Working Man's Advocate*, July 27, 1844.

[113]Royden Harrison, *Before the Socialists. Studies in Labour and Politics 1861–1881* (London, 1965), ch. 2, "British Labour and American Slavery."

plained in terms familiar to American workingmen, "When one listens to an Abolitionist one might think that outside of the blacks there was no slave within British rule. If these scoundrels entertained a sincere hatred against slavery they would begin by abolishing it at home."[114]

In the United States one of the most famous cycles of public debate on the question of "wage slavery" was printed in *The Liberator* in 1846–1847, with Wendell Phillips and William Lloyd Garrison at issue with Evans and William West, a New York labor leader who became prominent in the early 1850s. When Phillips argued that the abolitionists defined the concept of freedom as "self-ownership" which the Northern working class possessed, Evans responded that "men robbed of their lands are robbed of themselves most effectually." When Garrison found it ridiculous to argue that "it was worse for a man to be free than to be a slave, worse to work for *whom* he pleases, *when* he pleases, and *where* he pleases," West replied that it was "surpassing strange" that Garrison had "lived for forty years" and could still believe that a Northern laborer had such freedom. The substantive issues of the debate clearly counted, but more important was the attempt on both sides to establish the primacy of their respective causes: as Garrison put it, "what hope, nay what possibility is there, that, in a nation where it is reputable to steal men, the right of every man to a just portion of the soil will be conceded and enjoyed? . . . The deliverance of the slave must precede the redemption of the land."[115] Similar issues were debated in another, if less well-known, of these open debates in the columns of the *Working Man's Advocate* in July and August 1844 between Evans and Gerrit Smith, later the presidential candidate of the Liberty Party, the political wing of abolitionism. Once again, we can see how the labor movement used the

[114]*Ibid.*, 59.

[115]*The Liberator*, September 4, 1846; March 19, 26 and April 2, 1847. See Foner, "Abolitionism and the Laboı Movement," 264–65.

discourse of anti-slavery to draw attention to its situation and to demand redress, though in this case the exchange developed into a practical exemplification of the growing conflation of land reform and anti-slavery from the mid-1840s—a theme which has not had the attention it deserves.

Evans first accused Smith of being "one of the largest slaveholders in the United States" because he was "one of the largest landholders in the state." Wage-slavery should be abolished before turning southwards. Smith replied that he was "unspeakably sorry that you should justify the enslavement of your colored brothers. You will deny that you justify it. Nevertheless, you do justify it when you say that poverty is as bad as slavery, nay even identical with it." To this Evans retorted,

> You do not see that there is white slavery: you call it poverty. I must still, until further enlightened, maintain that the landless poor man is a slave: if not quite so degraded a slave as the black, still so near it that the difference is hardly worth bothering about. The one is a slave to a single master. The other to a master class.

Evans believed it "most proper to begin our abolition efforts with that form of slavery that is nearest home. Having accomplished this, we could with more effect, it seems to me, turn our attention to that at a distance."[116]

At one point in these exchanges Smith had asserted, "Convince me that a principle is right in the abstract, and I will reduce it to practice if I can."[117] It would seem that by 1846 Smith had indeed been convinced by the arguments of the land reformers. For in that year, and for the next six, until his election to Congress in 1852, he gave away parts of his extensive estates (estimated at approximately three-quarters of a million acres at this time) in New York state, de-

---

[116]*Working Man's Advocate*, July 6, 20, and 27, 1844.
[117]*Ibid.*, July 20, 1844.

puting friends and notables to serve on local committees to select worthy recipients of the land.[118] There were three separate distributions: to 3,000 free blacks in New York state; to 196 of the poor of Madison County around Smith's home in Peterboro; and in 1849, to 1,000 poor whites. To distribute land to 3,000 sober, propertyless blacks between the ages of twenty-one and sixty, Smith used four committees to gather names. The committee based in New York City included two notable leaders of the free black community, Dr. James McCune Smith, M.D. of the University of Glasgow, and Charles Bennett Ray, journalist and Methodist pastor of the Bethesda Congregational Church, New York.[119] And one of the committees with responsibility for the third distribution to "virtuous, landless and poor" white citizens of the state, to "be taken from the sexes in equal numbers," included Evans among its members. Each of the free black recipients was given a plot of about forty acres, most of it in Franklin and Essex counties in the Adirondacks.[120] As Smith explained "three thousand colored persons have received deeds of land from me, entirely

[118]See "Gifts of Land and Money 1846–1855" in the "Business and Land Records Subject File," Gerrit Smith Papers, George Arents Research Library, Syracuse University Library. Most of the material is similar to the following from Daniel B. Cady, Smith's uncle, dated July 10, 1849: "I believe that Mr. John M. Norton of the village of Johnson, Fulton County, is between the age of 21 and 60 years, that he is virtuous, landless and poor, and entirely clear of the vice of drinking intoxicating liquors." For an estimate of the extent of Smith's landholdings, see Harlow, *Gerrit Smith*, 249, 255.

[119]Smith apparently kept a book containing "the records of his . . . gifts of land to Negroes," but it was destroyed by fire in 1936. See Harlow, *Gerrit Smith*, 237.

[120]See "Business and Land Records," Land Book J (1844–1847). This includes a full enumeration of all blacks in receipt of gifts. Some 2,942 names are listed according to county of origin, along with the size of plot granted and its location.

free of all charge either for the land, or for the expense of the perfected deeds thereof."[121] In October 1848 the National Convention of Colored People, meeting at Troy, New York, expressed gratitude to Smith for the total gift of 140,000 acres.[122] In the following year the 1,000 whites were given lots of between thirty and sixty acres each.

The whole venture was unsuccessful. Much of the land Smith proposed to donate was too poor to farm, many of the recipients were too old or frail to cope with the rigors of up-state farming, and many of the donations were therefore converted to cash payments.[123] Indeed, in January 1850 Smith commuted all outstanding land grants to women to a $50 dole. Failure was prefigured in a circular of 1849 which warned the committees that "to guard the beneficiaries of your county against disappointment, I wish you would inform them, that most of the land is of an inferior quality: that it is probable that, in some instances it will prove unfit for farming; in some of little or no value either for farming or timber; and that it is possible . . . that, in some instances, my title will fail." Certainly Smith did not give up the best portions of his land, two-thirds of which he retained.[124]

Whatever the outcome, the episode is testimony to the persuasiveness of Evans and National Reform. Smith's biographer was perplexed and unclear about the origin and motivation of these schemes.[125] On his own admission, Smith had entertained the idea of distributing land for some time before their exchanges, but was probably provoked into a public demonstration of his own good faith by Evans' barbs in 1844. Apparently he had "cherished" a belief for

[121]Gerrit Smith Papers, "Gifts of Land and Money 1846–1855," circular dated May 1, 1849.

[122]Harlow, *Gerrit Smith*, 244–45.

[123]See "Gifts of Land and Money 1846–1855," Smith Papers. The file contains many orders for payment in lieu of land.

[124]Harlow, *Gerrit Smith*, 254.

[125]*Ibid.*, 252.

some years "that the individual owners of large tracts of farming land should divide them into lots of say, forty or fifty acres, and then give away the lots to such of their poor brethren as will reside on them."[126] Having converted Smith to the cause, National Reform had a champion in Congress: in July 1854, Smith introduced resolutions on the public lands in the House which included the assertion "that the right of all persons to the soil—to the great source of human subsistence— is as equal, as inherent and as sacred, as the right to life itself."[127] Smith's benefactions are richly suggestive of the links between land reform and the abolitionists' struggle. As Smith wrote later, catching a strand of argument that would be reworked by some of the Radical Republicans in the 1860s, "Land reform is the mightiest and most thorough of all anti-slavery measures. Abolish slavery and land monopoly will reproduce it. But abolish land monopoly, and make every man an acknowledged owner of the soil and there will be no room left for the return of slavery."[128]

V

Gerrit Smith's benevolence is one example of a more general trend: the gradual incorporation of land reform into the sectional struggle and, eventually, into the platform of the Republican Party. The National Reform Association chose, as a matter of strategy, to debate with abolitionists, to express its aims in the language of slavery and freedom, and to attach its own cause to those issues dividing North and South. In the process, in a notable, if unacknowledged and unappreciated example of success for the radical movement of this or any other period of American history, land reform merged into anti-

---

[126]*Working Man's Advocate*, July 6, 1844. See also O. B. Frothingham, *Life of Gerrit Smith* (New York, 1876), 110.

[127]Harlow, *Gerrit Smith*, 256–57.

[128]Devyr, *The Odd Book of the Nineteenth Century*, II, 106.

slavery—free land became "free soil"—and its chances of being enacted were greatly enhanced.

The process can be traced by examining the evolving meaning of certain key terms. In the mid-1840s, when the National Reformers talked or wrote of "free soil," they meant land given to settlers free of charge. Thus Evans publicized the success of the National Reform Association in *Young America* under the headline "A Free Soil—Progress of the Cause:" But the Mexican War and Wilmot Proviso introduced the distinction between free and slave soil, and by May 1848 an element of doubt had entered the labor press. *The Chronotype*, published in Boston, then sought to clarify that "by Free Soil, whatever others mean, we mean to express the great tradition that the soil was given to the race for their common benefit, and that every man who is willing to cultivate it has a right to the use of so much of it somewhere he can cultivate it, and no more."[129] By December of the same year the two different usages were being combined, however: a *Chronotype* correspondent argued that Van Buren's candidacy for the Free Soil Party would have been more successful in the previous month's presidential election if he had placed greater emphasis on free grants of land—the policy of National Reform: "It is free soil for white men as well as soil free from slavery that we advocate."[130] In the intervening August, indeed, one enthusiastic land reformer had written to Van Buren to ask him to endorse a homestead policy and had exclaimed in conclusion, "Free Soil to the Free Occupant—What a war cry for Free Men—Free Homes for Free Hands!" "Freedom" denoting land free of charge, and "freedom" denoting land outside slave cultivation had been conflated; two previously separate issues, sectional and class-based, were now being linked.[131]

---

[129]*The Chronotype*, May 6, 1848, quoted in Zahler, *Eastern Workingmen*, 107n.

[130]*Ibid.*, December 17, 1848.

[131]George M. Stephenson, *The Political History of the Public Lands* (New York, 1917), 137.

The politics of anti-slavery and the politics of homestead were now eliding. In 1848, the Liberty Party declared in favor of land reform and won the endorsement of the National Reform Association. Meanwhile the Free Soil Party sought to lure the votes of organized labor by championing Van Buren's past support for a ten-hour day and for *limited* land reform. In 1848 the Free Soilers declared in favor of free grants of the public lands "to actual settlers in consideration of the expenses they incur in making settlements in the wilderness . . . and of the public benefits resulting therefrom."[132] Four years later, the Free Soil party platform was more vigorously in favor of homesteads, but had shifted its grounds from the public service of settling on the frontier, to the argument of Evans and National Reform concerning the natural right to the land, for "all men have a natural right to a portion of the soil; and that, as the use of the soil is indispensable to life, the right of all men to the soil is as sacred as their right to life itself."[133] Land reform was popular with Free Soil voters: indeed, many candidates and activists tried to incorporate free land into the goals of the Free Soil party by focusing their local campaigns on the dangers of land monopoly as well as the extension of slavery. And in the other direction, during the 1848 campaign, several land reform journals "deserted the hopeless prospects of Gerrit Smith and joined the forces of Free Soil."[134] The conflation of two different "free soil" campaigns is well-illustrated in the biography of Alvan E. Bovay who was at one time secretary of National Reform. In the early 1850s he moved from New York to Ripon, Wisconsin, and there, in 1854, organized what is claimed to have been the first conference of Whigs, Democrats and Free-Soilers to have adopted the name "Republican Party."[135] In

[132]E. Stanwood, *History of Presidential Elections* (Boston, 1884), 175.
[133]Ibid., 188.
[134]Rayback, *Free Soil*, 265–66.
[135]Commons, "Horace Greeley and the Working Class Origins of the Republican Party," 484.

league with a local Democrat and a Free Soiler, Bovay organized a meeting on February 2, 1854, at which it was resolved "that if a bill then pending in the Senate to throw open to slavery the territories of Kansas and Nebraska should pass, the old party organization in Ripon should be cast-off, and a new party, to be called the Republican, formed on the sole issue of opposition to slavery extension."[136] A second meeting on March 20, after the passage of the bill, began that task. Although Bovay's actions in 1854 did not long remain unique, his real importance lies in the influence he exerted at this time over his long-standing friend in the land reform cause, Horace Greeley, in pushing him and the *New York Tribune* towards Republicanism.[137]

By the 1850s land reform was a sectional issue in the editorials of all Southern newspapers, the South needing no prompting to realize that a public domain divided into 160-acre tracts was no home for plantation cultivation.[138] The *Wilmington (N.C.) Daily Journal* spoke for the whole South in its judgment of May 1,1854 that "Of all the measures of legislation by which abolitionists seek to accomplish the ruin of the South, the Homestead Bill is, beyond comparison, the most iniquitous and most efficient for their evil purposes."[139] As Senator Mason of Virginia protested in the March 1860 debate on a Homestead bill, which Congress passed, but which was vetoed by President Buchanan, "it has no longer the narrow and contracted purpose of giving land to the landless . . . it has no longer the diminished character of a philanthropic exercise . . . it is a political engine, and

---

[136]See Charles M. Harvey, "Origin of the Republican Party," *The Chautauquan*, September 1897 extracted in Francis Curtis, *The Republican Party: A History of its Fifty Years' Existence and a Record of Its Measures and Leaders, 1854–1904*, 2 vols. (New York, 1904), I, 173–78.

[137]*Ibid.*, 177. See also Suzanne Schulze, *Horace Greeley: A Bio-Bibliography* (Westport, Conn., 1992), 27.

[138]Eric Foner, *Free Soil, Free Labor, Free Men*, 28, 236.

[139]Quoted in Stephenson, *Political History of the Public Lands*, 154–55.

a potent one."[140] Votes on homestead in Congress in the 1850s were almost perfect illustrations of sectional division. In the division on Galusha Grow's homestead bill of January 1859, which was carried in the House 120 to 76, only three votes were cast from slave states in its favor, and only six Northern Congressmen voted against it. In the following year, another bill introduced by Grow passed the House 115–65, but only one vote cast against it was from a free state, and only a single vote from a slave state was in its favor.[141]

As this process of conflation developed, so the National Reform Association diminished. Its publications ceased in 1849 and after about 1852 no more was heard of it. Individual land reformers stood on the sidelines as the Republican Party stole their clothes. Their grievance is evident in two letters from Devyr and Commerford in 1859 to the Democrat, Andrew Johnson, a tireless advocate of a Homestead Act from 1846, though in the interests of the poor whites of east Tennessee whom he represented, rather than the urban working class. Devyr began by pointing out that all the organizers of the land reform campaign were old-time Jacksonians. "When the National (Land) Reform Movement was organized in New York City in 1844, nearly all the men engaged in it were Democrats." And he expressed regret that the Democrats would go down to electoral defeat for opposing homesteads on sectional, pro-slavery grounds. Instead of supporting the proposal, they were allowing "the comparative bagatelle of whether a slave shall work on the hither or thither side of a line . . . to swallow up public attention and lose your presidential candidate such states as New York." But even in late 1859, at "the eleventh hour," if the Democrats would take up "this redeeming law" and oppose to the Republicans the "great primary principle of land reform" (for the Republican Party was not officially committed to homesteads

[140]*Congressional Globe* 36th Congress, 1st session, 1635.
[141]Benjamin H. Hibbard, A *History of the Public Land Policies* (New York, 1924), 375–77.

until the Chicago party convention in 1860), then enough free states could be carried to give the Democrats the presidency.

Devyr was convinced that a form of deception was being perpetrated by the great new Northern coalition, "For the Buffalo Men [Free Soilers] and their successors, the Republicans, *were* and *are* imposters. If the Democrats were indeed Democrats they could turn the tide against them." According to Devyr, "the Greeley Whigs made a show of favoring it—still more so did the Buffalo Platform men. Indeed, those impostors stole our friends and our name in 1848. *Ours was the 'Free Soil Party'* up to that time. They deceived us and drew from us nineteen-twentieths of our men."[142] As he later put it, "the contest was virtually won, when this slavery question carried the public thought away from it."[143] Many of the same points were made in Commerford's letter—the same conviction that slavery was irrelevant to the Eastern workingman, the same belief that it was homesteads and not anti-slavery that motivated the people of the North. "I know," he wrote, "that the Republicans attribute their success to other issues than the advocacy of the distribution of land among the people, but I am satisfied that they are mistaken." Despite this, Commerford changed his political allegiance, leaving the Democrats in 1859 and running as a Republican candidate for the House in 1860. As he explained, "I have made it a rule for the last twenty years to not support any man or party that was not in favor of giving the lands to the people, and I am afraid that in the next presidential contest I shall have to cast my ballot for the Republican candidate."[144]

How are we to understand this process of conflation, as the aims

---

[142]T. A. Devyr to Andrew Johnson, December 9, 1859, *The Papers of Andrew Johnson*, Leroy P. Graf and Ralph W. Haskins, eds., III, 1858–1860 (Knoxville, Tenn., 1972), 311–12.

[143]Devyr, *The Odd Book of the Nineteenth Century*, 115.

[144]John Commerford to Andrew Johnson, December 17, 1859, *The Papers of Andrew Johnson*, III, 357.

of land reformers were adopted, and then in 1862 enacted by the emergent Republican coalition? First, it must be appreciated that homesteads were never just advocated by Northeastern workingmen: squatters in the West who wanted legal title to their property, and Southern poor whites from upland areas in states like Virginia and Tennessee were also keen advocates. Nor was land reform exclusively the policy of the Republicans: Commerford and Devyr might lament the failure of the national Democratic party to adopt a homestead policy in 1859, but in the following year the Douglas Democrats, at least, "supported the measure as ardently as Republicans."[145] And land reform was not opposed by the South alone. Whigs had favored national integration rather than further dispersion, and worried over conflicts on the frontier with native Americans. Those who had favored Henry Clay's "American System" supported the *sale* of the public lands (rather than their free grant) and feared that rapid migration to the West would spread the young nation's human resources and capital too thinly for successful industrialization in the East.[146] Indeed, employers in the Northeast looked askance at a policy designed to draw off surplus labor and so raises wages. Large-scale Western farmers saw in "free land" a threat to the value of their private real estate and a likely source of competition among producers, resulting in lower prices all around. Nativists opposed any proposal that would have given free land to foreign immigrants.[147]

Reform of the public domain long pre-dated the National Reform Association, as well. The demand for free land for settlers was before Congress frequently from the mid-1820s when Thomas Hart Benton moved for an inquiry into the expediency of giving lands to settlers. The House committee on public lands reported in favor of such a policy in 1828 and Andrew Jackson added his support in his message

---

[145]Foner, *Free Soil, Free Labor, Free Men*, 175, 304.
[146]Howe, *The Political Culture of the American Whigs*, 138.
[147]Foner, *Free Soil, Free Labor, Free Men*, 233, 256.

of December 4, 1832. Although the concerted campaign for a homestead law began in Congress in 1846, when Felix Grundy McConnell of Alabama and Andrew Johnson both introduced homestead bills in the House, at which time the influence of the National Reformers was at its height, it would be erroneous to place undue emphasis on the part played by Evans and his fellows.[148] Indeed, the wave of states which passed homestead exemption laws between 1848 and 1852— some eighteen in all—demonstrates how broad was the movement for land reform at this time. Homestead exemption—always a component of National Reform's demands—generally protected the homestead from execution for certain kinds of debt, limited the owner's ability to dispose of it by requiring the consent of a spouse to its sale or mortgage, and regulated the inheritance of the homestead for the family's benefit. These laws have been interpreted recently as a defensive response by Northern and Western majorities to the "market revolution" that was threatening traditional household independence and stability. They show also how open were legislators and their constituents to attempts to protect and extend a society of small, secure producers on the land.[149] The National Reform Association was a successful propagandist for a policy that thus had many different supporters and which grew in significance as the sectional struggle intensified. Land reform on the public domain was never the sole property of New York artisans; they could not claim special rights over it, and the issue had a turbulent life of its own far beyond the concerns of workingmen. Devyr and Commerford were merely parochial in their protests: irrespective of their advocacy, the

[148]For a concise history of the struggle for a homestead law in Congress, see Hibbard, A History of the Public Land Policies, XVII, 347–85.

[149]Paul Goodman, "The Emergence of Homestead Exemption in the United States: Accommodation and Resistance to the Market Revolution 1840–1880," Journal of American History, LXXX (September 1993), 470–98.

question of the future of the public domain became central to the politics of America after the Mexican War, and once this occurred, conflation of "free land" with "free soil" was almost inevitable.

But it might still be argued that in the late 1840s and early 1850s tensions between labor and capital that had expressed themselves in the panacea of land reform, were diverted into sectionalism and anti-slavery. The author of a hostile article on the radical movement, published in *Atlantic Monthly* in 1859, was in no doubt, certainly, that in the preceding two decades "the slavery question" had helped purge American politics of the pernicious influence of "agrarianism" and had hence ensured "the freedom of our later party struggles from radical theories."[150] Many Republicans saw homesteads in the West as a means of conferring social as well as geographic mobility, and supported the policy just because it would take families out of the ranks of the urban working class and the poor, and transform them into the self-supporting, industrious and acquisitive citizens of Republican mythology. In this way, class tensions would ease.[151] It has also been argued that the crusade against slavery drew attention from the factory system, the new industrial regime, and the protests of workers, and "an entire generation was side-tracked."[152] Workers who had previously voted for workingmen's candidates in Northeastern cities like Lynn, switched allegiance to the Republicans. Victory in the Civil War consolidated this political support for Lincoln's party; and for a decade after the cessation of hostilities the issues of Reconstruction overshadowed questions of industrial reform. Thus, during "the most critical years of industrialisation," from the 1840s to the 1870s, "the United States was more keenly divided politically between industrialism and slavery than between industrial workers and industrial

[150]"Agrarianism," *Atlantic Monthly*, III, No. xviii (April 1859), 397.

[151]Foner, *Free Soil, Free Labor, Free Men*, 28–29.

[152]Alan Dawley, *Class and Community. The Industrial Revolution in Lynn* (Cambridge, Mass., 1976), 238.

capitalists."[153] As David Montgomery has argued, substantive class differences did exist in the 1860s and 1870s, but in the midst of a sectional crisis, no vocabulary, no central political language existed through which they could be expressed, acknowledged, and addressed.[154]

The National Reform Association might be held responsible, in part, for this lacuna. It had, after all, deliberately engaged in debate with the abolitionist movement, deliberately exploited that movement's language against it, sought to put its own gloss on the "master metaphor" of slavery, and paid the price in linguistic and then institutional incorporation. The language of radicalism was crowded out by the language of sectionalism. But this is to overlook two things: the very success of land reform, and the strategy that Evans devised. The setbacks to the fledgling labor organizations that he observed in 1837 in New York convinced him that industrial action on its own would never suffice to win for labor its just rewards, and that separate workingmen's parties were doomed to a marginal, impotent existence. Hence the decision to support any candidate or party who would endorse land reform. The strategy carried the risk, in other words, that land reformers would make unfamiliar alliances and be carried far from their immediate political context—that they might lose control of the issue itself, as occurred in the 1850s. But Evans judged it a price worth paying for success, and the remarkable outcome of this episode was the incorporation of the homestead plank in the Republicans' 1860 platform, and the Homestead Act that was signed by Lincoln on May 20, 1862.

The Act was not all that Evans, by then dead, would have wanted.

[153]Alan Dawley and Paul Faler, "Working-Class Culture and Politics in the Industrial Revolution: Sources of Loyalism and Rebellion," *Journal of Social History* (June 1976), 475–76.

[154]David Montgomery, *Beyond Equality: Labor and the Radical Republicans 1862–1872* (New York, 1967), *passim*.

Though it stipulated that no individual could acquire more than 160 acres, and it did provide exemption for the homestead from execution for all debts incurred prior to the issue of a patent for the land, it did not reserve the public domain for the settler alone, and it allowed for the commutation to a cash payment of the five-year residence requirement before valid title to the land was granted. It thus invited the wild speculation in millions of acres of Western land in subsequent years. The legislation was "hasty" and flawed by "fatal mistakes" as the chairman of the House Committee on Public Lands in 1862, George W. Julian, was to put it later. It was "a half-way measure instead of that complete reform in our land policy which was demanded" and gave cause to doubt "the boasted friendship of the Republican party for the landless poor."[155] Nevertheless, it was passed, and thousands of families did benefit from its provisions, and the National Reform Association deserves recognition for its part in helping on the national movement for homesteads—an achievement for the radical movement of these years whose influence on national affairs was otherwise very limited.[156]

Moreover, the strategy, if it carried the risk of incorporation, also offered the opportunity of influencing the national political movements that subsumed land reform in the 1850s. Ironically, a movement with roots in the Jacksonian Democratic party brought its influence to bear by virtue of its incorporation within the Republican coalition of the 1850s. Long ago, in 1909, John R. Commons tried to prove the "working class origins of the Republican Party." He argued that it "was not an anti-slavery party. It was a homestead party. On this point its position was identical with that of the workingmen. Only because slavery could not live on one-hundred-and-sixty-acre farms did the

[155]George W. Julian, *Political Recollections, 1840 to 1872* (Chicago, 1884), 216–18.

[156]For a far more pessimistic assessment of the movement's influence in the 1850s, see Wilentz, *Chants Democratic*, 394.

Republican party come into conflict with slavery."[157] Commons was almost certainly mistaken: the uniting principle of Republicanism was undoubtedly opposition to the extension of slavery, and his case is lacking in anything like enough evidence to make the argument in this strong form. While the Republican party was most popular in rural areas and the small towns of the North, it was at its least popular in the Eastern cities where the workingmen were to be found. But if we fall back to a weaker position in which we acknowledge the attractiveness of a homestead policy to thousands of Northern families, who simultaneously feared the reach of the slave power into the territories, and thus recognize that the homestead law of 1862 owed something considerable to the influence of radical groups during the complex process of political realignment in the 1850s, we may be nearer the truth. And this weaker position may be substantiated by casting forward and observing small indications that the influence of land reformers and their organizations did not cease with the passage of legislation in 1862.

There were land reform societies in the Northeast in the 1860s and 1870s and land reformers like Commerford, Masquerier, William West and Joshua K. Ingalls (prominent in the industrial congresses of the late 1840s) were active at their head.[158] Distribution of the public domain was a live issue for the Knights of Labor, and also for Henry George, who in *Progress and Poverty* reversed the direction of Atlantic radicalism and took land reform, in the shape of the single tax, back to Britain in the early 1880s. Above all, land reform continued to be an issue at the heart of national politics during Reconstruction, which would not have surprised the original land reformers themselves. Skidmore had observed in 1829 that those who traveled in the South noted the reluctance of slaves to take their freedom, even when it was

---

[157]Commons, "Horace Greeley and the Working Class Origins of the Republican Party," 488.

[158]Montgomery, *Beyond Equality*, 415.

offered, because "they would have no property; they therefore think they could not support themselves." Thus, "if with freedom they were presented with lands and other property also wherewith to obtain subsistence, the case would be very different and nothing could intervene to create dissension and disturbance."[159] And Evans had contended in one of his open letters to Gerrit Smith in 1844 "that to give the landless black the privilege of changing masters now possessed by the landless white would hardly be a benefit to him in exchange for his surety of support in sickness and old age."[160]

The relationship between land reform and emancipation, which the land reformers understood implicitly a generation and more before black freedom, thus leads us to those Radical Republicans of the 1860s who argued that the only guarantee of a complete social revolution in the defeated South was the distribution of planters' lands to the freedmen. Masquerier, writing in 1877, saluted three congressional advocates of homesteads in the 1850s and 1860s—Galusha Grow, Ben Wade and George W. Julian. In the case of Grow and Wade, they came from states, Pennsylvania and Ohio respectively, where land reform was a major issue in the late 1840s and early 1850s, and National Reform was notably successful. Grow, the law partner of David Wilmot from 1847, was the Republican Speaker of the House when the Homestead Law was passed in 1862. Julian, who had urged on Congress a homestead measure from the early 1850s, was an original Free-Soiler, present at the 1848 Buffalo convention, and was chairman of the House Committee on Public Lands when the Homestead bill became law. All three were likewise advocates of land redistribution in favor of the freedmen in the 1860s: "to extend the Homestead Law of 1862," in Julian's formulation, "to the forfeited and confiscated lands of Rebels . . . to deal with these lands as *public* lands, and parcel them out into small homesteads among the poor of

---

[159]Skidmore, *The Rights of Man to Property!*, 80.
[160]*Working Man's Advocate*, July 6, 1844.

the South, black and white."[161] As Sumner posed the problem to John Bright in May 1865, "can emancipation be carried out without usurping the lands of the slave-masters? We must see that the freedmen are established in the soil, and that they may be proprietors."[162] When Robert Dale Owen, a powerful influence on the Jacksonian workingmen's movement, and thirty years later the author of the final 1864 report of the American Freedmen's Enquiry Commission, asserted in that document in the tradition of National Reform that "no such thing as a free democratic society can exist in any country where all the lands are owned by one class and cultivated by another," the authentic voice of the old radicals and land reformers could be heard—only now it was the considered opinion of one of Lincoln's appointees.[163] Without wishing to exaggerate the influence of land reformers in the Republican party, or the degree to which radical ideas, in the confluence with national politics, were able to shape policy, a case could still be made in which the process of conflation we have examined did not simply eradicate labor radicalism, but gave it some longstanding if diffuse influence within the dominant political coalition of the next generation. Certainly George Julian, who must be considered a reliable witness on the Homestead Act, believed that the policy enacted in 1862 "was borrowed from the Free Soil platform of 1848 and the Land Reformers of New York."[164]

Eric Foner has written that American history needs an "inte-

---

[161]Julian, *Political Recollections*, 238.

[162]Sumner to Bright, May 13, 1865, quoted in Margaret Shortreed, "The Anti-Slavery Radicals: From Crusade to Revolution 1840–1868," *Past and Present*, 16 (1959), 78.

[163]R. W. Leopold, *Robert Dale Owen* (Cambridge, Mass., 1940), 362–63. See "Final Report of the American Freedmen's Inquiry Commission, to the Secretary of War," *Senate Executive Documents* (38th Congress, 1st Session, No. 53), 25–110.

[164]Julian, *Political Recollections*, 103.

grated approach incorporating both Thomas Jefferson and his slaves, Andrew Jackson and the Indians, Woodrow Wilson and the Wobblies in a continuing historical process, in which each group's experience is shaped in large measure by its relations to others."[165] The history of the early workingmen's movements has for too long been treated as a self-contained episode with limited import for other aspects of the nation's history, when a more integrated history, noting relationships and subtle interactions between groups and movements, and between high and low politics, is required. As this essay has sought to show, some American workingmen were able to exert influence by choosing their objectives and strategy with care, and by using political language with subtlety and craft. They learned to identify themselves, to themselves, in the language of British radicalism, and came to understand their historical position in relation to the experience of British workers. In interchange with others, they exploited the common heritage of all Americans in republican ideas. They presented their case in terms of the dominant discourse of sectionalism of the 1840s and 1850s. In the process they lost their separate identity and their movement, but gained their object, and may also have broadened the aims and perspectives of some elements of the great national party that absorbed their organization and program. Rather than lament yet another example of the incorporation of American radicalism, we may in this case note the modest success of a movement that helped to persuade and alter the mainstream.

[165]Eric Foner, *New York Times Book Review*, March 2, 1980, 31.

PART FOUR

Other Political Cultures

The Case of South Carolina:

Reflections on the Nature
of Political Culture

Rebecca Starr

The problem of political culture in early American studies has compounded silently since the term's introduction into the field in the late 1960s. Although widely used for the next thirty years, the term received almost no further analytical scrutiny. Several scholars, especially those in pursuit of a theory of national identity, have implicitly critiqued its limitations in case-study format,[1] but to date no systematic attempt to track a history or fully formulate a theory of the nature of political culture has appeared.

Perhaps the oversight is not surprising. Historians are not philosophers, and few professional philosophers choose to explain their insights through histories. Yet just as all sound ideas need concrete, illustrative material, proofs if you will, to demonstrate their explanatory power, so too do all good historical narratives require a clear explication of the theories upon which they rest. Following an intro-

---

[1]European scholars have led the way in this respect. See, for example, Keith Michael Baker, *Inventing the French Revolution: Essays on French Political Culture in the Eighteenth Century* (Cambridge, 1990); Linda Colley, *The Britons: Forging the Nation, 1707–1837* (New Haven, 1992); Harry T. Dickinson, *The Politics of the People in Eighteenth Century Britain* (New York, 1995); and Kathleen Wilson, *The Sense of the People: Politics, Culture, and Imperialism in England, 1715–1785* (Cambridge, 1995).

ductory section on the "problem" of South Carolina's famous radicalism, this essay concentrates first upon a conceptual analysis of political culture as it has come into use in the study of early America. Then, using the case of South Carolina's distinctive political culture to identify the term's analytical limitations, I attempt to reconfigure the concept in its functional rather than its descriptive character. Finally, I redefine the nature of political culture to argue that it is process, and not any particular content of a political culture that has determinative, shaping power.

This task, as often happens, was thrust upon me by the history I chose to analyze. South Carolina's political history simply wouldn't fit the model I inherited. I had to begin again. The essay that follows is the fruit of a root and branch reassessment of the "problem of political culture" in early American historiography, a task that proved a prerequisite to readdressing the "problem" of South Carolina.

Fascinated by the dramatically disruptive role of South Carolina in the events of the antebellum period, scholars have repeatedly tried to unravel the "problem of South Carolina."[2] As early as 1820, the state seemed to possess a unique (read deviant) political culture. Historians have long wondered why the state's politics were so obstructionist, its politicians so petulant. Although most have looked to the nineteenth century for its sources, the qualities later deemed "problematic" stood almost unnoticed and unremarked upon from about the mid-eighteenth century. This distinctive political culture whose flamboyant opposition politics dominated the antebellum scene in fact had quite undramatic beginnings in the colony's eighteenth-century commercial and political relationship with Great Britain.

---

[2]James M. Banner, Jr., "The Problem of South Carolina," in Stanley Elkins and Eric McKitrick, eds., *The Hofstadter Aegis: A Memorial* (New York, 1974), 60–93 summarizes the literature.

My reading of that relationship suggests that Carolina's leaders developed a pattern of interest-group practices and habits of mind that provided a psychological and methodological framework for the future.[3]

Having no assertable power in Parliament to push for legislation more favorable to the colony's considerable rice and indigo trade, Charleston's great merchants and lowcountry planters (who were also its provincial political leaders) resorted to economic power to bolster a weak political position. They established a trade lobby[4] in conjunction with British merchants and manufacturers concerned in the Carolina trade. As the lobby developed, and leadership passed from London to Charleston, tactics passed from simple influence to outright pressure.

As the Revolution approached, the lobby shifted its activities from commercial to political questions. Joining forces with the Rockingham whigs to press for a negotiated settlement to the crisis, Carolina leaders observed their Rockingham allies "secede" from Parliament for the remainder of the 1776 session, the ultimate parliamentary tactic of an outgunned minority. South Carolina's politics are not so irrational as they have been portrayed.

During the same period, the Charleston lobby learned that solidarity at home lent extra punch to its arguments. Knit together by kinship, friendship, and marriage, lowcountry elites enjoyed unusual social harmony, but economic divisions could erupt. When such internal conflicts arose, interests were quietly adjusted to retain an undivided front. From these pragmatic beginnings, Carolina leaders developed a body of political practices and habits of mind—a

[3]For a full treatment of these ideas, see Rebecca Starr, *A School for Politics: Commercial Lobbying and Political Culture in Early South Carolina* (Baltimore and London, 1998).

[4]Of course, the term "lobby" was not used in the eighteenth century. I use it here to refer to political activity pursued by groups joined by some interest, such as a common economic, religious, political, or ethnic interest.

practicing harmony at home, a radical style in national councils, and a concept of enlightened group interest—that came to typify South Carolina's politics at home and abroad. These habits accorded well with Carolina gentlemen's pragmatic view of society as a collection of competing interests and themselves as its natural leaders.

After independence, when the political community widened to include a diverse and underrepresented backcountry, strains in the legislature weakened traditional leadership. An emerging back-woods elite demanded greater say in state politics. Backcountry farmer and debtor discontent threatened a Shays's-like upheaval. Everywhere, violent disagreement over the handling of returning loyalists threatened to coalesce into divisive proto-political parties. Old elites needed a model for channeling popular unrest into the legislature where it could be defused within the traditional consti-tutional framework, without resorting to a reapportionment that would cost them their majority.

Carolina leaders had an available tradition to turn to. Using fa-miliar, lobby-learned tactics, they tooled the committee system of the lower house, balancing membership between the two sections to contain and diffuse tensions behind closed doors. Backcountry in-terests could find parity there. When an issue became too explosive to contain, committees counted signatures on opposing petitions, allowing a kind of referendum to rule, yet always within legislative discretion.[5]

In national councils, South Carolina delegates applied pressure politics to win concessions where they lacked voting muscle. For example, before the 1774 Continental Congress could pass an As-sociation barring exports and imports with England, rice had to be

---

[5]And see Rebecca Starr, "Parity without Equality: Representation 'Reform' in the South Carolina Legislature in the Early Republic, 1783–94," *Parlia-ments, Estates and Representation*, Vol. 17 (1997), 89–109.

exempted from the prohibition to forestall a walkout by the Carolina delegates. A similar hard line in the Federal Convention of 1787 forced delegates to delay giving Congress the power to prohibit the African slave trade until 1808 for fear that the Carolinians would not ratify the new Constitution.

Eventually, practice became policy. By 1800 brinkmanship politics marked South Carolina's leadership style in Congress, backed by a seemingly seamless political harmony at home. Eventually too, policy became philosophy, as John C. Calhoun distilled constitutional theory (the doctrine of the concurrent majority) from an analogous politics long practiced by his state's elite leaders. These processes and preconditions shaped a political culture that set South Carolina on a fateful trajectory for the nineteenth century.

Understanding the problem of South Carolina therefore came down to a problem of understanding the nature of political culture. Just what does that often used, but little explained, phrase mean? Political culture is usually defined as a cluster of values potentially organizable into meaningful world views.[6] But the available scholarship on the nature and operation of the concepts of political culture and its most usually studied organizer (or paradigm[7]), ideology, would not explain the case of South Carolina. The main task became the search for another master model. Is an "ideology" of one sort or another the only paradigm available to organize a political culture and to stock its shelves with values? What other master

---

[6]The main lines of this approach were worked out in the study of classical republicanism. For a summary of this literature, see Robert A. Shalhope in the *William and Mary Quarterly,* "Towards a Republican Synthesis: The Emergence of an Understanding of Republicanism in American Historiography," 3rd ser., XXIX (1972), 49–80; and "Republicanism and Early American Historiography," 3rd ser., XXXIX (1982), 334–56.

[7]A much criticized, but properly understood, extremely useful term, whose precision this essay hopes to re-excavate.

model might act as chief creator, selector, editor, and integrator of the contents of a society's political culture, might recognize and respond to as "problems" those contingent events which threaten its values, provide a pattern for handling those problems, and do all these operations simultaneously without reference to an explicit world view? My study of the origins of South Carolina's brand of opposition politics suggests that a habitual, patterned method of problem-solving behavior formulated in the commercial context became paradigmatic in future political contexts.[8] Put another way, the mind and methods of lobbying entered South Carolina's political culture and came to shape it.

I

Many scholars have come to use the terms "paradigm" and "ideology" as though they were interchangeable. But the ideological approach ignores the possibility that people become attached to their accustomed ways of doing things, continuing them long after the original, pragmatic reasons for devising those procedures have been forgotten. A method that continues to work on new sets of problems becomes valued for its own sake, and becomes a model for thinking and acting without first being transformed into abstract principle.[9]

Moreover, method, although nonreflective, can by virtue of long and familiar usage begin to collect a logic which seems to explain its utility and justify its continuation. That logic, when challenged, may then be forced from its deeply held but inchoate state into a fully articulated system of beliefs and supporting values. Until then,

---

[8] And compare to Joyce Appleby's remarks on a "modus operandi" in America's national political culture, this volume, 173.

[9] David A. Hollinger, "T. S. Kuhn's Theory of Science and Its Implications for History," collected in *The American Province: Studies in the History and Historiography of Ideas* (Bloomington, Ind., 1985), 114. This essay helped crystallize my thinking on the problem of pre-ideological paradigms.

the method operates nonverbally, processing problems in the same familiar, tried-and-found-again-to-be-true way, and through success and longevity, establishes an entrenched legitimacy.

As a concept, political culture has undergone a long and uneven definitional history. The term, first coined in the 1750s by J. G. Herder, equated to what we might now call "national character."[10] When taken up by twentieth-century scholars, political culture required a more precise definition, which raised three subsidiary questions: what is its nature, that is, its essential components; what does it do; and how does it do it?

Political scientists were the first to attempt a formal analysis of the concept in the late 1950s and early 1960s. They described it in a visual sense, as the setting for political action of all sorts and by all sorts. Several adopted the imagery of the theater. Political culture was the backdrop to the political stage on which political action takes place. In this scenario, political culture provides the options available to political actors and sets the boundaries beyond which they may not go. It also supplies their attitudes and influences the working of the political institutions they set up. For these scholars, political culture figured as the prevailing influence, but not the determinant of political action.[11]

One of the earliest studies of political culture (1956) supplied the definition still widely used among political scientists. Political

[10]J. G. Herder, *J. G. Herder on Social and Political Culture*, edited, translated and introduced by F. M. Bernard (Cambridge, 1969), 25.

[11]This early reliance on visual analogies later gave way to linguistic metaphors as the connections between political culture, political thought, and political discourse were more clearly worked out. Cf. the work of J. G. A. Pocock, esp. *Politics, Language and Time: Essays on Political Thought and History* (London, 1972) and *Virtue, Commerce and History: Essays on Political Thought and History, Chiefly in the Eighteenth Century* (Cambridge, 1985).

culture, according to Gabriel A. Almond, is "not a theory . . . but a set of variables" which make up society's "particular pattern of orientations to political actions."[12] In 1972 Dennis Kavanaugh further refined the term to "a shorthand expression to denote the emotional and attitudinal environment within which the political system operates."[13] Similarly, W. A. Rosenbaum's 1975 book-length study called it "a conceptual shorthand for feelings, thoughts, and behaviors we note or infer from watching men carry out their daily civic lives."[14]

While useful, all these descriptors lack a sense of integration or process. By 1986 the historian Christopher Thorne would redefine political culture in terms of a system. In Thorne's hands political culture became "a predominant pattern of widely proclaimed values which influences, but does not determine social and political behavior; a value system which can be seen to be operating at the levels of the community itself (that is, in relation to its fundamental political beliefs and 'rules of the game') of the regime (that is, the particular arrangement which regulate political demands, debates, and decisions) and of the immediate, day to day exercise of authority." The concept overlaps to some extent those of "national character" and "national style," while sharing a contextual relationship to the construct called "public opinion."[15] "Rules of the game" refers to values

[12]Gabriel A. Almond, "Comparative Political Systems," *Journal of Politics*, XVIII (1956), 396; and with Sidney Verba, eds., *The Civic Culture* (Princeton, 1963); and *The Civic Culture Revisited* (Boston, 198), chapter 1.

[13]Dennis Kavanaugh, *Political Culture* (London, 1972), 10.

[14]W. A. Rosenbaum, *Political Culture* (London, 1975), 8. The only other scholar to include behavior as an aspect of political culture is Richard R. Fagan, *The Transformation of Political Culture in Cuba* (Stanford, Calif., 1969), 5.

[15]Christopher Thorne, "American Political Culture and the Asian Frontier, 1943–1973," *Proceedings of the British Academy*, LXXII (1986), 339–94.

which respect legal procedures and established practices, and considers the rights of all game players.[16] This broadened definition gave the concept wider scope and greater intellectual coherence, but still fell short of identifying a working construction for all these elements. It was approximately at this time and at this point in the conceptual development of political culture that I began to puzzle on the problem of South Carolina. I soon realized that I must construct a more usable definition of political culture than I had inherited before I could continue. Marshaling all the relevant sources I could find, I read on.

I noted that, despite their differences, in the hands of both political scientists and historians, "values" figure as the basic components of political culture. Values, however, may be further delineated into two separate dimensions. At one level exist discrete values that are so fundamental and widely shared that they are never fully or systematically articulated, nor is their relationship to one another fully worked out. It is not necessary to do so, as they are so implicit to the society's fabric that they are simply assumed. Michael Polanyi calls this realm a society's "tacit dimension."[17] The tacit dimension may be all that is necessary in small, socially homogeneous societies (such as South Carolina's colonial lowcountry culture); societies knit together by kinship, ritual, and custom, where role assignments are exact and role expectations are known to all.

The political cultures of larger, more complex societies, however, while retaining a basic tacit dimension, must rely upon persuasion more than custom and ritual to communicate the community's ideals. The means of persuasion is chiefly by spoken and written language (although paintings, sculpture, music, and drama may also at

[16]Harold McCloskey, "Consensus and Ideology in American Politics," *American Political Science Review*, LVIII (1964), 364.
[17]Michael Polanyi, *The Tacit Dimension* (London, 1969).

times be political languages).[18] Thus, the second value dimension is that which is explicit, fully and systematically articulated in both the spacial and linguistic senses; that is, the values "fit together" into expressive and expressed sets of beliefs. This configuration of ideas is what most historians mean by an "ideology."[19] (But note that here, ideology is subsumed within the concept of political culture, and that a political culture may contain several ideologies, although one usually dominates.) If ideology is an overt text of a political culture, then the tacit dimension is its subtext.

Of these two dimensions, ideology is the most advanced, most formally thought out, the most visible, and intellectually the most available of the two discussed. It has certainly attracted by far the most scholarly attention. Yet I believed there had to be a third, largely unrecognized but critical feature to political culture—a methodological dynamic (introduced here in the case study of the South Carolina lobby) that is as systematic as ideology, but as implicit as an assumption. To continue the language metaphor, it is neither text nor subtext but a working grammar, a method, socially

[18]For the role of art as public discourse, see David A. Hollinger, "Historians and the Discourse of Intellectuals" in *American Province*, 142–43. For a brilliant analysis of a work of art as political discourse, see Quentin Skinner, "Ambrogio Lorenzetti: The Artist as Political Philosopher," *Proceedings of the British Academy*, LXXII (1986), 1–56.

[19]Ideology is used here in its theoretical sense, as a concept shaped by and expressive of the overall values of the society in which it is contained, not in the pejorative sense of a conscious selection of certain values while suppressing others to present a distortion for polemical purposes. See Clifford Geertz, "Ideology as a Cultural System" in *The Interpretation of Cultures: Selected Essays* (New York, 1973), esp. 193–200, 218–19. For a summary and interpretation of the literature on value, see Joyce Appleby's essay "Value and Society" in Jack P. Greene and J. R. Pole, eds., *Colonial British America: Essays in the New History of the Early Modern Era* (Baltimore, 1984), 290–316.

learned and nonverbal, whose authority is so deep as to need no reflection. (I will develop this methodological dynamic of political culture in Section II.)

How does the tacit dimension of political culture—the implicit and unarticulated value pool—operate with the explicit, highly thought out, expressive and language-borne belief system, and how does the whole of political culture fit together with and operate with a society's visible systems of political action and political structure? Political scientists appear to favor a structural-functional approach to these questions. Drawing on the work of Talcott Parsons, who envisioned culture as a system of subsystems (of which political culture is but one), and gluing the value dimensions together with the concept of congruence,[20] political scientists talk about an individual's or a group's "orientations" towards the various elements in the political system.[21] It is an integrative approach, but its problem, as Joyce Appleby points out, is getting it to move.[22] It has no mechanism to explain historical process. Parsons' analysis does account for how a society maintains itself and provides an adequate way to describe if not explain its character. This last permits comparisons between two or more political cultures across space, but it is too static to permit comparisons of a society's own political culture

[20]H. H. Eckstein, "A Theory of Stable Democracy" in *Division and Cohesion in a Democracy* (Princeton, 1966), 234, 241. Eckstein points out that no stable political society will display conflicting views of a fundamental value. If we take authority patterns, for example, one would not find an authoritarian form of government coexisting within a society displaying a prevailing pattern of permissive child-rearing practices.

[21]Talcott Parsons, *The Structure of Social Action* (New York, 1937); *The Social System* (New York, 1951); *Structure and Process in Modern Societies* (New York, 1960); and with Edward A. Shils *et al.*, *Toward a General Theory of Action* (Cambridge, Mass., 1951).

[22]"Value and Society" in Greene and Pole, eds., *Colonial British America*, 296.

across time. In other words the approach cannot account for development and change.

Not surprisingly, many historians eagerly turned to the work of the philosopher of physics Thomas Kuhn, whose model for scientific revolutions promised to account for both stability and change. First published in 1962, the Kuhnian thesis as adapted by historians describes a universal model of political culture consisting not only of a collection of values, but also a central control called a "paradigm." Kuhn's paradigm holds that human cultural activities (of which science is but one) are defined and controlled by tradition, and that "tradition consists of *sets of devices,* or principles, that have proven their ability to order the experience of a given social constituency."[23]

Kuhn himself cautioned that "Paradigms are not to be equated with theories. Most fundamentally, they are accepted concrete examples of scientific achievement, actual *problem-solutions* which scientists study with care and upon which they model their own work."[24] Whether Kuhn would exclude ideologies (being theories) as paradigms is irrelevant for our discussion. It is not so much his work, as what historians have made of it that concerns us here.

Historians of colonial America ignored Kuhn's emphasis on "sets of devices" and "problem-solutions" as a possible source for paradigms, and dwelt almost exclusively on his mention of abstract "principles." Remodeled by the cultural anthropologist Clifford Geertz and others, and renamed "ideology," this partial reading of Kuhn's ideas on paradigms came to dominate the social sciences. Timing assisted the "ideological" interpretation to find an overarch-

---

[23]Thomas S. Kuhn, *The Structure of Scientific Revolutions* (Chicago, 2nd ed., 1970), emphasis added. See also Hollinger, "Kuhn's Theory," *American Province,* 109 for clarification of the term "paradigm."

[24]Quoted in Pocock, *Politics, Language, and Time,* 14n (emphasis added).

ing acceptance among historians, thanks to the sudden and profound impact of the seminal work of Bernard Bailyn.

Bailyn, working contemporaneously (1960s) with Kuhn, and while editing the pamphlet literature of the American Revolution, recognized the potent explanatory power of a set of beliefs which he called "country ideology." He found these beliefs, articulated again and again in the writings of eighteenth-century British opposition writers, had been reformulated in the colonial American press. With his pathbreaking book *The Ideological Origins of the American Revolution*,[25] Bailyn introduced both political cultural and the ideological paradigm into early American studies, and through the influence of his work the pattern for the recovery of eighteenth-century American political thought was set. Bailyn not only introduced the paradigm theory, but the "Bailyn" paradigm theory into the historiography of early America. It is this version which has held a virtual interpretative hegemony ever since.

Writing about the same time as Bailyn, J. R. Pole's broadly conceived, comparative study of colonial America's political culture *Political Representation in England and the Origins of the American Republic*, focused on how its politics actually developed and worked.[26] His suggestive work on interest representation signaled the limited nature of the ideological approach, but this aspect of his work went largely unnoticed. The explanatory power of the ideological paradigm gripped the imagination of a generation of historians. The burst of scholarship on the secular ideology of republicanism alone generated so much literature as to be virtually unmanageable.[27] After

[25]Cambridge, Mass., 1967. For the influence of Bailyn's interpretation on early American historiography, see John M. Murrin, "Political Development" in Greene and Pole, eds., *Colonial British America*, 413–14.

[26]London and New York, 1966.

[27]See footnote 6. See also Lance Banning, "Jeffersonian Ideology Revisited: Liberal and Classical Ideas in the New Republic," *William and Mary*

protagonists of classical and liberal humanist varieties of republicanism had their say, claims for the contributions of religion (sacred ideology), and the Scottish Common Sense School (rational ideology)
were advanced. James Kloppenberg's 1987 attempt to synthesize the
outpourings for these three viewpoints was a signal that the debate
had become fragmented and the concept overworked. And while his
essay restored a needed coherence, it succeeds chiefly (and once
again) in classical terms, since he collects all these strands under the
rubric of "virtue."[28] Moreover, his analysis considers only formal, explicit thought systems, the ideas-based explanations that still dominate American historiography.

II

To restate the problem, what other master model may be at work
where ideology does not appear to account for political behavior?
Although he does not develop the point, the intellectual historian
David A. Hollinger's 1985 reexamination of Kuhn's theory revealed
that ideology may be only one of several paradigms that a society
may possess to perform the chore of organizing contingency.[29] "Organization," writes Hollinger, "may be achieved through a number
of modes and devices, ranging from formal institutions to *informal
habits* and from codes of abstract principles to concrete examples of

Quarterly, 3rd ser., XLIII (1986), 3–9 and Joyce Appleby, "Republicanism
in Old and New Contexts," *ibid.*, 20–24; and the essays collected in the
special issue, "Republicanism in the History and Historiography of the
United States," ed. Joyce Appleby, *American Quarterly*, XXXVII (1985),
461–598.

[28]James Kloppenberg, "The Virtues of Liberalism: Christianity, Republicanism, and Ethics in Early American Discourse," *Journal of American
History*, LXXIV (1987), 9–33.

[29]The next two paragraphs are drawn from Hollinger, "Kuhn's Theory," *American Province*, 109, 111 (emphasis added), 114.

how problems of a given class have been solved in the past." Moreover, "concrete examples [such as accepted, though informal, modes of problem solving] have a staying power *distinct* from the general principles they embody." He might also have added that habitual methods of proven utility have staying power regardless of whether they originally embodied any systematic principles at all.

Continuing the point, Hollinger stresses the significance that Kuhn attaches to those "elements of tradition that are prior to, or even apart from, principles, laws, and other conventionally 'rational' organizing devices. Certain specific achievements within the remembered history of a community may function as models for thinking and acting without first being transformed into abstract principles." Kuhn thus argued compellingly that historians should make it a practice to look for prototypes of this sort, especially when trying to explain the behavior of a community that seems not to be following any preformulated principles at all. "For example," notes Hollinger, "English colonists in America enslaved Africans long before the principle of lifetime, heritable, racial slavery was acknowledged by English Americans. The behavior of the colonists was influenced by precedent from social situations they regarded as analogous."

The paradigm as concrete, shared examples is, according to Kuhn's own final re-evaluation, the most important aspect of his theory.[30] It is important from our standpoint, too, because it opens up an epistemological explanation for political culture not previously explored by historians, and on which my analysis of political culture finally depends.

According to Kuhn, the knowledge embedded in and common to a community's complement of "exemplars" is prior to that enshrined in rules, laws, theories, or other transcendent abstractions. If that is true, it becomes important to understand how this knowl-

---

[30]See his "Postscript–1969" to the revised edition (1972).

edge is acquired. Kuhn proposes that while all stimuli have an independent reality that is immutable, they are received in the form of sensations. Sensations, as *socially* learned responses to stimuli, are thoroughly mutable, and as such may differ from community to community. For example, two people reared in different cultures may literally "see" different things when confronted by the same stimuli. This "seeing" is the process of perception. It is not an interpretative process, an unconscious version of what we do after perception has taken place. It is an involuntary, direct, stimulus-to-sensation route. We have no access to what we know here. It is tacit knowledge.

Interpretation (a process of evaluation) only begins when perception ends; therefore, the amount of interpretation needed to complete an evaluation by any given community depends on how thoroughly the perceptual job has been done. That thoroughness in turn depends drastically on the nature and amount of prior experience and training by exposure to such practices as have withstood the test of group use. Repeated use of accepted practices (the "exemplar") in analogous situations does the job of perception training. The more frequently and successfully each application of a model solves different sets of related problems, the more thoroughly tacit knowledge manages the situation and the less is "left over" to be interpreted. In this sense, method is deeper and is *a priori* to ideology.[31]

Let us now return to the idea that small homogeneous societies may dispense with formal theories while larger, more diverse ones must formulate a justification or some interpretation of the problem in order to achieve a consensus on values. The distinction between methodological (for small societies with tacit value systems) and ideological (for large, more diverse ones) paradigms may be seen as that between epistemology and hermeneutics. Hermeneutics relies upon languages to cope with the problems of social understanding.

---

[31]Kuhn, *Scientific Revolution*, 44–50; and in the "Postscript–1969," 175, 187–98.

Discourse, normal (understood as relevant by all), as well as abnormal (or one could say "revolutionary" since incommensurable with received wisdom) is the arena in which hermeneutics operates. It is not a new epistemology. Indeed it is not concerned with epistemology at all. It is not another way of knowing, but another way of coping.[32] Ideological (rhetorical) traditions spread patterns of thinking to cope with change. Methodological traditions spread ways of knowing. They facilitate outcomes. Viewed in this way, hermeneutic and epistemological traditions do not compete with one another, they help each other out.

I began this essay by describing an epistemological politics in an initially homogenous society, the lowcountry culture of South Carolina. After independence, when the political community widened, strains appeared. At times, when method alone could not handle problems presented by heterogeneity, hermeneutics became an additional way of coping. For example, when the backcountry and lowcountry split over the basis of representation in 1794, lowcountry leaders utilized republican rhetoric to argue for an equality of interests. In South Carolina, abnormal (revolutionary) discourse never overturned normal discourse. In the hands of its elite leaders, public discourse became instrumental, intended to spread consensus rather than open any serious line of inquiry. Most of the strain, however, was diffused nonverbally, within the workings of the legislature. The job of adjustment to contingent experience flowed largely from the method, not the debate.

III

In this essay I have argued (and it is a hypothesis that may be applicable to other political cultures) that by 1800 South Carolina had evolved a tradition commensurate with but distinct from that al-

[32]Richard Rorty, *Philosophy and the Mirror of Nature* (Princeton, 1979), 315–56.

ready worked out from social sources[33] that accounts for South Carolina's politics, its political culture, and to a certain extent its political structure, as well as for some of the politically mature principles that crystallized in the nineteenth century.

It is a tradition of informal habit and concrete example. A commercial analogue, the Carolina lobby, served as both prototype and precedent for a political method. Through multiple applications, the method collected a body of common and commonly agreed on, tacitly held characteristics, which became the basis of its identity as an "exemplar," or model, or paradigm. The method entered South Carolina's political culture at the critical period of its maturation from colonial dependency to assertive independence. But because it had its origins in the colonial condition, and retained the imprint of economic power linked to political powerlessness, it dragged with it certain aggressive features that made it a volatile formula for resolving conflict in the new republic. When joined to the republican imperative that its leaders demonstrate a selfless commitment to all the state's interests with no particular regard for their own, it could lead to acts that now appear reckless. As a model for brokering strains within state government, however, it proved a particularly stable and stabilizing tradition.

I have also argued that South Carolina's leaders' prevailing political values, its leadership style, and even some of John C. Calhoun's constitutional thought ultimately may be traced to this early set of practices. To say that deeply held convictions can have their origins in mere convention is to invite the outrage of the committed, regardless of the ideas and ideals they embrace. But it is also to suggest that we are freer than we supposed to embrace new ideas that

---

[33]The classic statement is Robert M. Weir, "'The Harmony We Were Famous For': An Interpretation of Pre-Revolutionary South Carolina Politics," *William and Mary Quarterly*, 3rd ser., XXVI (1969), 473–501.

appear more useful, or to have greater moral authority, and to let go of values that have become anomalous.[34]

My reading of the origins and character of South Carolina's politics rests upon a theory of political culture that may seem uninteresting, unimportant, and disturbingly detached. But accepting that convention can influence conviction may also free us from an unhelpful hostility toward the values of other peoples and other political cultures, since we can conclude they are similarly derived, similarly held, and are similarly dispensable as the world changes. If we can learn greater tolerance and a little patience from such a view, can it really be so dangerous?

[34]These final remarks are influenced by the reasoning in Joyce Appleby's essay, "The American Heritage: The Heirs and the Disinherited" in *Liberalism and Republicanism in the Historical Imagination* (Cambridge, Mass., 1992), esp. 229–31.

Jack Richon Pole:

A Scholar's Portfolio

The most visible signs of an academic's intellectual life are his education, his academic appointments, his awards, his publications, and his training of younger scholars. J. R. Pole graduated from Oxford University with first class honors in 1949, and from Princeton University in 1953, where his Ph.D. dissertation won the New Jersey Prize. He was a Lecturer in American History at University College, London (1953–63), a Reader in American History and Government at the University of Cambridge (1963–79), and Rhodes Professor of American History and Institutions at Oxford University (1979–89).

J. R. Pole's research awards and prizes include two Rockefeller Research Awards (1952, 1960), fellowship awards from the Commonwealth Fund (U.K.) for American Studies (1956); the American Philosophical Society (1957); the American Council of Learned Societies (1968); the Center for Advanced Study in the Behavioral Sciences at Stanford University (1969–70); the Woodrow Wilson International Center for Scholars (1978–79); a Leverhulme Research Professorship from the British Academy (1988); the Goleib Fellowship at New York University Law School (1990); a Senior Research Fellowship at the Institute of Commonwealth Studies, College of William and Mary (1991); a Visiting Fellowship at the Institute of Bill of Rights Law, Marshall-Wythe Law School (1991); and a Leverhulme Trust Emeritus Fellowship (1988–94). He won the Southern Historical Association's Charles W. Ramsdell Award for his article "Representation and Authority in Virginia" in 1959. In 1985 he was elected a Fellow of the British Academy, the highest distinction a British academic may receive from his peers.

Bibliography of Published Works by J. R. Pole

The following bibliography of J. R. Pole's published works includes books, essays, major review articles, special lectures, and occasional pieces (in that order) arranged by year. Specific reprints and foreign language items are not included. J. R. Pole was general editor of the *American Historical Documents* series (Harrap, London, 1972) and series editor (with Jack P. Greene) of *Early America: History, Context, Culture* (The Johns Hopkins University Press, 1991 ongoing). He has served on the editorial boards of the *William and Mary Quarterly* (1974–76), the *Cambridge Studies in the History and Theory of Politics* (1964–85), and the *Journal of American Studies* (1967–80).

ABBREVIATIONS

AHR	*American Historical Review*
JAH	*Journal of American History*
JSH	*Journal of Southern History*
PNJHA	*Proceedings* of the New Jersey Historical Association
WMQ	*William and Mary Quarterly*, 3rd series

1953

"The Suffrage in New Jersey, 1770–1807," PNJHA, January 1953.

1956

"Suffrage Reform and the American Revolution in New Jersey," PNJHA, July 1956.

"Jeffersonian Democracy and the Federalist Dilemma in New Jersey, 1798–1812," PNJHA, October 1956.

1957

"The Making of the Constitution" in H. C. Allen and C. P. Hill, eds., *British Essays in American History* (London, 1957).

1958

"Election Statistics in Pennsylvania 1790–1840," *Pennsylvania Magazine of History and Biography*, April 1958.

"Representation and Authority in Virginia from the Revolution to Reform," JSH, February 1958. 1959 Winner of the Charles W. Ramsdell Award, Southern Historical Association.

"Suffrage and Representation in Maryland from 1776 to 1810: A Statistical Note and Some Reflections" and "Election Statistics in North Carolina, to 1861," both in JSH, May 1958.

1959

Abraham Lincoln and the Working Classes of Britain (London, 1959).

1960

"Constitutional Reform and Election Statistics in Maryland, 1790–1812," *Maryland Historical Magazine*, December 1960.

1962

"Historians and the Problem of Early American Democracy," AHR, April 1962.

"Forward from McCarthyism: The Radical Right and the Conservative Norm," *Political Quarterly*, April-June 1962.

1964

Abraham Lincoln (Oxford, 1964).

1966

Political Representation in England and the Origins of the American Republic (London and New York, 1966).
"The Emergence of the Majority Principle in the American Revolution," *Etudes sur L'Histoire des Assemblées d'Etats, Faculté de Droit* (Paris, 1966).
Abraham Lincoln and the American Commitment (Cambridge, 1966).

1967

The Advance of Democracy (ed.; New York, 1967).
"The American Past: Is It Still Usable?," *Journal of American Studies*, April 1967.

1969

"Daniel J. Boorstin" in Marcus Cunliffe and Robin Winks, ed., *Pastmasters* (New York, 1969).
The Seventeenth Century: The Origins of Legislative Power (Charlottesville, Va., 1969).

1971

The Revolution in America: Documents of the Internal Development of America in the Revolutionary Era, 1754–1788 (ed.; London and Stanford, 1971).
The Meanings of American History (co-edited; Glenview, Ill., 1971).

1972

Foundations of American Independence, 1763–1815 (Indianapolis, 1972; Fontana edn., London, 1973).

1973

"The New History and the Sense of Social Purpose in American
Historical Writing." *Transactions* of the Royal Historical Society,
5th Series 23, 1973.

1974

"Of Mr. Booker T. Washington and Others," *The Historical Journal*,
1974.

1975

Slavery, Secession and Civil War (ed.; London, 1975).
The Decision for American Independence (Philadelphia, 1975; Lon-
don, 1977).
"Whigs, Tories and the Idea of Equality," in Esmond Wright, ed.,
A Tug of Loyalties (London, 1975).

1976

Equality in the Founding of the American Republic: A Complex Heritage
(B. K. Smith Lectures in History, Houston, 1976).

1977

The Idea of Union (Alexandria, Va., 1977).
"Slavery and Revolution: The Conscience of the Rich," *The Historical Journal*, 1977.

1978

The Pursuit of Equality in American History (Berkeley, 1978).
"The Judicial Campaign: An American Mode of Politics," Radio 3,
BBC, 13 March 1978.

1979

Paths to the American Past (New York, 1979).

1980

"The Language of American Presidents" in Leonard Michaels and Christopher Ricks, eds., *The State of the Language* (Berkeley, 1980).

1981

"Test Cricket Commentaries," *The Listener*, 17–24 December 1981.

1983

The Gift of Government: Political Responsibility from the English Restoration to American Independence (Athens, Ga., 1983).

1984

Colonial British America: Essays in the New History of the Early Modern Era (co-edited; Baltimore, 1984).
"Can the Past Survive the Future?," in *Democracy and Capitalism in America* (1983–84 Humanities Forum, Simon's Rock of Bard's College, Massachusetts, 1984).

1987

The American Constitution: For and Against. Documents of the Debate over Ratification (edited with an introduction; New York, 1987).

1988

"The Politics of the Word 'State' and its Relation to American Sovereignty" in *Parliaments, Estates and Representation*, 8 (part I), June 1988.
"Vocabolario Politico: Notes on the Word 'State' in the Anglo-American Tradition" in *Il Pensiero Politico* (Firenze, 1988).
"Ramadhin and Valentine," A review of Michael Manley, *A History of West Indies Cricket* and Garfield Sobers, *Sobers: Years at the Top*, *London Review of Books*, 13 October 1988.

"The Ancient World in the New Republic: The Founders' Use of History" in Rob Kroes and Eduard Van De Bilt, eds., *The U.S. Constitution After 200 Years* (Amsterdam, 1988).

"Equality: An American Dilemma" in Dennis Donoghue and Leslie Berlowitz, eds., *America in Theory* (New York, 1988).

1989

"What is Still Vital in the Political Thought of the Founders?" in R. C. Simmons, ed., *The American Constitution: the First Two Hundred Years* (Manchester, U.K., 1989).

"Misusage and Abusage," *The Times Higher Educational Supplement,* 9 July 1989.

1991

The Blackwell Encyclopedia of the American Revolution (edited with Jack P. Greene; Oxford, 1991), including essay "Equality."

"The American Revolution and the Early Federal Republic," *The Encyclopaedia Britannica* (Chicago, 1991).

"Mortuary Science: A Proposal" (with F. N. L. Robinson), *The Oxford Magazine*, 67 (Hilary, 1991).

1992

"The Individualist Foundations of American Constitutionalism" in Herman Belz, Ronald Hoffman and Peter J. Albert, eds., *To Form a More Perfect Union: The Critical Ideas of the Constitution* (Charlottesville, Va., 1992).

1993

The Pursuit of Equality in American History (revised and enlarged 2nd edn., Berkeley, 1993).

"Reflections on Law and the American Revolution," *WMQ*, January 1993.

"Further Reflections on Law and the American Revolution: A Comment on the Comments," WMQ, July 1993.

1994

"A Bad Case of Agoraphobia: Is There a Market Place of Ideas?," *The Times Literary Supplement*, 4 February 1994.

1995

"In Machiavelli's Fading Footprints," *The Historical Journal*, September 1995.
"The Origins of Congress" in Donald C. Bacon, Roger H. Davidson, Morton Keller, eds., *The Encyclopedia of the United States Congress*, 4 vols. (New York, 1995).

1997

"Colour Casting," *The Oxford Magazine*, 80 (Hilary, 1992).
"A Letter from Gamma Airlines," *The Oxford Magazine* 145 (Michaelmas, 1997).

1998

"Freedom of Speech, Right or Privilege" (Institute of United States Studies, London, 1998); reprinted as "Freedom of Speech: From Privilege to Right" in R. Cohen-Almagor, ed., *Challenges to Democracy: Essays in Honour and Memory of Isaiah Berlin* (Ashgate, Aldershot, 2000).
"On C. Vann Woodward" (on his 90th birthday), *Journal of American Studies*, 1998.

1999

"Some Problems of a Colonial Attorney General in a Multi-Cultural Society" in Angerer, Bader-Zaar and Grandner, eds., *Geschichte und Recht: Festschrift für Gerald Stourzh zum 70* (Vienna, 1999).

"The Individual; The Region; The Nation: Where Three Roads Meet" in Waldemar Zacharasiewicz, ed., *Remembering the Individual/ Regional/ National Past* (Vienna, 1999).

"Bicameralism and Republican Government in British North America and the United States" in H. W. Blom, W. P. Blockmans, and H. de Schepper, eds., *Bicameralism in Past and Present* (The Hague, 1999).

"A Target respectfully returns the Arrow" (reply on deference), JAH, December 1999.

2000

A Companion to the American Revolution (edited with Jack P. Greene; Oxford and Boston, 2000), including essays "Equality," "Law: Continuity and Reform," and Preface.

"How to Avoid a Coup d'etat: The Federalist and the American Constitution" in *Parliaments, Estates & Representation* 20 (2000).

"Richard Hofstadter: The Historian as Critic," in Robert A. Rutland, ed., *Clio's Best: Leading Historians of the United States, 1945–2000* (Columbia, Mo., 2000).

"Letter from Kingdom of Poland, Research Funding Council (1498) to Dr. Mickaus Kopemick," *Times Higher Education Supplement*, 2 June 2000.

FORTHCOMING

The Annotated Federalist (edited with Philip Bobbitt; 2001).

Doctoral Theses Supervised by J. R. Pole

Ph.D.s supervised at the University of Cambridge

1969—D. J. MacLeod, "Racial Attitudes in Revolutionary and Early National America"

1970—R. Harrison, "The Structure of Pennsylvania, 1876–1880"

1971—W. L. McIntosh, "The American Negro Faces European Immigration, 1830–1924"

1972—G. W. Martin, "Britain and the Future of British North America, 1837–1867"

1974—C. Shindler, "The Significance of the Cinema in American History, 1929–1941"

1974—J. R. Zvesper, "Republican Ideology and the Origins of American Party Government, 1789–1801"

1975—B. W. Collins, "The Politics of Particularism: Economic Issues in the Major Northern States of the U.S.A., 1857–1858"

1978—R. A. S. Atwood, "The Mercenaries from Hessen-Kassel in the America Revolution"

1978—P. M. Neiditch, "The Origins and Development of Andrew Jackson's Foreign Policy"

1978—E. S. Perry, "Time and the Land: The Work of American Historians during the Generation of the American Revolution"

1979—P. J. Augur, "The Cotton Famine 1861–1865: A Study of the Principal Cotton Towns during the American Civil War"

1979—W. F. Duker, "A History of the Writ of Habeas Corpus"

1981—M. D. Kaplanoff, "Making the South Solid: Politics and the Structure of Society in South Carolina, 1790–1815"

1981—D. D. Scarboro III, "An Honourable Peace: The Peace Movement in Civil War North Carolina"

1983—J. R. Oldfield, "The Life and Work of Alexander Crummell, 1819–1898"

D. Phil.s supervised at the University of Oxford

1987—R. J. Cook, "Puritans, Pragmatists and Progress: The Republican Coalition in Iowa, 1854–1878"

1987—A. W. Robertson, "Men and Measures: Election Rhetoric in Nineteenth Century Britain and the United States"

1990—R. K. Starr, "A School for Politics: Interest Group Strategies and the Formation of South Carolina's Political Culture, 1763–1794"

1991—C. E. Klafter, "Reason Over Precedents: The Origins of American Legal Thought"

1992—C. G. Suttlemyre, "Proprietary Policy and the Development of North Carolina, 1663–1729"

1993—R. B. Vernier, "Political Economy and Political Ideology: The Public Debt in 18th Century Britain and America"

1994—W. P. Mayo, "The Federal Bill of Rights and the States before the Fourteenth Amendment"

1998—P. L. Thompson, "Southern Pine Workers and the Rise of Capital in the New South"

Ph.D. Candidates at Cheltenham and Gloucester College of Higher Education (with Rebecca Starr)

Ian David Margeson, "Political Ideology and Loyalist Mentalité in Revolutionary America"

Contributors

JOYCE APPLEBY is Professor of History at the University of California, Los Angeles.

ANTHONY J. BADGER is Paul Mellon Professor of American History and Institutions, Cambridge University.

LAWRENCE GOLDMAN is a Fellow and Tutor in Modern History at St. Peter's College, Oxford.

JACK P. GREENE is Andrew W. Mellon Professor in the Humanities at The Johns Hopkins University.

J. G. A. POCOCK is Harry C. Black Emeritus Professor of History at The Johns Hopkins University.

ANDREW W. ROBERTSON is Associate Professor of History at Lehman College, City University of New York.

REBECCA STARR is Senior Lecturer at Cheltenham and Gloucester College of Higher Education in the United Kingdom.

RICHARD VERNIER teaches history at Purdue University at Calumet.

Index

abolitionist movement, 157–58, 201, 214–18, 219–20, 222. *See also* anti-slavery movement; Liberty Party
absolutism, 47
Adams, John, 88
Address to the Working Men of New England (Luther), 213
Agrarian Justice (Paine), 202
Almond, Gabriel A., 244
America. *See* United States
American Freedman's Enquiry Commission, 232
American Geography (Morse), 157
American National Trades' Union, 199
American Revolution, 2, 4, 5, 42, 106, 131, 158, 177–78, 179; ideological legacy, 179; ideological origins, 205; as opportunity for regeneration, 159; postwar economic contraction, 111–12; and regionalism, 158–60; and war debts, 91–92, 103, 105–6
Ames, Fisher, 123–24
Anderson, Benedict, 150
anti-slavery movement, 10, 196, 214, 219–23, 227. *See also* abolitionist movement; Liberty Party
Appleby, Joyce, 4, 7, 8, 247; and deference as "quark" term, 133–34
Articles of Confederation, 159, 160
Asbury, Francis, 170
Association of American Patriots for the Purpose of Forming a National Character, 166
Awl, 189

Bacon, Nathaniel, 47
Bagehot, Walter, 133
Bailyn, Bernard, 2, 249
balance of trade, 97
Bank of North America (BNA), 115–17
Baptists, 156, 173; Antimission, 169; Freewill, 169
barbares farouches, 34
Bates, John, 203
Benton, Thomas Hart, 225
Bingham, William, 119–20
Blackstone, Sir William, 49, 50–51, 54, 56, 63
Blackwell's Encyclopedia of the American Revolution, 134
Bland, Richard, 82
Bolles, Albert, 108
Bovary, Alvan E., 192, 221–22
Braduax, William E., 153
Bray, John Francis, 203
Breen, T. H., 140–41
Bright, John, 232
Brisbane, Albert, 190, 191
Brown, Charles Brockden, 165
Brown, Robert E., 132
Brownson, Orestes, 213
Buddhism, 27–28
Budsoists, 25, 26
Burke, Edmund, 41, 42
Burnett, William, 74

Calhoun, John C., 241, 254
Calvin's Case (Coke), 61–62
Calvinists, 169–70
Candidates, The (Munford), 139, 141, 144

Care, Henry, 51–53, 54
Carlile, Richard, 185
Carnegie, Andrew, 180
Carter, Landon, 139
Carter, Robert Wormeley, 139
Charles II, King, 76
Chartism, 203–5, 208–10
Chartist Land Company, 208–9
Chartist Land Plan, 210–11
Chase, Samuel, 146–47
Chauncy, Charles, 106
China, 23–24, 29, 30
Chronotype, The, 220
Clay, Henry, 225
Clopton, John, 145, 146, 151
Cluer, John C., 203
Coke, Sir Edward, 47, 49, 50, 51–52, 68–69
colonial courts, 137–38
Columbus, Christopher, 18, 21
Commentaries upon the Laws of England (Blackstone), 68, 103
Commerford, John, 187, 214, 225, 226, 230
Commons, John R., 182, 184, 229
Confucianism, 25, 26, 27, 43
Confucius, 23
Constantine, Emperor, 20
Constantinople, 18
Constitution (U.S.), 161, 162, 165, 173, 197
consuetudo Angliae, 49
Continental Congress: voting blocs in, 158, 159–60
Correspondent, The, 185
Crafts, N. F. R., 96
Craw v. Ramsey, 62
cultural nationalists, 165

da Gama, Vasco, 18
Daily Sentinel, 186
Davenant, Charles, 94, 97; and "political arithmetic," 94–95
Davies, Sir John, 47
Declaration of Independence, 157, 178, 196–98
Decline and Fall of the Roman Empire (Gibbon), 15–16, 20
deference: definition, 135; economic manifestations, 136; ethnographic, 136; political, 131–35, 139, 172. *See also* political culture, "deferential-participant"
de Guignes, Joseph, 26
deism, Enlightened, 23

Democrats, 223–24, 225, 229
Dening, Greg, 35
Devyr, Thomas Ainge, 199–200, 204, 225, 226
Diderot, Denis, 15, 16–17, 21, 26, 31–32
Douglas Democrats, 225
Dominicans, 21
Dulaney, Daniel, 64–65
Dupont, Samuel, 171
Dutton v. Howell, 62

E Pluribus Unum, ideological importance of, 153–54, 174
electioneering, 131–32, 138; and candidates, 141–42; and "courting," 139–40; and "treating," 142–43
England. *See* Great Britain
English Constitution, The (Bagehot), 133
English Liberties (Care), 68
English public debt, in the eighteenth century, 6, 7, 93–99, 109–10, 123, 129–30; defense of, 100–103; and development of political economy as a science, 94, 97, 100; postwar, 95; and the sinking fund, 93, 100, 104–5, 125, 127; and the Whig defense, 100–101
English settlements in North America, 46–47, 63, 64; and common law, 49–53, 78, 88–90; and crisis over independence, 87–88; and English identity, 56–57, 87; influence of English jurisprudence, 47–53, 68–69; and inherited rights, 60–68, 81–85, 87–88; of legislative authority and colonial assemblies, 70–80; in Maryland, 64–66; and metropolitan authority, 59–60, 73; and Parliament's jurisdiction over, 81–87, 90; and taxation, 80, 85–86
Essai sur les Moeurs (Voltaire), 20
Essay on the Right of Property in Land (Ogilvie), 203
Eurocentric history, 26, 44
Evans, Frederick William, 184, 195
Evans, George Henry, 184–86, 189, 191, 203, 207–8, 210, 214–15, 228, 231
Excellent Priviledge of Liberty & Property being the Birth-right Of the Free-born Subjects of England, 68

Federalists, 124, 162–63, 164–66, 167, 170
Ferral, John, 187
Findley, William, 127
Fisch, Jorg, 46

Foner, Eric, 201, 233
Formisano, Ronald, 131, 132, 134
Fortescue, Sir John, 47, 48–49, 55, 69; on monarchies, 48
Free Soil Party, 192, 220, 224
freeholders. *See* Virginia, and freeholders
French Revolution, 165; and American radicals, 162
Frick, Henry Clay, 180

Gallatin, Albert, 124, 128
Gammage, R. G., 210
Garrison, William Lloyd, 215
Geertz, Clifford, 248
George, Henry, 230
Gerry, Elbridge, 123
Gibbon, Edward, 5, 15–16
Goldman, Lawrence, 9, 10
Gooch, Sir William, 67–68
Gordon, Thomas, 52
Gore, Christopher, 124
Grand National Consolidated Trade Union, 199
Gray, John, 203, 205
Great Britain, 6, 39–40, 127, 162, 185, 205–6; and colonial charters, 82; and industrial capitalism, 200; and Parliament, 53–54, 76, 80; and the Sedition law (1792), 163; specific acts of Parliament, 54; working classes in, 211–12. *See also* English public debt, in the eighteenth century; English settlements in North America
Greece, 19, 23, 43
Greeley, Horace, 186, 188, 190, 194, 222
Greeley Whigs, 224
Greene, Jack P., 3, 5, 134–35, 138–39
Grenville, William, 103
Grow, Galusha, 192, 223, 231

Hale, Sir Matthew, 69
Hall, Charles, 203
Hamilton, Alexander, 86, 100, 106, 107; attacks on his financial policies, 123–30; financial policies, 118–22; on public credit, 120; Report on Public Credit, 125–26; as Secretary of the Treasury, 118, 124
Henderson, H. James, 158
Herder, J. D., 243
hermeneutics, 252–53
Histoire des Etablissements et du Commerce des Européens dans les Deux Indes. See Histoire des Deux Indes

Histoire des Deux Indes (Raynal), 5, 17 n.4, 15–18, 27–28, 32; and the African slave trade, 38–41; and *bons sauvages*, 31–34; and the buccaneers (*boucaniers*), 36–37; and civilizations of the Indian Ocean, 22–24; and Creoles, 37–39; and *encyclopédiste* history, 27; and enlightened philosophy, 20–21; and enlightenment as child of commerce, 34–36, 40; and Hindu culture, 22–23, 29; as *Histoire des Deux Mondes*, 30–31, 38; and "Hottentots," 28–29; and island culture, 24–26; and the New World (*nouveau monde*), 30–34, 37; on North American history, 42–43; and pre-Columbian populations, 33–34; and three sets of humans, 31; and the Spanish empire, 37–38. *See also* China; Eurocentric history; Greece; historiography, enlightened; Japan; Jesuits; magian religions
Histoire des Huns, Turcs et Mogols (de Guignes), 26
"Historians and the Problem of Early American Democracy," 132
historiography, enlightened, 20–22
History of the American Revolution (Ramsay), 156–57
Hodgskin, Thomas, 203, 205
Hollick, Frederick, 203
Hollinger, David A., 250–51
Homestead Act, 9, 10, 191, 192, 210, 222–23, 228–29, 231, 232
homestead exemption, 226
Hopkins, Stephen, 81
Houston, George, 185
Hume, David, 94, 97, 98, 99 n.12, 100, 126

Ideological Origins of the American Revolution (Bailyn), 249
imperialism, European, 45–47
Industrial Congress, 190
Ingalls, Joshua K., 230
Inquiry into the Principles of Political Oeconomy (Steuart), 101, 112
Isaac, Rhys, 136, 138

Jackson, Andrew, 184, 225–26, 233
Jackson, R. V., 96
Jacksonian Democrats, 229
Jacobins, 162
Jamaica, and English law, 63–64, 65–66, 70
James II, King, 70
Japan, 24–25; and *état policé*, 25; Tokugawa regime, 25–26

Jefferson, Thomas, 4, 83–84, 117, 126–27, 160, 161, 163, 164, 166, 193, 233; and revivalist support, 169–70; and Westward Mill Library Society, 153–56
Jesuits, 21, 27, 33–34
Johnson, Andrew, 223, 226
Jones, Gareth Stedman, 204–5, 206–7
Jones, Sir William, 76
Jordan, Daniel, 141, 152
Julian, George W., 229, 231, 232

Kavanaugh, Dennis, 244
Keith, William, 66
Kent, James, 89, 90
King, Rufus, 124
Kloppenberg, James, 250
Knight, James, 78
Knox, William, 63, 66, 67
Krause, Paul, 180
Kuhn, Thomas, 248, 250–52; and "exemplars," 251; and interpretation, 252

Labor: Its History and Prospects (Owens), 201
labor movement, 182–83, 199–201, 206–7, 215; and European corruption, 201–2. *See also* trade unions
L'Histoire de Jesus Christ (d'Holbach), 185
land reform, 10, 191–92, 194–95, 198, 202–4, 209–10, 211, 221, 224, 226–27; and language of political discourse, 213. *See also* anti-slavery movement; National Reform Association; republicanism
Laudibus Legum Angliae, De (Fortescue), 47
lex non scripta, 49
Liberator, The, 200
Liberty Party, 192, 215, 221
Lloyd, Thomas, 204
Locke, John, 53, 97; and Constitutions of Carolina, 32
Loco-Foco Party, 185, 187
Logan, George, 127
London Workingmen's Association, 209; and the People's Charter, 209
Louis XVI, King, 162
Luther, Seth, 213

Macaulay, Catherine, 105
Macfarlane, Robert, 200
Madison, James, 138, 161, 193
magian religions, 23
Magna Charta, 51–52, 64
Mamluk Egypt, 18
Man, The, 186
Manicheism, 26

Marina, Dona, 33
Marshall, John, 145, 146
Marx, Karl, 208
Maryland Assembly, 58
Mason, George, 148, 222
Masquerier, Lewis, 191, 197, 230, 231
Massachusetts *Body of Liberties* (1641), 59
Mathias, Peter, 96–97
McConnell, Felix Grundy, 226
McMechen, Alexander, 146–47
Mechanics' Free Press, 184
Mechanics Mutual Protection Society, 200
Methodists, 156, 169
methodological/ideological paradigm distinction, 252
Miller, Samuel, 171
modus operandi, 173, 242 n.8
Monroe, James, 117
Montgomery, David, 228
Morris, Gouverneur, 107, 121
Morris, Robert, 100, 106, 107, 108–11, 116
Morse, Jedediah, 157
Munford, George Wythe, 144–45
Munford, Robert, 139, 152
Murray, Joseph, 78

National Land Company, 209
National Reform Association, 9, 10, 181–82, 186–92, 209, 219, 221, 223–26, 229; founding members, 203–4
National Reform movement. *See* National Reform Association
National Reform Union, 189
National Trades' Union, 184
nativism, 167, 172, 225
Navigation Act (1696), 70
Netherlands, The, 47
New England Association of Farmers, Mechanics, and Other Working Men, 182
New Haven Gazette, 115
New York City, pauperism in, 195
New York Daily Tribune, 190
New York Tribune, 186
New York Working Men's Party, 207–8
Northern Star, 209
Northwest Ordinance, 160

O'Brien, Bronterre, 211, 214–15
O'Brien, Patrick, 96
Oceana (Harrington), 135
O'Connor, Feargus, 211
Offen, Benjamin, 203
Office and Authority of a Justice of the Peace (Webb), 68

"oriental despotism," 28–29
Otis, James, 76
Ottoman Empire, 18–19
Our Natural Rights (Devyr), 204
Owen, Robert Dale, 185, 200, 201–2

Paine, Thomas, 106, 203
paper money, 116–17
paradigm, 241 n.7, 242. *See also* Kuhn, Thomas
Parsons, Talcott, 247
Pendleton, Edmund, 142
Pessen, Edward, 203
Phillips, Wendell, 200–201, 215
philosophy of history, 21
Pitt, Sir William, 93, 105
Pocock, J. G. A., 3–5, 134, 135
Polanyi, Michael, 245
Pole, J. R., 2–3, 105, 132–35, 141, 151, 177–79, 249
political culture: American, 1–12, 237–38, 249; British, 2, 177; "deferential-participant," 131, 132 n.2, 150, 152; definition, 243–45; and ideology, 246 n.19; 246–47, 248–50; in the South, 11–12; and tradition, 248; and values, 245–46. *See also* South Carolina, political culture; Virginia, political culture
political economy, 6–7, 94, 97, 113–16. *See also* Bank of North America; English public debt, in the eighteenth century, and development of political economy as a science
Political Representation in England and the Origins of the American Republic (Pole), 2–3, 133, 249
political theory, Enlightened, 24
Postlethwayt, Malachy, 99
Price, Richard, 104, 106, 125
Progress and Poverty (George), 230
Pursuit of Equality in American History, The (Pole), 178
Pyne, James, 187, 203

Quakers, 43, 159
quantity theory of money, 97

Radical, The, 186
radicalism, 10, 199–200, 204–8, 212, 232, 233
Radicalism of the American Revolution, The (Wood), 135
Ramsay, David, 8–9, 89–90, 156, 165
Rawson, Edward, 74

Ray, Charles Bennett, 217
Raynal, Guillaume-Thomas, 15, 16–17, 26
Reconstruction, 227
Reconstruction of Society (Masquerier), 197
Report to Congress on Public Credit (1782), 110–11
republicanism, 158, 159, 179–81, 192, 194, 198–99, 213, 230; expansive, 160, 174; "worker," 212
Republicans, 10, 163, 164, 167, 212, 221–22, 223–24, 227–28, 229–30; critique of Federalist fiscal policy, 118–19; ideology, 198–99; Jeffersonian, 163–64, 170; and the national debt, 124–25, 126–27; Radical, 219, 231. *See also* republicanism
Ricardian Socialists, 203
Ricci, Matteo, 27
Right of the Inhabitants of Maryland to the Benefit of the English Laws (Dulaney), 64–65
Rights of Man to Property, The (Skidmore), 183
Risjord, Norman K., 148
Robertson, Andrew, 7–8, 163
Rockingham Whigs, 239
Rodgers, Daniel, 181
Rosenbaum, W. A., 244
Rousseau, Jean-Jacques, 31, 34
Ryckman, L. W., 190

sabbatarianism, 167, 172
Saville, John, 210
Scottish Common Sense School, 250
Second Institute (Coke), 68
Second Treatise (Locke), 53
sectionalism, 213, 227, 233
Seven Years' War, 95, 105–6
Shower, Sir Bartholomew, 62
Sidney, Algernon, 54
Skidmore, Thomas, 183, 202
slave economies, 40–41
slavery, 38–39, 157, 160, 167, 216, 229–31, 250. *See also* anti-slavery movement
Smilie, John, 117
Smith, Adam, 6, 7, 94, 97, 102, 115, 116–17, 129; on interest rate, 110
Smith, Gerritt, 190, 192, 215–19, 231
Smith, James McCune, 217
Smith, William, 76
"Society, Ideology and Politics: An Analysis of the Political Culture of Mid-Eighteenth Century Virginia," 134
Sombart, Werner, 179

South Carolina: and brinkmanship policy, 241; political culture, 11, 12, 238, 240–42, 253–55; relationship with Great Britain, 238–39; and trade lobby, 239, 239 n.4
Southwest Ordinance, 160
Spence, Thomas, 202
Sri Lanka, 26
Statute de tallagio non cencedendo, 51
Steuart, Sir James, 94, 101, 106, 116, 117, 124
Stone, Barton, 173
Supplément au Voyage de Bougainville (Diderot), 32
Sydnor, Charles, 146

Taycosama, 25
Third Institute (Coke), 69
Thompson, Dorothy, 210
Thompson, William, 203
Thorne, Christopher, 244
Tibet, and the Lamaist religion, 26
Tlaxcalans, 33
trade unions, 182–83, 203–4, 207
Transformation of Virginia, 1740–1790, The (Isaac), 136
Treaty of Paris (1763), 63
Trenchard, John, 52
True Workingman, 189
Tucker, Henry St. George, 138, 140
Tucker, Nathaniel Beverly, 143

Union, The, 187
United States: and British public finance as a model for emulation, 106, 109–10; and Chartist emigration, 203–4; commercial prosperity, 163; and the gentry, 173; land sales, 165; literacy in, 163; and modernization, 157; national identity, 167, 174; nationalist movement in political economy, 107–13, 114–16; pauperism in, 195; perception of Britain in aftermath of Seven Years' War, 105–6; population, 171; post-Revolutionary morality, 168; and public debt, 95, 106–7, 121–22; publishing in, 155–56, 170–71; religious freedom, 169; and transformation of religion, 168–69, 170; voluntary associations in, 166–67, 171. *See also* American Revolution; Bank of North America; Constitution (U.S.); cultural nationalists; French Revolution, and American radicals; Hamilton,
Alexander; labor movement; Jefferson, Thomas; radicalism; republicanism
Universal Dictionary of Trade and Commerce (Postlethwayt), 99–100

Van Buren, Martin, 192, 220
Van Rensselaer estates, 187, 187 n.25
Vaughan, John, 62
Vernier, Richard, 6, 7
View of the Progress of Society in Europe (Robertson), 20
Virginia: political culture, 131–32, 134, 144–45, 150–52; and freeholders, 139, 142, 151–52; political issues, 147–49; polling periods, 136–37; and the print community, 150, 150 n.42. *See also* deference; electioneering
Virginia Company of London, 57; and representative Virginia Assembly, 57–58
virtue, as a political value, 158–59
Voice of Industry, 189, 213

Wade, Ben, 231
wage-slavery, 215–16
Wallace, Robert, 101
Walpole, Sir Robert, 98, 99 n.12, 125
Washington, George, 164, 192; Neutrality policy, 163
Wealth and Misery (Owen), 200
Wealth of Nations (Smith), 6, 97–98, 102–3, 115, 129
Weaver, Charles Daniel, 204
Webb, George, 68
Webster, Noah, 165
Webster, Pelatiah, 108
West, William, 215, 230
Westward Mill Library Society, 153–56, 166
Whigs/Whig Party, 52, 124, 177, 201, 225. *See also* Greeley Whigs; Rockingham Whigs
Wilmington Daily Journal, 222
Wilmot, David, 231
Wilmot Proviso, 220
Wilson, James, 83, 89, 90, 107, 114, 116
Wilson, Woodrow, 233
Windt, John, 187
Wirt, William, 140
Wood, Gordon S., 134
Working Man's Advocate, 185, 186, 192, 194, 209, 215
Wright, Frances, 185
Wyche, James, 153

Young America, 186, 189, 209